SPECIAL events

FOR YOUTH GROUPS

THE ideas LIBRARY

THE IDEAS LIBRARY

Administration, Publicity, & Fundraising
Camps, Retreats, Missions, & Service Ideas
Creative Meetings, Bible Lessons, & Worship Ideas
Crowd Breakers & Mixers
Discussion & Lesson Starters
Discussion & Lesson Starters 2
Drama, Skits, & Sketches
Games
Games 2
Holiday Ideas
Special Events

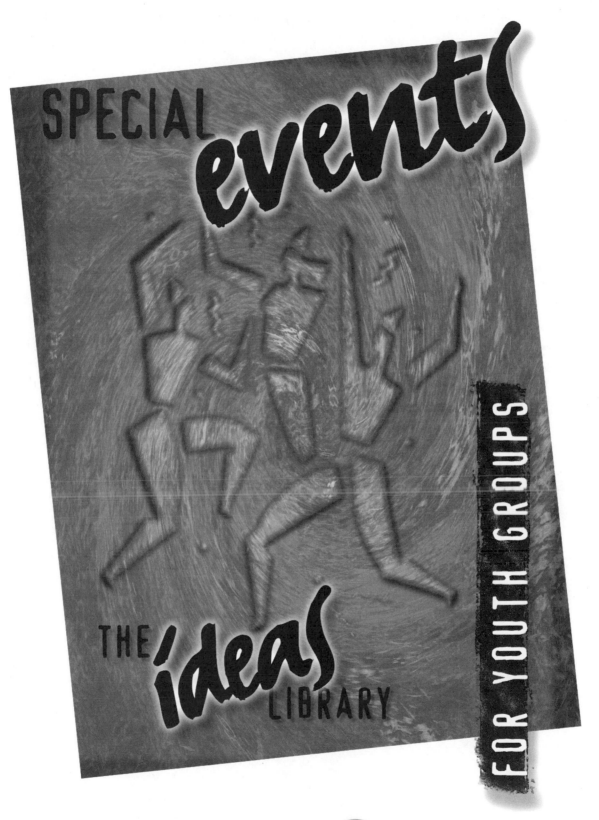

SPECIAL events

THE ideas LIBRARY

FOR YOUTH GROUPS

ZondervanPublishingHouse
Grand Rapids, Michigan
A Division of HarperCollins*Publishers*

Special Events

Youth Specialties Books, 1224 Greenfield Dr., El Cajon, CA 92021, are published by Zondervan Publishing House, 5300 Patterson Ave. S.E., Grand Rapids, MI 49530.

Project editor: Vicki Newby
Cover and interior design: Curt Sell
Art director: Mark Rayburn

ISBN 0-310-22040-8

Printed in the United States of America

97 98 99 00 01/ /5 4 3 2--

CONTENTS

THEME EVENTS

FOOD EVENTS

SPECIAL EVENTS WITH A POINT

OUTINGS & OVERNIGHTERS

RACES & RALLIES

OTHER PARTIES & SPECIAL EVENTS

So what special event have you created lately?

Are your kids still talking last month's big event? Youth Specialties pays $25 (and in some cases, more) for unpublished, field-tested ideas that have worked for you.

You've probably been in youth work long enough to realize that sanitary, theoretical, tidy ideas aren't what in-the-trenches youth workers are looking for. They want—*you* want—imagination and take-'em-by-surprise novelty in meetings, parties, and other events. Ideas that have been tested and tempered and improved in the very real, very adolescent world you work in.

So here's what to do:

• Sit down at your computer, get your special event out of your head and onto your hard drive, then e-mail it to ideas@youthspecialties.com. Or print it off and fax it to 619-440-4939 (Attn: Ideas).
• If you need to include diagrams, photos, art, or samples that help explain your idea, stick it all in an envelope and mail it to our street address: Ideas, 1224 Greenfield Dr., El Cajon, CA 92021-3399.
• Be sure to include your name and all your addresses and numbers.
• Let us have about three months to give your idea a thumbs up or down*, and a little longer for your 25 bucks.

*Hey, no offense intended if your idea isn't accepted. It's just that our fussy Ideas Library editor has these *really* meticulous standards. If the special event isn't creative, original, and just plain fun in an utterly wild or delightful way, she'll reject it (reluctantly, though, because she has a tender heart). Sorry. But we figure you deserve only the best ideas.

ALPHABETICAL LIST
OF EVERY IDEA IN THIS BOOK

GAMES & SPORTS EVENTS

GAMES & SPORTS EVENTS

The thrilll of victory and the agony of defeat can be yours with a well-planned game night or sports event. For the most part, you don't have to be a jock to have fun playing these. For games that are part of a larger theme event, see "Theme Events" on page 95.

ALL-CHURCH OLYMPICS

Here's a way for your church to have its own summer Olympic games. Place participants in nations or countries (or just make the youth group one country and the rest of the church the other country).

Create an Olympic committee to organize and schedule events over a period of a month, with different events slated for each week. Kick things off with an opening ceremony; finish with a closing ceremony. Purchase or create awards (gold, silver, and bronze medals) for the winners in each event.

Events can include both individual and team competition—volleyball, racquetball, tennis, pool, bowling, ping-pong, tug-of-war, Frisbee throwing, cow chip tossing, anything that you can think up. Provide horseshoes and dart games for the more sedentary crowd, relays and bike contests for children, and especially competitive games for teens and active adults. These Olympics can truly perk up a dull summer and draw together your entire congregation. *John Herbert Jaffry*

BAT AND PUTT NIGHT

Rent a miniature golf course and batting cages in your area for about two hours so you can have it to yourselves. Create extra excitement by guaranteeing special prizes for all winners. Here's how to arrange your competition:

Divide your teens into groups at different competitive levels:(junior high girls, junior high boys, senior high girls, senior high boys) so that each person competes with those near his or her own level. The competitions can be arranged in several categories such as—

- Golf score for whole round
- Holes-in-one
- Best score left-handed
- Highest number of strokes on one hole
- Highest number of strokes for a whole round

(These last two categories are for those who aren't as skilled as the others.)

If you have batting cages, you can add two more categories to your competition:

- Most hits in 25 tries
- Most consecutive hits

For each category you should award four

minor prizes. Then four grand prizes should be awarded to the kids who have done the best in all categories. To determine this you have to establish a system of points awarded for their scores: number of hits, holes-in-one, and so on.

Or you could ask if the owner of the golf and batting course will give you some free passes (assuming that you pay him a fair price for your evening's fun). If he does, you can award them to kids who meet the challenges you set before them, such as making a certain putt or making holes-in-one. Another aspect of having a successful evening rests in your ability to sell it to the kids. Advertise it with posters saying "First Annual (City or youth group name) Golf Open and Batting Championships." Build it up, excite the kids, and prepare to have a great time. *Doug Graham*

BICYCLE PEDALMONIUM DAY

This is a fun event that can involve the entire youth department in an exciting day full of bike activities.

• **Bicycle Olympics.** Divide the group into four competing groups if you have junior high through college age involved: junior high boys, junior high girls, senior high and college boys, senior high and college girls. Points and prizes can be awarded the winners in each division.

Some sample events:

–**100-Yard Dash.** A race for time. Use a stopwatch.

–**20-Lap Endurance Race.** Should be about five miles on a regular quarter-mile track. Award points to first through fifth places.

–**Bicycle Demolition.** Have all bike riders form a circle about 100 feet in diameter. They may each have all the water balloons they can carry (stuffed in shirts, pockets, etc.). When the whistle blows, they all interweave in the circle and let each other have it!

–**Bike Jousting.** Bike riders ride toward each other in parallel lanes. Each rider gets a water balloon. The object is to ride by your opponent and hit him with the balloon, without getting hit yourself. Winners advance.

–**Bike Pack.** See how many can fit on a bike and still go 10 feet.

–**Figure Eight Race.** Set up a figure-eight track. Contestants ride it, one at a time, for best clocked time.

–**Obstacle Race.** Set up a track with obstacles — mud, trees, or whatever — to make riding difficult. Include anything you want. The rougher the better. From a starting point, bikes compete for time. On the trail have a Long Jump (4-inch log that the bike must jump over), Tight Rope (a 2x6 that is 12 feet long and about six inches off the ground), a Limbo Branch (low tree branch or board about 10 inches above the handle bars), and a Tire Weave (eight or ten old tires set up in a row about six feet apart). The one who completes the course in the fastest time wins. You can make penalties for those who mess up on some of the obstacles.

–**Baton Relay.** Ride bikes across the parking lot and hand off baton to next rider on the team.

–**Slalom Race.** Time kids as they ride bikes through a slalom course. Have a stopwatch on hand.

–**Snail Race.** Mark off a narrow trail and riders must try to stay in the trail and ride as slowly as possible. Feet may not touch the ground. The rider with the longest time wins.

–**Straw Race.** Place coke bottles all over the parking lot with drinking straws in them. Bike riders must ride up to the bottles, pick up the straws with their bare toes, then reach down with their hands and take it from their toes.

• **Bike Road Rally.** This is a simple treasure hunt event in which teams of three to four bike riders must follow clues to reach a final destination. By arranging for the teams to go different routes, yet ending up at the same place, they won't be able to follow each other. The first team to finish the course is declared the winner. This should take about an hour.

• **Bike Tour.** Last on the activity list is a bike ride to a not-too-distant park or beach for a hamburger and hot-dog feed.

Make sure participants have appropriate safety gear. *Ken Etley, Roger Disque and Nancy Thompson*

BOWLING AWARDS

Does your youth group enjoy bowling? If so, here's how to make an average bowling night much more interesting. Print up some awards like the one pictured here, and give them for categories like these:

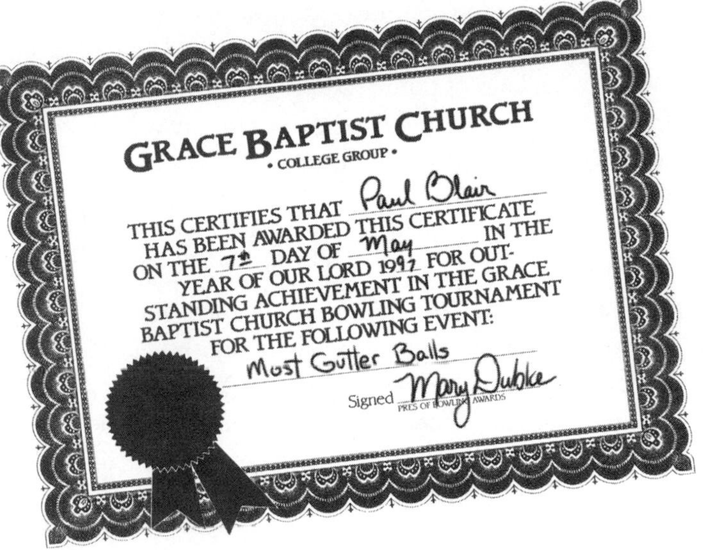

GRACE BAPTIST CHURCH
• COLLEGE GROUP •

THIS CERTIFIES THAT Paul Blair HAS BEEN AWARDED THIS CERTIFICATE ON THE 7th DAY OF May IN THE YEAR OF OUR LORD 1997 FOR OUTSTANDING ACHIEVEMENT IN THE GRACE BAPTIST CHURCH BOWLING TOURNAMENT FOR THE FOLLOWING EVENT:
Most Gutter Balls

Signed Mary Dubke
PRES OF BOWLING AWARDS

- Most strikes
- Low game
- Most expressionless bowler
- Greatest hope for the pro tour
- Most creative shot of the night
- Best form (male/female)
- Most gutter balls
- High game (male/female)
- Sore loser award

Paul E.B. Gruhn

SUMMER BLIZZARD BLAST

These special event ideas for hot days are built around snow and ice themes. Give teams names such as The Icicles, The Snowdrifts, The Snowflakes, and so on. Here are some sample games you can play:

- **Snowball Fight.** Teams wad up stacks of newspaper into snowballs and throw them into the other team's territory. The team with the least amount of snow in its territory at the end of the game is the winner.
- **Ice Melting Contest.** Each team receives a block of ice. Players must try to melt the block using only their hands (rubbing it). The ice is weighed at the beginning of the game and after the game. The ice block that has lost the most weight wins. The game can go for about ten to fifteen minutes.
- **Mining for Marbles.** Team members try to find marbles hidden in a large pan of crushed ice...using only their toes.
- **Ski Relay.** Make skis (old shoes nailed to strips of wood) and have the kids put them on and race in them. You can do this also with snowshoes.
- **Snowman Feed.** Hold a pie-eating contest using lots of whipped cream. No hands are allowed.

If done during the winter, or if you live somewhere near snow, then you can add some authentic snow games. Refreshments can include varieties of ice cream, snow cones, iced tea, and so on. Use your own creativity and this event can be a lot of fun. *Robert McDonald*

CARD TABLE GAME NIGHT

Here is just the event for a night when it's raining or snowing and there is no place to go. Before the kids come, set up one card table for every three or four kids you are expecting. Place one table at the front of the room where the teller and the leader can sit. Have at least one game per table. The games must be for three to four players and be such that a winner may be determined in some way at the end of 15 minutes. If you have more games than you need, that's okay. Just save them until later and exchange them for other games. When the kids come in they are instructed to find an empty chair around one of the game tables until all the chairs have been taken. Each table has 15 minutes to play their game.

When the bell rings at the end of the period, play must stop. The winners at each table report to the teller who has a large stack of red, white, and blue poker chips. The chips are awarded to the winners as follows:

- First place: 6 reds or 3 blues (tie—3 reds or 12 whites each)
- Second place: 3 reds or 12 whites (tie—6 whites each)
- Chip values: 1 blue equals 2 reds or 8 whites; 1 red equals 4 whites.

There can be only three or four players per game per period, (no more or no less) and no one can stay at the same game for two consecutive periods. The nonwinners stay at their tables long enough to re-organize the game for the next group of players and the play begins when all the players have settled down to their new game. At the end of the evening you can award prizes to those with the most chips...or you can have an auction (using the chips as money) which allows everyone to take something home. *Joel Guillemette*

Couch Potato Race

More than just a race, this event can entertain participants and spectators (no pun intended) for the better part of an afternoon. The heart of the event is the race itself, in which two or three couch potatoes each recline on a couch that is pushed like crazy down the race course by their team. Get some old, donated, or Salvation Army sofas that have casters, can have casters attached to them, or that can be firmly strapped to a piano dolly or mechanic's creeper dolly. Lay out a course with lime, chalk, or speed cones.

Conduct several types of races, all with the couch potato theme. In addition to the straightforward speed race, collect some old living-room furniture destined for the dumpster and set up an obstacle course that teams must push their sofas through. Introduce this race as a realistic exercise for a couch potato in quickly navigating his way around coffee tables, stacks of TV *Guides*, and piles of pop cans from the TV room into the kitchen for more food during commercials.

The enthusiasm rises when teams create their customized vehicles, adopt team names and costumes (all relating to couches, potatoes, TV, or the junk food consumed while watching it), and participate in the preliminary contests (most authentic imitation of a couch potato, cheerleaders' competition, most outlandish team costume, etc.).

After the races award appropriate couch potato prizes—couch potato games, stuffed couch potato toys, bags of potato chips, gift certificates for french fries, and packages of other munchies known to be inhaled by couch potatoes. *Jeannie Duckworth*

Guinness Games

Here's a great idea that can become an annual event for your youth group. Have a day of contests in which kids try to set a world's record à la *The Guinness Book of World Records*. However, kids do not compete against the Guinness book but against themselves. The first year, records are set and the following year kids try to break those records. They become the new record holders for the next year. Here are a few sample contests:

- **Eating Contests** (amount of food eaten within time limit)
  - Hamburgers
  - Tacos
  - Bananas
  - Marshmallows
  - Lemon Wedges
  - Onions
- **Endurance Contests** (time)
  - Standing on your head
  - Running in place
  - Talking
  - Stare down
  - Pogo Stick Jumping
  - Dribbling a basketball
  - Keeping eyes open without blinking

- **Skill Contests**
  - Free-throw shooting (percentage of shots)
  - Burping (number in succession)
  - Frisbee throwing (distance)
  - Bubble blowing (number in succession)
  - Marshmallow throwing (distance)
  - Various games (highest scores)
- **Other Contests**
  - Hula Hoop Pack
  - Marshmallows stuffed in mouth (number)

You may want to create boys' and girls' categories in the athletic contests. Kids can pay an entry fee and sign up for whatever events they would like to try. Trophies can be presented to the new record holders. *Robert Brown*

Croquet Party

An annual, formal croquet party just may become a highlight of the year! High schoolers will really enjoy the classiness of the event.

Secure a house that has a large lawn and a formal-looking place to meet—a manicured garden, plush living room, elegant patio. The formal gardens of a city park will always work if you have no formal house. Send formal invitations to everyone in the group a few weeks ahead of time. Dress, of course, is formal.

At the party have enough sets of croquet wickets set up to accommodate everyone. As they enter the yard, they are introduced to others by the butler (an adult sponsor). Waiters (more sponsors) circulate, serving Perrier water, cheese, and fruit. (You actually need only one bottle of Perrier per tray for appearance's sake—you can fill up their glasses with water, 7-Up, or club soda.) Supply classical background music from either a stereo or an actual string quartet—composed of your own students, if possible.

You are cordially invited to
A Croquet Party
on Wednesday Evening, Six O'clock,
August 16
at the Estate of
Sarah Fillmore
8264 Oak Street
Only the finest mineral water and
cheeses will be served.
(Formal Dress)

When everyone has arrived, begin the croquet games. Become familiar with the rules prior to the party so you can advise the less knowledgeable. When all but one player is eliminated, everyone retires to the garden or living room for a poetry reading. Prior to the party, assign a variety of humorous and more serious poetry, perhaps including the lyrics to a few popular Christian songs.

End the party on a rowdy note by returning to the lawn for a few chuckers of polo. The girls, wielding croquet mallets, ride their polo ponies (the guys) and attempt to shoot a croquet ball into the goals.

Be sure to shoot lots of pictures so you can

show slides of the party at the next youth group meeting. Formal prom-type photos make nice gifts, too. *Keith Wright*

GOOFY GOLF

For a junior high or high school party, build your own miniature golf course. Purchase nine tin putting cups from a sporting goods store or golf pro shop. Ask kids to bring putters and golf balls or borrow

putters and purchase inexpensive golf balls. A local golf course may have some old putters they could let you use. Then set up a nine-hole miniature golf course. Build it in your church basement, youth room, or gym. Create ramps, water traps—even run the course down sets of stairs. Use tape on the floor for tee-off boxes. Use old 2x4s for banking the balls (save the woodwork). Make a night of it and have tournament prizes and score cards. Kids love the fun and competition! *Steve Ziemke*

FUN FAIR

This activity is good for a whole night's fun and involves creativity, skill, and competition. Tell everybody coming to the evening to bring various items such as hammers, nails, string, paper, buckets, etc., but don't tell them why. Each person must also bring $.50. As players arrive, exchange their $.50 for fifty pennies. Have the kids group themselves in teams of two to four people. Then tell them they have one hour in which to think up and build a game booth for their team.

Various items such as balloons, paper, tacks, etc. can be provided and the participants are allowed to return home for any needed items. At the end of the hour, open the Fun Fair. Everybody (except those running games) is then free to go around and try the other booths, using up their fifty pennies. Team members are not allowed to try their own booths. The winning team is the one who, after an hour and a half or so, has gained the most money. Examples of booths are a simple penny toss into an ash tray, a dart throwing at a water balloon, a horror house, a water balloon tossed at an individual, a ball in the bucket, a penny shove, and a jail where you pay one cent to have a friend captured and held in jail for one minute. *Brett Cane*

MINI-MASTERS TOURNAMENT

Hold a golf tournament just like the pros, only do it on a miniature golf course. Have each person play three rounds with the totals posted on a big blackboard after each round. Give trophies to the winners in both the guys' and girls' divisions for first, second, and third places. You might try to secure a miniature golf course for a flat fee so the kids can play cheaper. *John Davis*

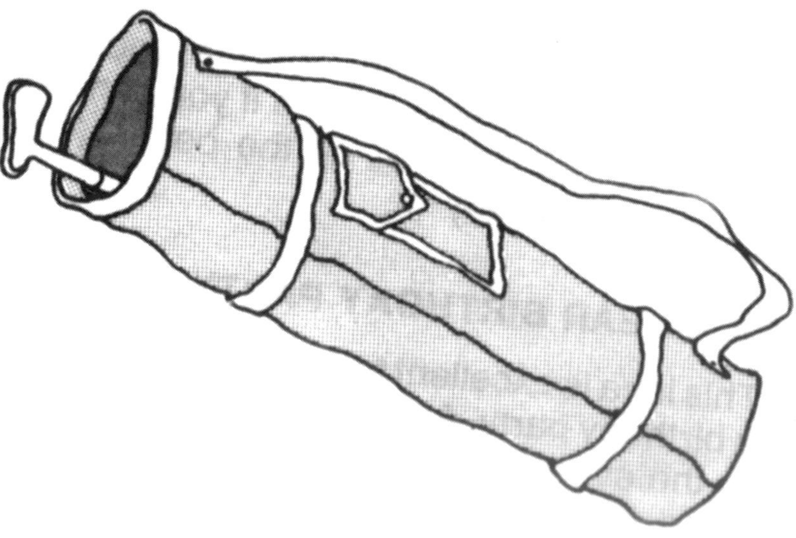

Dye Fights

This is a very successful party or special event that can really draw a crowd. Have all your kids meet out on a play field or vacant lot and supply them with either squirt guns or water balloons. The water is mixed with food dye, so when you get hit with water you also get colored (you dye!). This can be done a number of ways, but usually a big free-for-all is the most fun. At the end, whoever is the least dyed wins. To fill up water balloons, put a little dye in the balloon first, then add water. After the fight, have all the kids meet at a local hamburger stand for food. People who see them won't believe their eyes. *Von Trutschler*

He-Man Olympics

The purpose of this event is to build relationships between fathers and sons, or between men and teens whose dads may not be around for one reason or another. Try to conduct this event just before Father's Day. This all-day event includes lots of games and activities for fathers and sons. Fathers who have a son in the fourth grade or above are eligible to attend. Men in the church who would like to sponsor or adopt a son for the day can also attend. A father who has more than one eligible son should flip a coin to determine which son he will team up with. The others can be adopted for the day.

Here are some sample events:

• **Scripture Search.** Father and son pairs must find as many Scriptures as possible that refer to fathers, sons, or men. Verses must be written out with the Scripture references. Set a time limit and don't allow anyone to use a concordance.

• **Two on Two Volleyball.** Set up a round robin volleyball tournament with each pair playing volleyball against another pair for three minutes each. The pair scoring the most points in three minutes wins.

• **The Great Hunting Trip.** Each pair gets two slingshots and ten Ping Pong balls. Set up some cardboard animals that will fall over if hit with a Ping Pong ball. You could set this up so that the animals are in different rooms and the pair is led around by a guide. (Outfit them with safari hats, etc.) The larger the animal, the fewer points it is worth. The

object is to score as many points as possible with your ten ping pong balls.

•**Stock Car Race.** Set up a track around the church parking lot. The son drives (steers) a VW Bug and the father must push it around the racetrack. Each pair is timed.

• **Handyman Game.** This event is designed to bring out the handiness of each father and son. Give each pair a long piece of wood, a saw, and a few other tools (hammers, nails, etc.). Allow them a certain amount of time to make something useful. Finished products are judged by an impartial panel for points.

• **Optional Events.** Invent other father/son events such as a fishing contest, a tire changing contest, a home-run hitting contest, or whatever. Also plan activities for the non-athletic types.

Wrap up the day with a banquet (maybe invite mothers and sisters) and award trophies or prizes for different categories. Have a special speaker talk on the subject of fatherhood, the family, or men from the Bible.

You can also adapt this event for mothers and daughters. *Bill Wertz*

Hurricane Party

There is no socially redeeming value to this event. It's just a dirty, messy, mushy collection of gross games and sludgy stunts. And your kids will love every minute of it! Tell them to wear old clothes—very old clothes. And plan on getting gooped yourself. Award a million points to the winner of each event, and throw in one or two games worth a million and one points so a team could win by a single point. Cleaning up between games is forbidden.

• **Hair Sculpting.** Players team up and sculpt each other's hair with shaving cream. Sponsors judge the

weirdest looking team. Now everyone looks equally loony for the rest of the event.

• **Night-Crawler Hunt.** For this relay bury gummi worms in chocolate-pudding mud, one mud pit per team. Players must find and eat a worm before returning to their team lines. Extra effect is gained by not telling players exactly what they'll find in the mud and by requiring teams to eat the mud, too, before the game ends.

• **Balloon Bust.** Players must sit on shaving-cream-filled balloons in this relay. If you place the chairs close to each other, the exploding balloon splatters shaving cream on other players, too.

• **Grab-Bag Relay.** Another relay in which players must eat whatever they grab out of a sack. Add some dog biscuits to the bags, as well as cans of tuna and cat food—but with switched labels.

• **Party Poopers.** These are the losers, of course. Have a treat prepared for them: a big batch of doggie doo-doo made of chocolate pudding and crumbled Saltines squeezed through a tube or paper cone to make—well, you know, piles of the stuff. One pile per party pooper—to eat, that is.

There are all sorts of similar games that warm the hearts of vindictive youth leaders. When the Hurricane is over and everyone is gooped to the max, let them hose off. (Devious youth workers have been known to bombard their kids at this point with flour.) *Becky Ross*

INSTANT REPLAY

To attract a lot of kids to an after-the-football-game social on a Friday night, videotape an earlier big game of the season and invite kids to view it at your social. Try to secure permission to place one camera in the press box at the stadium and another on the sidelines for some close-up shots. You can also tape the halftime activities (marching band, cheerleaders, etc.). If this is advertised well, you will attract a lot of kids and automatically gain an audience with the football teams, the bands, the drill team, the cheerleaders, and others. This kind of event is an excellent way to introduce your youth program to the community and to make good contacts. Serve refreshments and provide a festive ambiance after the game for everyone. *Chris Liebrum*

LATE GREAT SKATE

Here's one way to put new life into the old roller-skating party that used to be so popular. First make arrangements to rent a roller rink for your own private use. Usually you can get one for a flat rate plus skate rentals. Also, make sure you have the freedom to plan your own skating program rather than being confined to the normal "all skate, couples only, grand march" kind of thing. You might want to consider an all-night skate that starts around midnight and goes until dawn. Roller rinks are easier to get at such ridiculous hours.

The basic idea is to play all sorts of games on skates to add a dimension of fun. Races, relays, ball games—all can be done on skates. Just be sure that the games are not too rough in order to avoid injuries.

Some sample roller-skating games:

• **Rag Tag.** Players hang rags out of their back pockets or out of their pants. On a signal they all start skating in the same direction. The object of the game is to grab someone else's rag without having yours taken by another skater. Once your rag is gone, you are out of the race. Awards are given for most rags grabbed by one person, and for whoever stayed longest in the game.

• **Obstacle Course Relay.** Set up an obstacle course through which the skaters must skate. The first team to have each of its members skate through it one at a time is the winner.

• **Triple Skate.** Have everyone skate around the rink in threes. No passing is allowed. On a signal, the skater in the middle, or on the right or left, moves up to the next threesome. This is good as a mixer.
• **Scooter Race.** Have one kid down on his haunches who is pushed by another skater. Set a number of laps for the race.
• **Tumbleweed.** Have all the skaters go down to a squat when the music stops or when the whistle blows. This will tire them quickly.
• **One-legged Race.** Skaters race, skating with only one skate on. The other foot is used to push.
• **London Bridge.** For each team, have two skaters stand opposite each other, grab hands, and form a bridge that other skaters can skate under. Each team then lines up and on a signal, begins skating under their bridge. Once under the bridge, each skater circles around and goes through again, as many times as possible before the time limit is up. There should be a counter standing by the bridge, counting the skaters as they pass under the bridge. The team that gets the most skaters under the bridge in the time limit wins.

There are many other possibilities, of course. For breathers, you might want to show some films, serve sandwiches and refreshments, or whatever else you can get away with. *Ron Richey*

MILK CARTON BOAT RACE

Here's a good game for camp competition between cabin groups. Each team is given several cardboard

milk cartons and a roll of duct tape and instructed to build a boat using only the milk cartons and tape.

Points should be given for:
• Number of cartons used
• Originality
• Number of pounds of weight the boat will support in water without sinking or capsizing
• Winner of race (200-300 yards)

Excitement should be built up during the week until the judging and race on the last day of camp. *Ron Elliot*

NERF FESTIVAL

There is now a wide assortment of Nerf balls and toys on the market. Why not collect a variety of these and have a Nerf Festival? Invite all of the kids to bring any Nerf toys they have. You may also want to go out and purchase a few of your own. There are Nerf frisbees, footballs, basketballs, baseballs, dart guns, and much more. Organize different kinds of ball games, football passing contests, shooting contests, relays, and anything else you can think of. There are hundreds of games that can incorporate the use of Nerf balls, and with a little creativity, you might be able to create a few new ones of your own. *Idi Owen*

NONVIOLENT SOFTBALL LEAGUE

Sometimes church softball leagues fail to achieve the fellowship and positive interaction between church members that was originally intended. In fact, the intense competitiveness of the game often leads to arguments, hurt feelings, and even fights between players. As a summer project, your youth group might attempt to organize a more enjoyable and constructive softball league centered around different game rules. One group, for example, amended the rules so that each team pitched to itself, no stealing or bunting was allowed, and no cleats could be worn. Think up additional rules that could be helpful to your league. *Dave Sauder*

ODDBALL OLYMPICS

Here is another approach to an Olympic-type event featuring all kinds of wild and crazy games. Have the students divide into teams (countries) and compete against each other for the gold medal. Here are some suggested events you can use.

• **Balloon Hurl.** This is simply shot-putting with a big balloon. Draw a circle on the floor or ground in which the hurler must stay, and give him a balloon to shot-put for distance. This can really be unpredictable when done outside on a breezy day.

• **Olympic Egg-Tossing.** Draw a line on the ground and put down distance markers at one- or two-yard intervals. Each team has two tossers who stand on the line two yards apart to begin with, and toss the raw egg back and forth once. They may then elect to step backwards one yard on both sides and toss again. If the egg breaks they lose half the distance they have gone so far. They may stop at anytime after a successful toss, and their score is recorded.

• **Iced-T Race.** Guys on each team wear T-shirts that are tucked in and tied around the waist with a belt or rope. A bucket of ice is dumped into the guys' T-shirts (down the neck), and they must run around a goal and back. Several guys do this, each time carrying the same ice inside their shirts. The last guy dumps the ice back into the bucket and the team that has the most ice still in their bucket wins.

• **Balloon Juggling.** This one is best as an indoor game. Each contestant stands in the middle of a big pile of blown-up balloons. The goal of the game is for the player to get as many balloons up in the air as possible, holding them up off the ground. When the time limit is up, count how many balloons are up. Give each person three tries and take the best score. *Lawrence Stewart*

Olympic Marathon

Divide your entire group into teams. Each team gets a copy of the marathon route (like the one on page 23) and enters the names of their team members in the blanks. A team leader reads the entire route to the team prior to starting and explains the rules.

The marathon is simply a very complicated relay which each team must complete, step by step, following the directions on the route sheet directly. A banana is used as a baton and is passed on, person to person. The entire team is always, with the participants in action, cheering them on. The example below was used in a large church building, but this can be used anywhere, such as a camp, etc.

Give the following instructions to each team:

• The banana must accompany the participant at all times. It must be handed to the person who is in the next event.

• Inside the building there will only be fast walking (no running allowed). Anyone who runs will have to begin his event over again.

• All begin by taking stations.

• If there are extra kids on your team, then they are the ones who will be led blindfolded in step 7.

• Do not begin the event until you have received the banana!

• Fill in the blanks with names of members of your team.

Bill Flanagan

Out-of-Egypt Olympics

For this wacky theme event, first name each team after one of Israel's 12 tribes (though there are 13 names—remember?).

• **People Pyramids.** Build a pyramid using only people who fit certain criteria. For instance, call out, "Use seven people with white socks" or "...with birthdays in the summer" or "...with long hair."

• **Leap Frog.** Relay teams race leap-frog style in memory of the frog plague.

• **Mummy Making.** Each team selects a victim to be wrapped in toilet paper until no part of the victim is showing.

• **Bug Bobbing.** Let a tray of red punch represent the Red Sea—then dump in a bag of Gummi Bugs. In this relay players must run up to the tray, bob for a bug, and return to their teams.

• **Horse Racing.** Riding piggyback on blindfolded Egyptian "horses," players coach their mounts through a sea of water balloons.

• **Speed-Eating Egyptian Treats.** The Israelites were always complaining about the food they left behind in Egypt. Let three volunteers from each team try to

THE OLYMPIC MARATHON!

INSTRUCTIONS

- The banana must accompany the participant at all times. It must be handed to the person who is in the next event.
- Inside the building there will only be fast walking (no running allowed). Anyone who runs will have to begin his event over again.
- All begin by taking stations.
- If there are extra kids on your team, then they are the ones who will be led blindfolded in step #7.
- Do not begin the event until you have received the banana!
- Fill in the blanks with names of members of your team.

1. _________ starts behind metal line just outside starting door (on sidewalk). He rides tricycle to curb line on alley (passes baton).
2. _________ walks on stilts to first floor of Hansen Hall, walks swiftly to top of stairs.
3. _________ sits on top stair and goes down to basement, sitting down, one step at a time. At the bottom of the stairs, she picks up a matchbox with her nose, hops on left foot through first door on the right, to where her teammate is. She passes the matchbox from her nose to her teammate's nose.
4. _________, who just got the matchbox on his nose, says loudly and distinctly:

   Peter Piper picked a peck of pickled peppers.
   A peck of pickled peppers, Peter Piper picked.
   If Peter Piper picked a peck of pickled peppers,
   Where's the peck of pickled peppers Peter Piper picked?
5. _________ and _________ do a wheelbarrow race. Stop by door of Room 103.
6. _________ goes into 103, picks up the broom handle, stands it up straight, holds onto it, turns around it rapidly 20 times, sets it down, and steps over it.
7. _________ verbally directs _________ blindfolded people through an obstacle course and back to Room 106.
8. _________ runs to blackboard in 106, draws a picture of an elephant, and signs her name.
9. _________ stands at bottom of stairs and eats half of a peanut butter sandwich. No liquid may be used.
10. ________ crosses Main Street but may not cross if there is a car as near as the yield sign. He then shoots and makes 5 baskets. Same for return.
11. ________ goes to Youth Department Office and wraps _________ with an entire roll of TP. The wrapped-up person must run out into the hall, where his teammates take off his TP and put it all in the wastebasket.
12. ________ grabs the sack at bottom of stairs and puts on old clothes at first landing. Carrying the sack, he runs outside to the corner of Main and Weber, then back to the door by the alley. Player takes off old clothes just inside that door and puts them back in the sack.
13. ________ pops balloons while walking or sitting, going down steps, to the Pepsi machine.
14. ________ untapes $1, buys pop, and drinks it.
15. ________, ________, ________, ________, ________, and ________, in Canteen, make a pyramid. The person on the top has to unpeel and eat the banana without falling.

eat some of these delicacies at high speed: an onion, a clove of garlic, and a cucumber (all of them small).

• **Manna.** "WHAT IS IT?!" will be the players' cry as they grab a foil-wrapped food item, unwrap it, and eat it as quickly as possible before running back to tag the next player on the team. Wrap carrots, crackers, Twinkies, marshmallows, and apples.

• **O, Ye of Little Faith.** Some people crossing the Red Sea didn't have much faith. Maybe they carried inner tubes—just in case. Make a relay out of cramming a tube over two people who must run to a point and back again before surrendering the tube to the next pair on their team.

• **Into the Promised Land.** The goal of this scavenger hunt is to bring back the biggest sample of everything on the list you compile. Give points to the teams with the longest piece of grass, the biggest pine cone, the largest leaf, and so on. *Lynne Hartke*

SEGA OLYMPICS

Now that so many people play these games, why not have an evening of competition and fun with them? Set up a roomful of video and computer games, or set up a few games at each of several locations. Provide team or individual competition. Print up in advance some score sheets with the name of each game and a place for scores to be recorded. Set up a rotation system so that everyone has a chance to play equally on each game.

This can also be done at a video arcade if you can get permission to take over one of those places for a night or if you can get a special deal on the tokens used in them. Promote it well, serve refreshments, and provide prizes for the best scores, worst scores, etc. You might also select a few secret scores in advance and put them in sealed envelopes. Award prizes to players who come closest to those scores. *Tom Hopewell*

SPOONS TOURNAMENT

This is a spinoff of the card game Spoons. Students really enjoy playing this simple game, so why not put on a tournament to see who the real champions are?

To make the tournament a big success, send out personal invitations for the First Annual Invitational Spoons Tournament, and offer prizes to the winners. It's so crazy that most students will enjoy the novelty of the whole thing.

Start the preliminary rounds in a large room with four or more teams of five or more kids each. Have each team eliminate people one at a time until only two are left from each team. Those two will be the team representatives for the final round.

For the finals go to a different area and have the finalists sit around a table with spotlights shining directly on the table. Have someone in a referee shirt be the dealer. Use new decks of cards and think of other details that might enhance the drama of competition. Present a team trophy and individual prizes for the top three finishers.

Something like this can be an annual event, and you can keep adding names to your trophy year after year. If promoted properly a Spoons Tournament can be a very successful and fun evening. This concept can work, by the way, for almost every kind of game that kids enjoy playing, regardless of skill or athletic ability—and everyone can be involved. *Brian Vreisman*

STROBE MANIA NIGHT

Get a strobe light and play games with it. Most strobes have an adjustment for higher and lower sequencing (greater or lesser intervals between flashes), which makes the following activities fun—especially if you videotape them and replay them for the kids.

• **Creature Feature.** Set the strobe at a high rate and position it about 40 feet from where the kids do their thing. For the trick to work you need total darkness. Have the kids shuffle their feet across the room as rapidly as they can, one at a time. The rest of the group watches as the strobe is turned on. The result is the illusion that the person floats across the room. See who can do it the best. Creativity and video replay make this one a lot of fun.

• **Surprise Tag.** Set the strobe at a low rate. Have kids move from place to place, and the result is that they appear to mysteriously move from one spot to another.

• **Trampoline Delight.** Use a small exercise trampoline and cover it with a piece of dark cloth. Then have the kids do the Creature Feature (above) and end by bouncing up on the trampoline. They'll appear to suddenly shoot up into the air. *David Washburn*

Tin Horn Rodeo

This event was successfully pulled off by a youth group in Texas. It may not be quite as practical for a youth group in New Jersey, but with a little creativity...why not? After all a tin horn rodeo is a rodeo for city-slickers. It calls for the use of one or more horses (real ones) and some real live goats and pigs, which really aren't that hard to come up with. You will also need to find a good location that has a rodeo feel to it, like a fenced-in corral. If you can't come up with any of the above, think of some substitutes that might work. It might even make the whole thing crazier!

Emphasize the cowboy theme. Have everyone wear boots and western attire, play country music, serve a western barbecue, stage mock gunfights, etc. The rodeo can be the main event, with competition for great prizes—new belt buckles, cowboy hats, trophies, or whatever. Rodeo events can include the following:

- **Boot Scramble.** Pile up your boots, select teams, return to a starting line, race to the pile, find your boots, put them on and return to the starting line. Have teams sit down to show when their entire team has crossed the line. First team to sit down wins the event.
- **Rodeo Rider.** You need a real horse and two actual riders. One person rides the horse bareback and the other person leads the horse in a cloverleaf pattern around three oil drums, as they do at real rodeos. The only difference is that at each barrel the person leading the horse stops and hands a water balloon to the rider. Fastest time wins. A two-second penalty is given if a balloon drops or bursts.
- **Goat Tie.** Stake a goat out in the middle of the arena on a 20 foot rope. The event is run like a calf roping event in the rodeo. Use two kids—one to catch the goat and hold it while the other one ties three of its legs. This is a good event to team older kids with younger ones. The event is timed. Shortest time wins the event.
- **Rescue.** You need four people per team for this game. One teammate rides the horse bareback, another teammate leads the horse. From a starting line they race to the first barrel where a third teammate is waiting. The rider jumps off the horse, the person who led the horse gets on, and the third person now leads the horse. They move to the next barrel where the fourth teammate is waiting. Again, the rider jumps off, the old leader gets on, and the fourth teammate now leads the horse to the finish line. The event is timed. Shortest time wins.
- **Milking Contest.** Stake a goat out in the middle and tie a surgical glove filled with water around its middle. Place a small stool next to it for the team member to sit on and a small cup or pail underneath the goat. At the signal the contestant must milk the glove to fill the cup. Be sure the fingers of the gloves have pinholes in them. Time the event and the shortest time wins.

- **Cow Chip Toss.** Take a 20-pound bag of flour and mark off an area of the arena in semicircles, much like that when the discus is thrown. Semi-circles should be marked at 10-foot distances. Mark a large enough area to toss a chip, usually 60 feet or so. Mark a throw line. Have several members of a team line up and toss a chip. A measuring tape of at least 10 feet or more should be on hand to measure the distance. Most of the chips are good for at least two tosses. Farthest toss wins, or you can combine the totals of all the team members. Largest total wins.
- **Greased Pig Chase.** Grease a pig with Vaseline and let it loose at one end of the arena. It's best to divide the kids up into age groups and let each group have an individual chase. The object is to catch the pig and bring it back across the finish line. The team members who get it back across the line win.

Elene Harger

Tin Man Triathlon

This is a scaled-down version of the famous Iron Man Triathlon. It is not only a test of endurance, but an opportunity for kids to help one another reach a tough goal. Any high schooler can enter the event, participating in one event or all three. You can promote participation with Tin Man T-shirts, buttons, or posters.

The course should be challenging, such as a half-mile swim, a 20- to 30-mile bike ride and a two- to four-mile run. But the emphasis should not be on winning as much as helping one another finish the course. It shouldn't be too grueling if they spend a few weeks on conditioning, but make sure you have on hand a nurse, salt pills, and plenty of a sports drink or water.

You might want to top off the Tin Man with a spaghetti feast. Try to get a Christian professional athlete to be a special speaker. *Keith King and Steve Fortosis*

TRANSGENERATIONAL BASKETBALL

Here's a great way to get your whole church involved in a recreation activity that allows for minimum competition and maximum fellowship.

Set up a mixed intramural tournament involving men, women, and youth all on the same team. Each team would consist of two men (adult, college, or high school), one woman (adult, college, or high school), one junior high girl and one junior high guy.

Use regular basketball rules with these restrictions:

- No fast break on offense.
- No full court pressure on defense.
- Everyone on the team gets to play.

The more teams you have the greater your fellowship will be. Plan a round robin tournament and the last night have refreshments provided for everyone. *Tom Prather*

TRIKE OLYMPICS

This event can be held in the church parking lot, a large driveway, or perhaps a tennis court. The area should be large, flat, and smooth. Mark off the race courses in advance. Have a green flag for "go," a yellow one for "caution," and a black and white checkered one for the winner. Gather tricycles—one for each team—or have teams bring their own. (Set a maximum wheel size.) Have pliers and an adjustable wrench on hand to tighten wheels if necessary.

Here are some events to get you started:

- **Indy 500.** Race 500 yards around an oval track, as many laps as it takes.
- **Drag Strip Races.** Race for fastest time, clocking each driver separately.
- **Endurance Race.** Race with one person sitting on the trike with legs over the handlebars. A second person pushes from behind with one foot on the back of the trike and with hands on the handlebars.
- **Egg Pass.** Have a relay race with riders bringing a raw egg along for the ride.
- **Dizzyhead Race.** Spin the riders around three times before they take off toward the finish line. You can blindfold them first and point them in the right direction for a bigger challenge.

- **Backward Race.** Have contestants sit on the trikes facing backward.

Award ribbons for each event and team trophies for overall winners. This event works best with older kids because their size makes riding trikes so ridiculous. *Robert Rainey and Ron Wilburn*

TURTLE TOURNAMENT

For this special event you will need to obtain a number of live turtles. Large turtles are best, but the smaller miniature turtles can be used if the large ones are unavailable. You should have one turtle for every four kids. That constitutes a Turtle Team.

Turtle events can include the following:

- **Turtle Decorating Contest.** Provide paint, dye, paper, ribbon, or whatever and have each team decorate their turtle within a given time limit. Judge for the best job and award points.
- **Turtle Races.** Draw concentric circles on the ground with the largest at about 15 feet in diameter. Place the turtles in the center circle and let them

run in any direction. The turtle which travels the farthest from the center in the time limit is the winner.

• **Turtle Tricks.** Each team is given ten minutes to teach, train, or force their turtle to do a trick. Props may be used and judges give points for creativity, ingenuity, and whether or not the turtle accomplishes the trick.

• **Turtle Chariot Races.** Each team is given cardboard, paper, tape, wheels, etc., and they must construct a chariot and hook it up to their turtle. Judge for the best chariots and then have a race on a track of your choosing.

Keep a tote board with the team names (have each team name their turtles) and their running point total. Have a starting gun, checkered flag, judges with clipboards, etc. Provide trophies for the winners and try to create a derby-day atmosphere. *Dave Gilliam*

WAR OF THE WORLDS

This is an outdoor game. Have kids come in their grubbies. Meet in a vacant lot or a big back yard that can be messed up. Rope off an arena 20 feet square or so, and explain that all the war games will be conducted inside that square. Create two teams of guys to compete against each other and two teams of girls. Make sure that you have plenty of ammunition for the number of players you expect.

Conduct these war games in rounds. The teams stand in their corners of the arena (as in a boxing match) and the ammo is placed in the center. At the sound of the whistle, opponents run to the ammo and begin to break it on their opponents until the next whistle sounds.

• Round 1—Water Balloons
• Round 2—Tomatoes
• Round 3—Eggs
• Round 4—Flour
• Round 5—Mud

Make sure kids don't bring any personal ammo. At the end of each round kids return to their corners while you set up the next round of ammo. You might be able to get free spoiled merchandise from your local grocer for these games. Mix the mud up ahead of time. Dump it in the arena with buckets or a wheelbarrow. Put the flour in small lunch bags and give one bag to each player. Rounds should be one minute in length.

Kids may wear anything they want for protection, such as safety helmets, raincoats, kneepads, etc. The winner is the cleanest team when it's all over.

Make sure players understand that no one is allowed to throw the ammo. Kids must break the ammo on their opponents. Have plenty of game supervisors on hand, especially if you have a large number of kids or a lot of new kids. Try to shoot video of the war games; replay it later after everyone is cleaned up (hose kids down with a garden hose).

PLUNGE PARTY

This is a great idea for a creative swimming party. Divide into teams. Mark ten starting places around the pool numbered one to 10 with the numbers clearly visible. One team member stands at each station. When team members take their turns, they must wear lifeguard hats (or some other hat) while participating in the event. The hat must be passed to the next person in line before he or she may perform the event. The following is done by the team members (each does a different event, one after the other for time):

• Swim across the pool with an egg balanced on a spoon. If the egg falls the swimmer must retrieve it and continue. The team with the best total time wins. Penalty seconds can be given for holding the egg, not making the distance underwater, and so forth.
• Dive to the bottom of the pool and retrieve a brick.
• Cross the pool hand-over-hand from a rope suspended over the water.
• Swim across the pool with a balloon or beach ball tied to one ankle.
• Two contestants have one ankle tied together and must swim in tandem across the pool.
• Sit in an inner tube and hand-paddle backward across the pool; the tube must then be placed over a stake before the next team member starts.
• Dive and swim underwater across the pool (side to side).
• Dunk the youth director in the pool. Either have a regular dunking machine or some target the contestant must hit with a ball. The clothed youth director can then be pushed backward off the diving board.

• Put on a large pair of pants, buckle the belt, and put on a long-sleeve sweatshirt. The contestant must then swim across the pool with a beach ball for buoyancy and toss the ball through designated goal posts. When the ball goes through the goal posts, the clock stops.

Here are some other games you can add to the event or substitute above:

• **Candy Grab.** Toss wrapped candy in the pool (a lot) and kids jump into the pool and see who can retrieve the most.

• **Block Nudge.** Nudge a block (children's wooden alphabet type) with your nose to the other side of the pool.

• **Frog Sub.** The opposite of leapfrog. Kids pair off and alternate going through the other person's legs.

• **Jelly Fish Float.** Float with face in the water with a 20-second time limit.

• **Candle Race.** Light a candle and carry it across the pool (swimming or walking) and back. If the candle goes out, go back to the start and light it again.

• **Dog-Paddle Race.** Kids dog-paddle back and forth or make a four-man relay.

• **Back Float.** Kids float on their backs for time.

• **Tread Water.** Kids tread water (deep end) for longest time.

• **Somersault Race.** Kids swim across the pool, but every time the whistle is blown, they must do a somersault in the water, then continue swimming.

• **Balloon Nudge.** A balloon is nudged across the pool with the head or by splashing it.

• **Punchbowl Party.** For an unusual swimming party, pour half a quart of red food coloring into your pool, stir well, add ice blocks and warm bodies and you have the world's largest punch bowl. You can use the ice blocks for ice sitting contests, or ice soccer (both teams try to get the ice block to their end of the pool). Food coloring does not stain tile and comes out with regular chemicals in about three to five minutes. *Ed Bender, Glen Richardson, and Rick Bundschuh*

WHEELBARROW OLYMPICS

Divide all the kids into equal teams of eight to 10. Each team should have a wheelbarrow. Try to obtain wheelbarrows that are equally matched in size and weight and are well-built. This event should be held on a grassy field for best results. The following wheelbarrow games can then be played:

• **Wheelbarrow Relay.** Teams line up and team members pair off. One person rides in the wheelbarrow, and the other pushes. On the starting signal the wheelbarrow and rider is pushed to a marker about 25 feet away and the two players trade places— the rider becomes the pusher and vice versa. Then the next two team members do the same thing, and so on. The first team to finish is the winner. If the wheelbarrow topples over, they must start over. If the teams are small, do it this way: Players One and Two race up and back, then Player Three gets in the wheelbarrow and is pushed up and back by Player Two. Then Player Three gets out and becomes the pusher, and Player Four gets in and rides—you get the idea.

• **Wheelbarrow Tube Race.** This is a relay, similar to the preceding one except that at the marker there is an inner tube, and the players must squeeze through the tube together before returning to the team.

• **Wheelbarrow Jousting.** Draw a circle with chalk powder or a rope about 15-20 feet in diameter on the ground. Two players from each team get in the circle with a wheelbarrow, one pushing and one riding on his knees. The object of this competition is to remain in the circle and try to upset the opposition. Wheelbarrows cannot touch (they are out if they do) and the riders cannot touch either of the wheelbarrows. Riders can touch each other and the pushers, but no hitting or using the fists in a slugging manner is allowed. The last wheelbarrow to remain in the circle is the winner.

• **Three-Man Relay.** Three members of each team compete at a time with the wheelbarrow. One person rides and the other two push, with one person on each handle. For added fun the rider must stand in the wheelbarrow. No squatting or touching the wheelbarrow with his hands is allowed.

• **Hand Wheelbarrow.** This is the old wheelbarrow race minus a wheelbarrow. Two kids at a time from each team compete in this one. One kid lies down on the ground, face down, in a pushup position, and the other person holds her feet like a wheelbarrow while she walks on her hands. Each pair races to a point and back.

• **Wheelbarrow Hop.** This is another relay with two members from each team competing at a time. Place the wheelbarrow at the starting line with the handles facing away from the team and toward the goal. One player stands on the left side of the wheelbarrow and one player stands on the right, both players facing the finish line. On a signal the player on the left side of the wheelbarrow places his right leg into the wheelbarrow and the player on the right side places her left leg into the wheelbarrow. They grasp the handles in front of them and hop to the goal and back. Penalties are given if anything but the wheel or the players' outer feet touch the ground. *Nelson Enns*

WHICH CLASS RULES?

For a fun, spirited outreach that involves your group's teens as well as their friends, throw this class-competition event two or three times a year. If your group is composed of kids from several schools, adapt it for interschool competition (Which School Rules?). Be sure you are well organized and have plenty of adult help. Here are the rules and points:

1. For each competition the points are as follows:

1st place	**500 pts.**
2nd place	**400 pts.**
3rd place	**300 pts.**
4th place	**200 pts.**

2. Points are awarded to each class for the following:
• The number of students wearing their class color (100 pts. each).
• The number of your class members who are new tonight (150 pts. each).
• The banner promoting your class.
• The class cheer performed by all class members, judged on clarity, volume, and originality.
3. All decisions by judges are final.
4. If there is a question, only the team captain can talk to the emcee.
5. The class with the most points at the end of all competition will be awarded a trophy, which means that THEIR CLASS RULES!, at least until the next Which Class Rules? night.

After the games but before the final scores are announced and refreshments are served, teens from your group can give their testimonies and an adult can speak briefly from 1 Corinthians 9:24 or a similar passage.

An emcee for the evening can explain the games:

• **Blindfold Relay.** Lead your blindfolded partner through the obstacle course without touching each other. If you touch you must start over.
• **Wheelbarrow Relay.** One driver, one wheelbarrow. If the driver drops the wheelbarrow, you must start over.
• **Strobe-Light Volleyball.** Station 12 players on the court to play by strobe light. Rotate players on and off the court every five points. Play to 11.

For the following events, one guy and one girl from each team must compete. The same person cannot do more than one event.

• **Longest headstand.** Everyone starts at same time.
• **Loudest burp.** Use a microphone.
• **Most push-ups.** No more than five seconds between push-ups.
• **Fastest dresser.** Completely—buttons buttoned, shoelaces tied—and with no help from team members.
• **Biggest bubble.** Two-minute limit.

David Smith

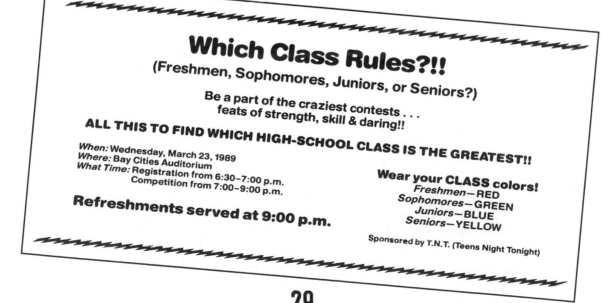

Which Class Rules?!!
(Freshmen, Sophomores, Juniors, or Seniors?)
Be a part of the craziest contests . . .
feats of strength, skill & daring!!
ALL THIS TO FIND WHICH HIGH-SCHOOL CLASS IS THE GREATEST!!

When: Wednesday, March 23, 1989
Where: Bay Cities Auditorium
What Time: Registration from 6:30–7:00 p.m.
Competition from 7:00–9:00 p.m.

Refreshments served at 9:00 p.m.

Wear your CLASS colors!
Freshmen—RED
Sophomores—GREEN
Juniors—BLUE
Seniors—YELLOW

Sponsored by T.N.T. (Teens Night Tonight)

WINTER OLYMPICS

If you happen to be fortunate (or unfortunate) enough to live in an area where it snows, the Winter Olympics is a great event that can involve everyone. The games listed below are best played on warmer days when the snow is starting to melt and the sun is shining. A large area such as a football field or park area would be ideal.

• **Three-Person Ski Race.** For this event you will need to make a few pairs of simple three-person skis.

Each ski is made out of a one-inch-thick board 6 feet long by 6 inches wide. With the front end rounded, use three bands of inner tube—bicycle inner tubes work great—for the footholds. Secure the bands to the sides of the skis with an extra piece of wood to prevent the rubber from tearing at the nail. Make sure you have the bands just tight enough across the skis so that a person's foot can get in with boots. Be sure to bring along an extra band or two and a hammer and nails. Teams can race against the clock, against each other, or relay style.

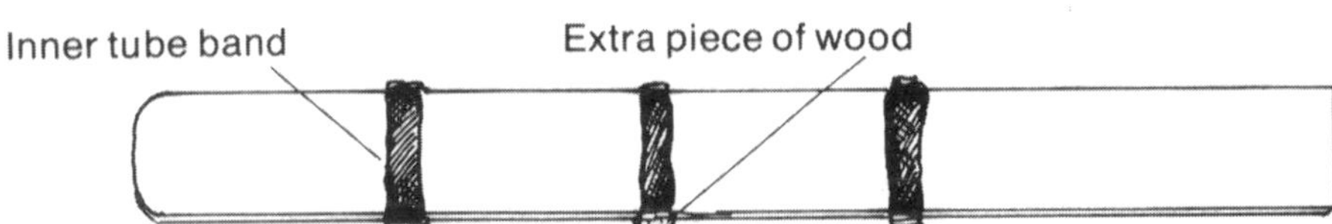

• **Stilt Relay.** Each team member races on stilts as far as they can for 30 seconds. The next team member takes over from that point. Falling forward is not counted in the distance.

• **Sled Spring.** One person (usually the smallest) sits on a sled while the rest of the team pulls them with a 20-foot rope. The race course can be straight, up and back, or obstacle.

• **Snow Mountain.** Teams compete to make the highest mountain of snow. Five minutes is plenty of time.

• **Snowball Throw.** Kids throw snowballs for distance (have sponsors stand just outside of range for incentive) and accuracy (through tire or other object).

• **Snow Creation.** Have each team build a figure out of snow to be judged for its artistic quality.

• **Snowmobile Slalom.** Team members are pulled behind a snowmobile on a giant inner tube and try to grab flags stuck in the snow without falling off the tube. Be sure to keep the speed down.

• **Snowshoe Games.** Try races, obstacle-course runs, and soccer games on snowshoes. The results can be a lot of fun.

The key to a successful Winter Olympics is to be well-prepared and keep the event short and alive. Ice-cold young people don't cooperate very well.

If you want to have more fun, but everyone is frozen, move into a nice, warm building for indoor winter Olympic games. Warm up with hot chocolate and a fire first. Then try these indoor versions of winter sports classics.

• **Biathlon.** Make cross-country skis for indoor use with some cardboard and masking tape. Just cut long strips of cardboard for the skis, and tape an old pair of shoes to them for the boots. Then set up your course with three or so shooting stations along the way. Arm your biathletes with water guns. At each station sits one of their teammates with lit candle in mouth. The biathlete shoots out the candle flame, skis on to repeat the process at the next stations, then skis to the finish.

• **Downhill Slalom.** This is a wonderful event if you have access to a long staircase. Make slalom gates out of short dowels with construction paper hung on one end to look like a flag. Tape these onto the stair railing so the flags hang into the path of the downhiller—like this:

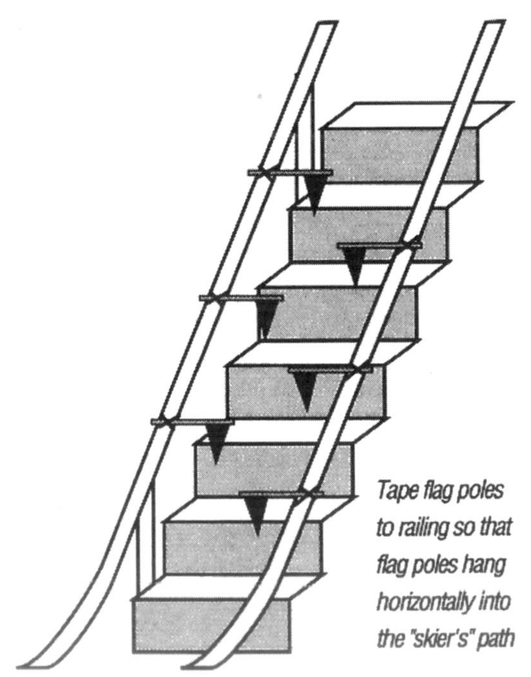

Tape flag poles to railing so that flag poles hang horizontally into the "skier's" path

To discourage kids from racing down the stairs and breaking their necks, don't make this a timed event. Instead, let the challenge be for each skier to ski down the stairs with a mouthful of water, which goes into an empty bucket at the bottom. The team to reach the bottom with the most water is declared the winner.

• **Ski Jump.** In this ingenuity contest give each team a Ping-Pong ball (with a picture of a skier drawn on it), a piece of poster board, and a roll of Scotch tape. Each team must develop the best way to propel their skier the farthest distance. And just so it's legal to call it ski jump, give them a ski to jump. In order for it to be a legal jump, the skier must at least make the length of the ski. *Alan D. Michael, Pat McGlone, and Gordon Swenson*

SNOW PENTATHLON

Divide into teams of eight, and have the following five events set up. Teams must compete in each event to achieve the best time. The teams proceed from one event right on to the next. Some of these games may be kind of rough, so take care that they are well-supervised to ensure safety. You may want to change the rules slightly to one or more of them, if they seem too difficult for your group.

• **Stand-Up-and-Go.** The eight team members are tied tightly together at the waist to form a circle. They begin by sitting on the snow facing out. At a signal they must all stand up together without touching the snow with their hands.

• **Slalom.** Remaining tied together in a circle, they must pass through the starting gate and run (or walk) through a slalom course marked with ski poles stuck in the snow. They must pass on alternate sides of each successive ski pole. If a ski pole is knocked down, the team must return to the starting gate and begin again.

• **Tubecide.** The team may now untie between two of the team members and stretch out in a straight line. They are given two inner tubes which they must take to the top of the tubing run and come down the run as a team on the two tubes. Use caution on this one if the run is quite steep or fast—someone could be dragged quite a distance if they fall off the tube.

• **Hill Roll.** Remaining hooked together in a straight line the team must now travel from the top of a small hill to the bottom of the hill without standing on their feet. At the bottom they may stand up and untie from each other.

• **Octa-Ski.** Two 2x6 pieces of lumber each have short rope loops attached to them at one foot intervals. Each team member must place a foot through a loop on each ski and the team skis the final 200 feet to the finish line.

Usually we forget who won the event but remember the teamwork, competitive spirit, and effort, which are more important than winning anyway.

If you like, you can also race individually or in teams. Try categories such as men and women's singles, men and women's doubles, mixed doubles, stunt riding, slalom, etc.

Award points for distance and form. Poor form criteria include wipeouts, turning the inner tube while riding it down the hill, closing eyes, and so on. Stunt riding is based on originality and distance. *Orv Gingerich*

WRECK IN THE STREET

First of all, get permission from the local police department to block off a side street near your church. They will usually be glad to supply barricades. Begin the activities with typical street games, such as wheelbarrow races, tricycle races, sack races, ice slide (one sits on block of ice while next player pushes), etc.

After about an hour take a refreshment break. During this time the young people prepare ammo for the battle. Then everyone gathers for the wreck-in-the-street battles using water balloons, shaving cream, water paint, and eggs. Usually the fire department will be glad to wash the streets for you. If not—good luck!

The kids will talk about this for a long time. The neighbors will, too! It can become an annual event. *Randall Perry*

SEAFOOD SPECIAL

A number of events can be developed by using frogs, crabs, turtles, snails, etc. Of course, the traditional frog-jumping contest is always a winner, but many other ideas can be adapted: turtle races, crab races, turtle football (first one to cross opposing team's goal line). What makes these events appealing is the publicity and elaborateness. Each contestant or team should have a week to choose and train their entry. Each entry should be elaborately decorated or painted. The judge should dress accordingly with loud horns, whistles, and guns to start and finish the race.

BARNYARD OLYMPICS

City folks and country folks alike enjoy activities with a rural theme. Add your own ideas to these games with a rustic twist:

• **Hay Toss.** Open up a bale of hay and give a handful of hay to each player. The winner is the one who throws the hay the farthest. (There is a way to throw hay to make it travel father than you think. Experiment!)

• **Egg Scramble.** Bring two dozen wooden eggs and a few raw eggs. Using barriers or tape, create a chicken coop with nooks and crannies for hiding eggs. It should be about 20 yards from one end to the other. Divide the group into two or more teams. One team at a time enters the coop; half the team searches for eggs at one end of the coop, and the other half searches on the opposite side. When players find an egg, they must throw it across the coop to their teammates who must catch it. If they don't catch the eggs, they have to do the toss over again until it is successful. The team who has all of their eggs found and tossed wins. The catch, of course, is the few real eggs. Have paper towels on hand to clean up the inevitable mess.

• **Hen-Scratching Relay.** Divide your group into two teams and have them make two single-file lines with a pile of blocks at the head of each line (one block per person). On "Go!" the first players in line must pick up one block with their mouths, carry it across the barnyard to the nest, and return to tag the next players in line. Play continues until the nest is full of eggs. The last player to deliver a block must sit on the nest and cackle, along with the rest of his or her teammates. The first team to cackle is the winning team.

• **Barnyard-Animal Relay.** Divide the group into teams. Tape down a starting line and, across the room, a finish line. Have each member of each team perform the following actions in the sequence listed. Each player performs the actions when the teammate just ahead has completed the last action and crossed the line.

Dog: Roll over and bark
Rooster: Stand up, cock hands under arms, and crow
Pig: Lie on back, wiggle, and oink
Cow: Get on all fours and moo loudly
Horse: Gallop to the finish line while neighing

• **Cow-Trough Relay.** Best played outdoors, this game requires a large trough, several boxes of oatmeal, brown food coloring, large paper cups, lots of bananas, and a five-gallon bucket for each team.In the trough mix the oatmeal with water, smashed bananas, and food coloring. Place the trough in the vicinity of the starting line and the buckets about 100 yards away from the trough. Divide the group into teams, and give paper cups to all players. At the signal all the players run to the trough, fill up their cups, and then attempt to get to their team's bucket to dump the contents. The first team to fill their bucket wins. To guarantee a mess of fun, be sure to leave the oatmeal runny and make appropriate barnyard comments about the smell, color, texture, and so on.

• **Cow Chip Glide.** This is the urban version using Frisbees. Each contestant competes to see who can throw the Frisbee the farthest distance. Each person gets three chances.

• **Corn Cob Fling.** You begin with a large cardboard box (washing machine or refrigerator box). The front of the box is cut away, and the box is painted brown to resemble the outhouse of former days. A chair facing the door is placed inside. Each contestant is given six corn cobs and told to take his/her seat inside the box and throw the cobs over his/her shoulder as close to the bullseye as possible. (A washtub can be used as the target.) The person who gets the closest to the target wins the event.

• **Barnyard Dash.** One of the most coveted skills on the farm is the ability to run through the barnyard without stepping into something (if you know what we mean by something). Place some tires in a staggered manner and tell the contestants that they must run the course by putting a foot into each tire as fast as they can. The winner is the one that can run the course in the shortest amount of time. One thing you forget to tell the contestants: there is a mud puddle under one of the tires. *Dale D. Hardy and Bob Messer*

AMERICAN GLADIATORS COMPETITION

Cash in on the popularity of "American Gladiators" with a summer-long competition or a special event tournament. Some of these games require skill and athletic ability, but some are based on dumb luck. Award points as follows:

First place	25 points
Second place	20 points
Third place	15 points
Fourth place	10 points
Fifth place	5 points
Sixth place	3 points
Seventh place	2 points

Organize these gladiatorial games as a competition between either individuals or teams.

First, all participants choose gladiator names. Do your best to dissuade the kids from using the TV names. Be creative! Use adults or older teens as the "house gladiators."

• **Soar.** Contestants make paper airplanes of their own designs, then launch them toward a target (say, a Frisbee on the floor). Decide whether you'll note where the plane first touches ground, or where the plane comes to rest. The craft nearest the target wins.

• **Tug-of-War.** Students compete with a house gladiator. Award points according to how long the competitors hold out.

• **Shot Put.** "Put" a bowling ball as you would a shot. The most distance wins.

• **On a Roll.** Teens roll a car tire across the church parking lot. Award points by the length of time they can keep the tire rolling upright.

• **Hot Air Balloon.** Contestants blow bubbles with bubble gum or bubble soap. Judges determine biggest bubble.

• **Bombs Away.** From a high spot, like a stairway landing or stabilized ladder, kids throw croquet balls toward a target. Closest hits win.

• **Jumpin' Jehoshaphat.** Kids throw croquet balls into a bucket while jumping on a trampoline. Award five points for each ball in the bucket.

• **Deflate.** Toss bowling pins (purchased from or donated by the local bowling alley) into the middle of a car tire from 10 feet away. Award five points for each pin that stays in the tire.

• **Standing Tall.** Compete for longest time walking on stilts. If you have more than one teen who can stay up indefinitely (30 seconds or more), let them compete in timed races for points.

• **Punt the Panda.** Kick a stuffed animal toward a target. Closest animal (with the most stuffing still inside) wins.

• **Batter Up.** A house gladiator pitches baseballs to batting youth group members. Mark off the field into five zones that radiate out and away from home plate:

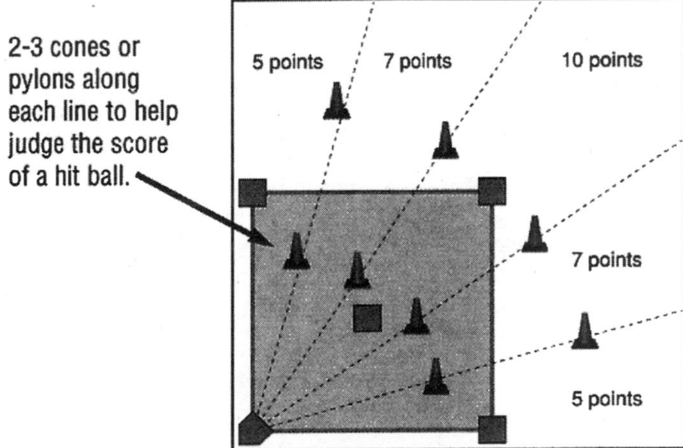
2-3 cones or pylons along each line to help judge the score of a hit ball.
5 points
7 points
10 points
7 points
5 points

• A hit up the middle: 10 points
• Slightly wide to the right or left: 7 points
• Outside zones on either end: 5 points

One round consists of 10 pitches per batter, whether hits, strikes, or misses. Play two rounds.

• **Power Ball.** Mark off a 25- by 50-foot playing field

in a grassy area. Set a five-gallon bucket at each of the four corners, and one in the center. Fill two barrels with water balloons and set one barrel just outside each end of the playing field. Designate a scorekeeper.

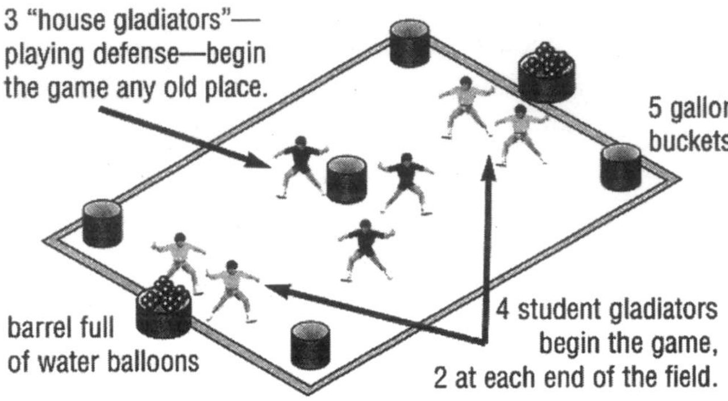

Four student gladiators try to get up to six water balloons into the buckets—in spite of the best efforts of *three* house gladiators, who try to break the balloons before they land in the buckets. Students must stay within boundaries except for trips to the balloon-storage buckets in order to restock. Two kids begin play near the barrel at one end, while the other two begin at the other end.

Physical contact isn't exactly prohibited, but outlaw deliberate knocking down of other players. Set a time limit of a minute or so for each round.

• **Assault.** Mount a target on a raised platform at one end of a 40- by 80-foot playing field. Example: a Hula Hoop covered with paper propped up in the back of a pickup truck. Have a second target ready and waiting.

Now for the barriers. Four tables will do. Arrange them like this:

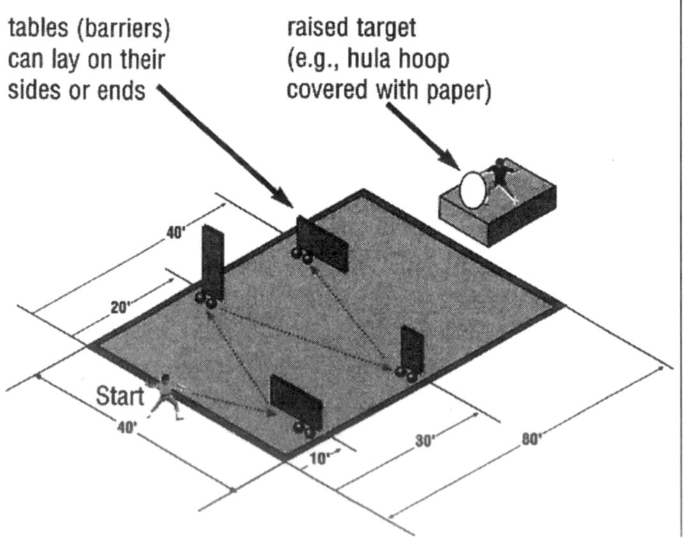

Before each round of play, place two balls (four-square, volleyball, football, Nerf, etc.) behind each barrier.

Each student gladiator (wearing headgear and goggles) has a one-minute time limit. Starting at the back end of the field, about 10 feet away from the first barrier, she runs to the first barrier, throws the two balls she finds there at the target, runs to the next barrier, and so on. All the while she is doing her best to avoid being hit by balls thrown at her by the house gladiator up on the platform. If the runner has thrown all eight balls, has not been hit by a tennis ball, and still has time left, she may run to touch the target—at which time you have a winner!

Award five points to runners for each ball they throw at the target, and 25 bonus points each time they hit it. If several players hit the target, rank them in order of the least number of throws.

Have the waiting players fan out at the back of the field to retrieve tennis balls.

COMMANDO CHURCH

During your next lock-in—or during a dark evening at the church—teach about spiritual warfare from Ephesians 6:10-18.

As the kids get bored with your traditional message, tell them it's time to jump into battle. Explain the rules of war before proceeding to the sanctuary, where it's pitch black and you're broadcasting taped sound effects of war. Set up a guard tower between or on top of the pews in a central location. Jail is in an adjacent room. Assign several students to be guards. The head guard stands in the tower with a searchlight (flashlight).

The kids maneuver in, over, around, and under the pews and furnishings, trying to reach the secret operative, to whom they give a password and receive a token (cut-up coffee stirrers work great). The secret operative could be right under the guard tower. Then they make their way back to base, receive credit for the tokens, and go on another mission.

Meanwhile, the head guard watches for movement and shines the light on vulnerable players. Players hit by the light freeze and are escorted by other guards to the jail. After a designated time, the guards can release the prisoners back into the game. The head guard may hold an air raid, during which the flashlight is left off for 10 seconds to ensure that students can get through to the secret operative.

After the game you can draw many spiritual parallels, including that spiritual warfare is conducted in the sanctuary, among other places—by prayer, praise, etc. *Bruce Lininger*

FRISBEE FROLIC

For this special event, all you need is an open field and a few Frisbees. Divide the group into teams and play the following Frisbee games:

• **Distance Frisbee.** Line teams up in columns behind a line. Each player gets three throws for distance. After each person throws the Frisbee, a judge marks the spot. The thrower retrieves the Frisbee for the next person in line. Farthest throw and the team with the best combined total wins.

• **Accuracy Frisbee.** The teams stay lined up in their columns behind the line and a tire is set upright about 25 feet away from each team. One by one, the team members try to toss the Frisbee through the tire. Again, they retrieve their own Frisbee and return it to the next person in line. The most successful throw wins. Or, each person continues throwing until successful, and the first team to finish wins.

• **Team Toss Frisbee.** Line up two teams opposite each other about 20 feet apart. The first person on one team throws to the first person on the other team who tosses the Frisbee back to the second person on the first team, who throws it back to the second person on the second team, and so on—like this:

Team One ● ● ● ● ● ● ● ● ● ● ● ● ● ● ● ●

↓↗↓↗↓↗↓ etc.

Team Two ● ● ● ● ● ● ● ● ● ● ● ● ● ● ● ●

The thrower's team scores a point if the catcher drops the Frisbee and the catcher's team scores a point if the thrower tosses the Frisbee beyond the reach of the catcher who must keep his feet planted. There should be a neutral judge for each game. You can play to a certain score or until everyone has thrown the Frisbee four or five times.

• **Crazy Legs Frisbee.** The teams line up in columns behind a starting line and there is a finish line 20 feet away. Each team has one Frisbee. The first person places the Frisbee between his knees and runs to the finish line where he tosses the Frisbee back to the next person. If the Frisbee is not caught, the thrower must go back and do the whole routine all over again. First team with all its members across the finish line wins.

• **Frisbee Water Brigade.** Teams are lined up in columns behind a starting line. Each team has a Frisbee (should be the same size for each team), a large pan of water by the starting line, and a wide mouth quart jar about 20 feet away. The object is to get as much water in the jar as quickly as possible by carrying it in the Frisbee. The team that fills the jar the most times in two minutes wins. Obstacles such as chairs to cross, or stairways, etc. add to the fun.

• **Frisbee Stand-Off.** You need one expendable Frisbee for this one. The object is to get as many people as possible with their feet partially or wholly on the Frisbee or with their weight completely supported by people on the Frisbee. Give them two minutes to practice, and then a one minute period to get the people on. At the end of the time limit, count them. The team with the most wins.

• **Freestyle Frisbee.** This is for the hot dogs. You can have one or two participants from each team demonstrate their best freestyle Frisbee throw. This could be around the back, under the leg, over the head, double skip, boomerang, or any other kind of fancy or crazy shot. A panel of distinguished and expert judges determine the winners.

• **Accuracy.** Using a garden hose or rope placed on the ground, make a semicircle around an object, such as a garbage can, at which each participant will throw. Place the object about 15 feet from all points on the semi-circle. All of the competitors throw at the same time. Each person gets two throws at each distance. Those who hit the object at that distance remain in the game. Those who miss it after two attempts are out. The object is then moved back three feet and each person left in the competition again gets two chances to hit it once. If the group is small they can throw individually rather than at the same time.

• **Distance.** Each person throws against those in the

same grade and of the same sex. Stretch a hose or rope out to make a straight line. From behind the line all throw at the same time unless the group is small. A judge will determine whose Frisbee went the greatest distance when it came to rest.

• **Boomerang.** All can compete together in this event. Have all the competitors line up in a straight line behind the marker facing into the wind. At a signal everyone throws a Frisbee at least 15 feet into the air at an angle so that it will come back in a boomerang fashion. The person who throws the Frisbee that returns the closest to the throwing line is the winner.

• **Single Frisbee Catch.** Have the participants pick a partner with whom they can compete. Two markers are stretched parallel to each other about 15 feet apart. One partner stands behind one marker and the other partner stands behind the other marker directly opposite him. Only one Frisbee is needed for each pair. Have all the Frisbees on one side. At a signal all of those on one side throw their Frisbees to their partners on the other side, who must catch it without crossing the marker. Those who do not catch it leave the game with their partner. After each throw one marker is moved back about three feet.

• **Double Frisbee Catch.** This is somewhat more difficult than the above events. Keeping the same partners, have each person take a Frisbee. Again make two parallel lines but about 10 feet apart. The rules are the same as the Single Frisbee Catch except that each person throws his Frisbee at the same time and each partner must catch the other's Frisbee. Emphasize that all Frisbees are to be thrown at the same time when the signal is given.

• **Doubles Distance.** One partner from each pair lines up at a starting point. Each throws the Frisbee as far as possible in a straight line away from the starting point. Then his partner stands exactly where the Frisbee landed, and at the signal each of the other partners throws the Frisbee as far as possible. The pair with the greatest combined distance is the winner.

• **Opposite-Handed Variation.** In the above events lefties throw right-handed and vice versa.

Jim Berkley, Dave Strople, and Samuel Hoyt

MUD BOWL

Your students will have no trouble inviting their friends to this gig. Mud Bowl requires land where a pit can be dug and where you (or another operator) can use a tractor or rototiller. Once the pit is dug you will need to drench it. (This takes *lots* of water.) Leave the water on for the entire night before the event, if possible, to soak the area completely.

Tell kids to come with—

- Old, old clothes on.
- Trashed tennis shoes (if they aren't trashed when they come, they'll be trashed by the end of Mud Bowl).
- A set of clean clothes and extra shoes.
- A plastic trash bag for their muddy clothes.

Equipment you'll need:

- a big ball
- volleyball net and standards
- inflated inner tubes
- eggs
- rolled-up newspapers
- pantyhose cut in half
- cinder blocks, and wood pallets (or skids) to set the blocks on
- a railroad tie
- old pillows with pillowcases
- hay bales
- firewood, matches, lighter fluid
- food
- paper plates and plasticwear
- a water source and hoses
- camera or camcorder

Now let the Mud Bowl games begin—all documented by an adult assigned to video and take still photos of the events. Games usually last about two hours.

• **Big Ball Volleyball.** Starting with this enables everyone to get muddy at least up to their calves—which is nothing compared to what's coming...

• **American Eagle.** No volleyball equipment? Then start the mud ball rolling with this classic field game, adapted to a mud pit. Several players stand in the middle of the pit, and the rest on the sides of the pit. At the signal all the outside players run from one side of the pit to the other. Those in the middle try to tag the runners. Tagged runners join the chasers in the middle. Continue until the last player is tagged.

• **Tube Tug.** Place seven or eight inflated inner tubes in the middle of the pit. Divide the kids into two teams, each line about 25 feet away from and on opposite sides of the mud pit. At a signal they all run to grab the tubes and bring them back to their own sides. Award points for each tube retrieved. Play several rounds, varying the teams each round: freshmen and sophomores against juniors and seniors, males against females, everyone against the juniors—whatever works for your group.
• **Egg Smash.** Needed per player: a rolled-up newspaper, one raw egg per round, one pantyhose leg each. Kids tie the eggs on top of their heads with the pantyhose. At a signal, teens use their newspapers to protect their eggs from being smashed while they work at smashing the eggs of other players. For one of the rounds, play with teams of three or four.
• **Jousting.** On a pallet, stack cinder blocks four high (the pallet is to give the blocks some stability in the mud). Build another block-and-pallet tower six feet or so away. Then bridge across the two stacks of blocks with a railroad tie. Teens compete against each other by sitting on the railroad tie and using a pillow to knock the other player into the mud. To keep it somewhat fair, try to match up opponents by height and weight. For safety's sake, you may want to put hay bales around the pallets or have sponsors stand in front of them so kids don't hit the cinder blocks when they fall.
• **Mud Packing.** Divide into teams and have them cover one member of their team completely with mud, except for the head, of course. Judge for the best job.
• **Mud Sculptures.** See which team can create the most recognizable form out of mud within a specified time limit.
• **Mud Ball.** Use your imagination here. The best ballgame to play is a variation of football, with tackling in the mud, etc. Any other ballgame can also be played.
• **Mud Jumping.** Set up a track or ramp and have students jump for distance into the mud. Splat.
• **Group Picture.** About this point in the Bowl, let the photographer get a group shot. Participants will be muddy enough for a memorable shot, but still recognizable.
• **Free for All.** After the group shot, explain whatever rules of Free for All you want to establish. Basically, kids should follow at least a muddy version of the Golden Rule. Let students who don't want to participate a chance to get out of the pit. Blow your whistle to signal the start. A Free for All is good usually for only five to 10 minutes.
• **Cleanup.** When Mud Bowl games are over, it's time for everyone to get cleaned up—and it may take a while if your group's on the large side. Have at least two water hoses available. Figure each teen will require five minutes at the hose. Make sure there are facilities for males and females to change clothes in. Parents will love you if you urge their kids to take responsibility for washing their own clothes as soon as they get home, instead of leaving them in a sodden heap in the garage.

A supper—and maybe singing around a campfire—is a fun way to end the Mud Bowl. And start planning Mud Bowl II for next year! *Joel M. Barber and Larry Lawrence*

SHOPPING MALL TAG

This game is simple and lots of fun. Get permission to play it in the mall first, otherwise you can play this at any busy location. After taking the group to the mall, give each person a blank index card. Two of the cards will have holes punched in them. Whoever receives them are It, but they won't tell anyone who they are.

When the game begins, everyone gets about five minutes to scatter and hide, but they must stay inside the mall at all times and not interfere with shoppers or salespeople or merchandise. The Its can begin tagging people after five minutes are up. When kids get tagged, they must go with It to one of the youth sponsors who is stationed in a designated place in the mall. The sponsor will punch the tagged kid's cards, making them Its also. They have to try to tag others. Set a time limit and have everyone reassemble at a designated site.

The winners are those who weren't tagged or It who tagged the most people. Every time It brings someone in to have his card punched, It also receives another hole. By the way, running is grounds for disqualification.

Winners can be rewarded with gift certificates to the food court. *Bill Curry*

WORLD'S LARGEST PILLOW FIGHT

For this event you will need a gym or a room large enough to accommodate a lot of action and which will be easy to clean. Each kid brings a pillow from home and sits on it during preliminary activities. Music, crowd breakers, a speaker, etc., are all good at the beginning of your meeting. At the close the pillow fight takes place.

Boundaries are marked on the floor, and no one out-of-bounds can participate. No furniture pillows are allowed (big foam-type) and check to make sure kids don't put rocks, etc., in the pillow cases. When the whistle blows everyone starts swinging pillows for one minute. When the whistle blows ending the first period, everyone must sit down on their pillow immediately. The last one to do so gets a penalty (pie in the face). Those who have had it are given the opportunity to leave the fight.

The fight continues in one-minute periods until everyone is pooped-out or their pillow breaks. If a person's pillow breaks, he is automatically out. Of course a giant feather mess is left behind which can be cleaned up with large industrial-type vacuums. In smaller pillow fights ordinary vacuum cleaners will work.

FEATHER GLADIATORS

Divide the group into teams and ask all players to get their pillows. Allow teams to choose their names. Assign a scorekeeper to write the teams' names on a chalkboard or marker board and keep score. Since this can get wild, have players remove their glasses before you begin.

Play the following games.

- **Use Your Head Relay.** Players take turns racing around a fixed object, such as a chair, at the opposite side of the room. During the first round, players balance pillows on their heads (no hands allowed).
- **Waddle Relay.** Runners hold the pillows between their knees (no hands allowed).
- **Cushy Caterpillar Slalom.** Next direct the entire

team to race at the same time, moving like a huge caterpillar with a pillow between each pair of players. They cannot touch the pillows with their hands, but must hold onto each other. Line up several chairs between the starting and ending points so that the caterpillars wind in and out. Do not make the caterpillars too long to avoid a domino effect if someone falls.

• **Goliath Clone War.** Have each team pick a Goliath. Have two Goliaths stand blindfolded on a low bench. With helpers standing by for safety, each tries to knock the other off the bench with his pillow.

• **Dodge Pillow.** Like dodgeball. Two teams on opposite sides of a line throw pillows at each other. If hit—even if kids catch the pillows—they're out. Exception: on each team's side are two pieces of paper. Anyone standing on the paper when catching a pillow puts the thrower out. A player may stand on a paper no longer than three seconds at a time. Game is over when one team loses all its players.

• **Flamingo Free-for-All.** Your standard pillow fight, though on only one foot. When a player's flamingo foot touches the ground, he's out.

• **Pillow Hockey.** Like hockey or soccer, only with a playground ball as a puck and pillows as sticks.

• **Target Shoot.** Place a target on a table and line up the kids behind a line 20 feet away with their pillows as projectiles.

• **Obstacle Course.** Set up simple obstacles that must be run by the kids in pairs as they hold a pillow between their heads without using their hands.

• **Hat Whap.** After players make hats for themselves out of newspaper sheets, the object is to whap the hats off others while trying to keep yours on. Kids cannot hold their hats on with their hands. They're out when their hats are whapped off their heads.

• **War Log.** Robin Hood and Little John on the log bridge, only with pillows instead of quarterstaves. Kids fight one-on-one, a pair at a time, on a log or bench or 2x4.

• **Indian Pillow.** Adapt Indian wrestling (two players, their right hands grasped in a handshake, and their right feet touching on the outside edge—the object is to make either foot of the opponent move) by allowing wrestlers to hang on to pillows in their free, left hands. The first player to move a foot is out.

• **Free-for-All Finale.** Limit this no-holds-barred pillow fight to three minutes.

Jim Walton and Kelvin Lustick

SCAVENGER HUNTS

SCAVENGER HUNTS

What better way to prepare your kids for the harsh realities of life than by having them beg, borrow, and scrounge for a bagful of eminently worthless items? The rules of a scavenger hunt are simple; the variations, endless. (For treasure hunts, where there's just one thing to search for instead of a bunch of things, see the next section, "Treasure Hunts," on page 71).

A to Z Scavenger Hunt

Each of your five or six teams needs a vehicle as well as a responsible, licensed driver. Determine what time each team must return to the starting point. The goal: to collect evidence from 26 shops and stores they visit—one store for each letter of the alphabet (**A**rby's, **B**lockbuster Video, **C**loth World, etc.).

- Each letter is given a random point value before the teams venture out.
- Letters such as Q or Z should be assigned a higher value than the more common letters, such as A or T, since they might be more difficult to locate.
- Evidence from the stores can be a business card, a bag imprinted with the business's name, a matchbook, etc.

Upon their return teams total their scores and a winner is declared. Deduct one point for every minute a team is delayed beyond the time limit.

Cheryl Ehlers

Aging Scavenger Hunt

Divide into teams and give each one a list of years from the present year working backwards for about thirty years (1997, 1996, etc.). Kids must scavenge for items (license plates, coins, drivers' licenses, books with readable copyright dates printed in them, deeds, certificates, and so on) with the dates marked on them indelibly. You can specify that only one item per date is allowed or that only one kind of item per team is allowed. In other words if the team brings back a book with the date 1974 printed on it, they cannot use a book for any other date. This forces them to be a little more creative than bringing back a whole pile of books. Set a time limit. The team that returns with the most acceptable items wins. *Dan Brandell*

Action Scavenger Hunt

Each person or team receives the list on page 45 and goes door-to-door as in a normal scavenger hunt. At each house the person at the door is asked to perform one of the actions on the list. If they comply the item can be crossed off. The team with the most crossed off at the end of the time limit, or the first team to complete the entire list, is the winner. Only one item may be done at each house. For added fun have them take along video cameras and capture it all on tape. *Larry Maland*

Back-to-School Scavenger Hunt

On page 46 you'll find the list of "school supplies." Create groups and assign an adult sponsor to drive each group around. You can stipulate that groups can go to only their own homes for the supplies. Whatever you do, make sure all of the items are returned following the hunt as some of them may be expensive. *Dale Hill*

Auto-Graph Scavenger Hunt

For this scavenger hunt, give each small group some white letter-size sheets of paper and a copy of page 47. The list includes different kinds of cars and other vehicles which have wheels or tires. The idea is to get each vehicle to run over a white sheet of paper so that the imprint of the tire tread is left on the paper. Each auto-graph is then verified by the signature of the owner of the vehicle or by the youth sponsor who accompanies each scavenger hunt group.

You may make certain vehicles worth more points if they are obviously more difficult to obtain. In addition to the suggestions below, it's a good idea to list the cars of specific people in your congregation, which means the kids will have to go to the people's homes to try and get them to drive their car over the piece of paper. *Dan Naramor*

Blackbeard's Treasure Scavenger Hunt

Give your students the list of piratical items on page 48. As in all scavenger hunts, define the boundaries and the deadline, then let them loose to board and pillage various homes for the donated items.

Your teenage cutthroats can use the occasion to leave fliers, brochures, or newsletters about upcoming events, regular meeting times, etc. For extra pizazz design a flier especially for distribution during the scavenger hunt and title it Treasure Map, which can be anything from directions to your church or youth group event to a gospel message.

When kids return with the booty, pour all the drinks they've collected into one punch bowl, and voila—Pirate Punch. With any luck, it will taste surprisingly good. *Steve Smoker*

Bible Scavenger Hunt

With the help of their Bibles, players first must decode the numbers to determine what it is they have to find. For example, 1-22-1-12-9 means Old Testament (1)—New Testament is signified by (2)—Song of Solomon (the 22nd book), chapter 1, verse 12, and the 9th word in the verse—that is, perfume. (This example was taken from the New International Version. Be sure your kids use only the version you designed the code around.)

For starters you can send the kids after fruit (2-3-13-7-23), snow (1-25-51-7-18), bread (2-1-26-26-7), and a footstool (2-19-1-13-21).

Len and Sheryl DiCicco

Auto-Graph Scavenger Hunt

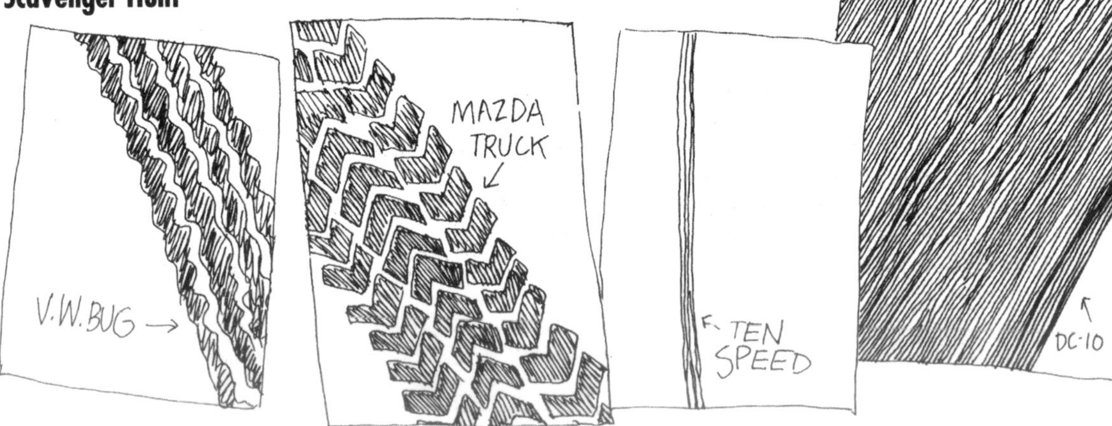

ACTION SCAVENGER HUNT

1. Sing two verses of "Old MacDonald."
2. Do 10 jumping jacks.
3. Recite John 3:16.
4. Name five movies currently playing at local theaters.
5. Yodel something.
6. Run around your house.
7. Start your car's engine and honk the horn.
8. Take our picture.
9. Whistle "Yankee Doodle" all the way through.
10. Say the Pledge of Allegiance.
11. Give us a guided tour of your back yard.
12. Autograph the bottom of our feet.
13. Say "bad blood" 10 times very fast.
14. Burp.
15. Do a somersault.

ACTION SCAVENGER HUNT

1. Sing two verses of "Old MacDonald."
2. Do 10 jumping jacks.
3. Recite John 3:16.
4. Name five movies currently playing at local theaters.
5. Yodel something.
6. Run around your house.
7. Start your car's engine and honk the horn.
8. Take our picture.
9. Whistle "Yankee Doodle" all the way through.
10. Say the Pledge of Allegiance.
11. Give us a guided tour of your back yard.
12. Autograph the bottom of our feet.
13. Say "bad blood" 10 times very fast.
14. Burp.
15. Do a somersault.

Back-to-School Scavenger Hunt

School Supply List

- ❒ Pencils—100 points. Limit 25. 500 extra points for the longest, shortest, and fattest pencils. 50 extra points for pencils with a company name or product printed on them.
- ❒ Rulers—300 points. Limit 5. 500 extra points for the longest ruler.
- ❒ Lunch box—500 points. Limit 1. 1,000 extra points for the most original decoration.
- ❒ Thermos—500 points. Limit 1. 300 extra points if it leaks.
- ❒ Sandwich—200 points. Limit 1. 500 extra points for the one with the most condiments.
- ❒ Erasers—200 points. Limit 5. 500 extra points for the biggest one.
- ❒ Notebook binders—300 points. Limit 5. 500 extra points for the thickest.
- ❒ Gym shorts—300 points. Limit 2. 500 extra points for the largest and the smallest size.
- ❒ Athletic shoe—300 points. Limit 1. 500 extra points for the smelliest.
- ❒ Folders—200 points. Limit 5. 100 points extra for ones with pockets; 500 extra for the most artistic one.
- ❒ Stack of notebook paper—Lose 500 points if the stack is less than six inches thick.
- ❒ Paper clips—25 points. Limit 25. 300 extra points for the largest one.
- ❒ Pen with erasable ink—500 points. Limit 1.
- ❒ Dictionary—1,000 points. Limit 1. 1,000 extra points for the biggest one.
- ❒ Thesaurus—1,000 points. Limit 1. 1,000 extra points for Roget's.

Auto-Graph Scavenger Hunt

- A 1957 Chevy
- Any car with the numbers 4, 5, and 6 in the license plate number.
- A church bus
- A blue Ford
- An ambulance
- A scooter
- A 1980 Firebird
- An orange Toyota pickup
- A car with less than 500 miles on the speedometer
- Any car that has just crossed over the river bridge
- A lawnmower
- A maid's cart at the Holiday Inn
- A fire truck
- Any car that has just driven over a banana
- A garbage truck
- A mountain bike
- ____________________
- ____________________
- ____________________
- ____________________

Auto-Graph Scavenger Hunt

- A 1957 Chevy
- Any car with the numbers 4, 5, and 6 in the license plate number.
- A church bus
- A blue Ford
- An ambulance
- A scooter
- A 1980 Firebird
- An orange Toyota pickup
- A car with less than 500 miles on the speedometer
- Any car that has just crossed over the river bridge
- A lawnmower
- A maid's cart at the Holiday Inn
- A fire truck
- Any car that has just driven over a banana
- A garbage truck
- A mountain bike
- ____________________
- ____________________
- ____________________
- ____________________

BLACKBEARD'S TREASURE SCAVENGER HUNT

- ☐ Bread and water
- ☐ "Yo, ho, ho, and a bottle of—" four bottles of any soft drink
- ☐ Picture of a pirate
- ☐ Crow or parrot (real or pretend)
- ☐ Bandanna
- ☐ Polka-dotted head scarf
- ☐ Sea shell
- ☐ A message in a bottle
- ☐ Cannon ball (any ball will do)
- ☐ Container of beach sand
- ☐ Silver coin
- ☐ Treasure chest (any box will do)
- ☐ String of jewels or pearls (real or fake)
- ☐ Polly wants a **cracker**!
- ☐ Fish
- ☐ Large loop earring
- ☐ Walk the **plank**!
- ☐ Spade or shovel
- ☐ Button
- ☐ Orange or lime
- ☐ Eye patch (real or toy)
- ☐ Captain **Hook**
- ☐ Autograph of someone who wants to be a pirate
- ☐ Model of a boat
- ☐ Rope
- ☐ Flag
- ☐ Skull and crossbones
- ☐ Pistol (toy)
- ☐ Anything off a boat
- ☐ Chain
- ☐ Three strands of blonde hair from a fair maiden
- ☐ Ring
- ☐ Hurricane tracking chart
- ☐ Map
- ☐ Anything a pirate would use that is not on this list
- ☐ Prisoner

Bible Scavenger Hunt with a Splash

A week before the meeting, tell your kids that there's a chance they'll get wet at the next meeting. Then set about to collect everyday objects mentioned in the Bible that carry spiritual symbolism:

- A key (the keys of the kingdom)
- A shepherd's staff (not so common these days, but it reminds us that "we all, like sheep, have gone astray" or "feed my sheep")
- A pitcher of water (the Samaritan woman at the well, living water, etc.)

...or a coin, a loaf of bread, etc.—common items that have clear biblical meanings.

Hide your collection outside on the church property before the kids arrive. Fill two balloons with water for each item that is hidden, plus a few extras just in case some break—and to give you an opportunity to toss a balloon or two yourself. Put the balloons into buckets. Set up a staging area with a table and chairs for you and any associates. You'll get wet, too, but why get soaked standing when you can get soaked sitting?

When the kids arrive, tell them there are lots of objects hidden around the property, objects they wouldn't normally find there. Clearly define the boundaries of the hunt. When they find such items, they should bring them to the staging area and give them to a sponsor. Then they must state something of the Scripture that relates to the item or quote a Scripture verse that mentions or alludes to the item.

If they can do this without prompting, they get two water balloons and are free to attack the other hunters or adult leaders. If they need help thinking of a biblical meaning to the object they find, go ahead and give them clues until they get it, in which case the kids get *one* balloon, and the adult who helped them gets the other one.

After all the objects have been found and turned in, or when the balloon supply is depleted, get together to explore how so much in life around us points us to spiritual truth. *Pete Mueller*

Comparison Scavenger Hunt

This is a great outdoor or camp game. Have an unusual scavenger hunt in which teams search for and bring back weird items such as the following:

- **The biggest piece of wood they can find**
- **The oldest nickel**
- **The smelliest sock**
- **The heaviest rock**
- **The most worn out shoe (or tire)**
- **The rustiest tin can**
- **The ugliest picture**
- **The biggest leaf**
- **The heaviest book**

Set a time limit for the search. Once all the teams have returned with all their treasures, have them display each item for comparison. Award points to first and second place winners in the various categories.

Cereal Scavenger Hunt

To get ready for this scavenger hunt, make a list of breakfast cereals and assign different point values to each. Break up the group into teams and give each team a list of the cereals along with Baggies and pens. Then send the teams into a residential area to

collect in their Baggies as many kinds of cereals as they can, marking off their lists as they go. They may not go to a store for any of the cereals, and they may get only one kind of cereal from each house.

Meet back at the church at a specific time. Provide bowls and spoons and milk and crunch away. Be sure to have a prize for the winning team. *Julie Suess*

FUNGUS HUNT

This scavenger hunt has shenanigans to do rather than objects to collect. Divide up into carloads, give each group a copy of page 51, set a time limit, and

MAM, COULD YOU TELL ME WHERE THE LAMPS ARE?

offer a prize to the group completing the most items. (Be sure to identify a person for item number 14.) The driver or any adult can be the judge to make sure the group doesn't cheat. Items can be taken in any order. *Mark Stofle*

MAGAZINE SCAVENGER HUNT

Divide your group into teams of two or three persons each and give each group a combination of old magazines. Then give them a list of various items, photos, names, etc., that could be found in the magazines. As soon as a group finds one of the items, they cut it out then continue to collect as many items as they can in the time limit. The list can be long or short depending on the time. Some of the items will be found in several magazines while others in only one. You can make the list as difficult as you want. The winner is the team with the most items found. *Michael Thiel*

GALAXY SCAVENGER HUNT

Give kids a list of nonsensical items to find—like these from the science fiction trilogy *The Hitchhiker's Guide to the Galaxy* by Douglas Adams. Familiarity with the stories isn't necessary to play.

When they return with objects to fit the outlandish names, they must explain their choices.

- **S.E.P.**
- **Lux-o-vals and retracto-nullifiers**
- **A glass of jynnan tonnyx with a twist of lemon**
- **Sens-o-tape**
- **Joo jantze 200 super chromatic peril sensitive eyeglasses**
- **Cosmovid thinkpix home brain box**
- **G-branded bistromatic boxers**
- **Informational illusionary inflater**
- **Xanthis restruction destabilizer zenon emitter**
- **Velvet paisley-covered chesterfield**

Mark Ziehr

GROTESQUE SCAVENGER HUNT

Hold this crazy scavenger hunt at any time during the year, but it's special fun at Halloween. Like most scavenger hunts, kids are divided into teams and sent out with a list of items to bring back. Here is the list:

- **1/4 cup or more of ketchup**
- **1 raw egg**
- **1 bone (any kind)**
- **1/4 cup or more of mustard (or horseradish)**
- **1/2 cup of leftover vegetables (any kind)**
- **1/2 cup flour**
- **Any portion of Jell-O or pudding**
- **Two inches of toothpaste**
- **Any portion of leftover meat (any kind)**
- **1/2 cup of leftover coffee or tea**

Each team should be sent out with 10 plastic sandwich bags that zip closed to hold one item each. Each team should also appoint a captain who must be courageous and daring. The captain can organize the scavenger hunt.

After the teams return with the items from the list, the next stage of the event may begin. Seat the captains behind a long table. Place a bowl in front of each captain. The rest of each captain's team stands 20 feet away at a starting line, facing the captain. Each team member must bring one of the bags collected on the scavenger hunt and one at a time deposit the contents into the bowl. The egg must be cracked and the shell thrown away.

Fungus Hunt

1. Go to a donut shop and buy a donut of your choice. The donut must be brought back to the church with a bite taken out of it by the person who sold the donut to you.
2. Get the entire group to a McDonald's and stand under or near the Golden Arches for one whole minute.
3. Get 30 marshmallows from a single block of homes—they must be brought back to the church and they can be various sizes. Limit five marshmallows per house.
4. Get the whole group to sit in a tree for one full minute.
5. Go to a fellow team member's house. File quietly inside and sit down at the kitchen table. In unison ask, "What's for dinner mom?" As soon as the mother comes out of shock, file out.
6. Go to an ice cream place, order a milkshake, and ask if it could be made without ice cream.
7. At a fairly long red signal, everyone get out of the car and run around it once and then get back in before the light turns green.
8. Buy a mushy greeting card.
9. Go to a grocery store and have each member of the group go up to the same checker and ask her where you would find a box of prunes. Space yourselves so she doesn't know you are all together. Be sure to thank her each time she tells you.
10. Go to any department store. Go up to a sales clerk and ask him where to find an item that is right across the aisle from him. Be serious when you ask.
11. Go to a fellow team member's house. Everyone file into the bathroom, shut the door, flush the toilet, and then file back out.
12. Go to a Taco Bell and have everyone get down on their hands and knees and pretend they're all looking for someone's lost contact lens. Keep this up for three minutes.
13. Go to a restaurant and have everyone gather around the waitress of your choice and sing "For she's a jolly good waitress."
14. Go to ____________'s house and have each person shake hands with him or her. As you shake his hands, each person must say, "I AM SOOO GLAD TO SEE YOU!"
15. Try to stuff everyone who is riding in your car into a phone booth.
16. Go to the mall and ask a tall, bald man what time it is.
17. Go to a gas station and seriously ask directions to the place right across the street from that particular gas station.
18. Get a pair of swim fins and walk through a department store holding hands with the person in the middle of your group wearing the swim fins.
19. Go stand in front of City Hall and sing "My Country 'Tis of Thee" with your hand placed over your heart.
20. Buy an orange and get the checker at the market to autograph it for you.

After all the contents of all ten bags are in the bowl, the last person must stir the whole mess around ten times and feed one big spoonful to the team captain. After the captain swallows it, he must stand up and shout, "My compliments to the chef!" The first team to complete this wins.

A slightly simpler version of this would be to skip the scavenger hunt and to provide all the ingredients for the teams. That way you would have a little more control over the cleanliness of the food items. Of course if you choose to go with the scavenger hunt, lay down some rules like only one food item per house may be collected; no item can come from the garbage, and so on. *Gary Harris*

HUNT FOR RED OCTOBER

Inspired by Tom Clancy's novel of the same name, this October scavenger hunt (see page 53) requires teams of five or so (plus one adult per team) to find as many of the following red items as they can in 60 minutes. If you want, assign different point values to items based on the amount of ingenuity needed to obtain them. *Terry Martinson*

KNOW YOUR CHURCH SCAVENGER HUNT

With this hunt you can teach your teens about the church property, especially if the youth room is on the fringe of your church facilities. Before you tell them about the hunt to come, take your students on a brief tour of the church campus, pointing out tidbits they may not be aware of:

- **Whatever church information lies on the table in the foyer or lobby**
- **Sunday school rooms**
- **Nursery**
- **Location of Bibles**
- **Library**
- **Public phones and phone books**
- **Volunteer workroom**
- **Sanctuary (hey, this might be virgin territory for kids who come only to youth group)**
- **Kitchen or pantry**
- **Prayer-request cards**
- **Church's roadside sign**
- **Pastoral offices**
- **Where new-member information is stored and processed.**

Be sure to include information they should know for the hunt. What you're doing, of course, is not merely prepping them for a game, but revealing to them all the parts of a church's ministry to its members and its community.

Distribute copies of page 54—and use the extra space at the end to add other items in your church building kids can hunt for, so that participants become familiar with the physical layout of the rooms, what aspects of ministry are planned or conducted in those rooms, and any other relevant or interesting information about the physical plant. Be sure to unlock doors into areas you want them to have access to and *lock* doors you don't want them to open.

Send them on the scavenger hunt in pairs with a pillow case to collect their goodies. Some items, like phone books that have limited availability, or signatures, need only be noted on the list, not lugged around in the pillow case.

After everyone returns have the teams share what they found. As the final phase of the hunt, students return all the items to their proper places. *Leslie R. Fordahl*

CHURCH SERVICE SCAVENGER HUNT

Give copies of the Church Service Scavenger Hunt (page 56) to your students just prior to a church service. (Choose a relatively informal service for this activity—one that doesn't require uninterrupted

Hunt for RED October

You have 60 minutes to find—and bring back with you—as many of the following **RED** items as you can!

- ❐ **Red onion**
- ❐ **Red button**
- ❐ **Red lollipop**
- ❐ **One red cent**
- ❐ **Red balloon**
- ❐ **Boy wearing red lipstick**
- ❐ **Red toothpick**
- ❐ **Red shoelace**
- ❐ **Red paper plate or cup**
- ❐ **Red pencil**
- ❐ **Lobster bib**
- ❐ **Child in red pajamas**
- ❐ **Red apple**
- ❐ **Red Sox baseball card**
- ❐ **Red ticket or ticket stub**
- ❐ **Red kidney bean**
- ❐ **Red crayon**
- ❐ **Firefighter's autograph**
- ❐ **Picture of a submarine**
- ❐ **Candy wrapped in red foil**
- ❐ **Red Hot**
- ❐ **Boy with red nail polish**
- ❐ **12 inches of red string or tape**
- ❐ **Newspaper that has been read**
- ❐ **Paint chart with three shades of red**
- ❐ **Test or assignment corrected in red**
- ❐ **Red place mat or napkin**
- ❐ **Radish**
- ❐ **Red bandanna**
- ❐ **Red matchbook**
- ❐ **Red birthday party hat**
- ❐ **Six inches of red ribbon**
- ❐ **Red birthday candle**
- ❐ **Picture of Santa Claus**
- ❐ **Red barrette**
- ❐ **Red comb or toothbrush**
- ❐ **Red licorice**
- ❐ **Red feather**
- ❐ **Red stamp**
- ❐ **Red Band-Aid**
- ❐ **A copy of *The Scarlet Letter***
- ❐ **Red game piece**
- ❐ **Red potato**
- ❐ **Valentine**
- ❐ **Red M & M**
- ❐ **Red marble**
- ❐ **Red cabbage**
- ❐ **Red plastic spoon**
- ❐ **Six ounces of tomato paste**
- ❐ **Piece of red construction paper**
- ❐ **Red food coloring**

Hunt for RED October

You have 60 minutes to find—and bring back with you—as many of the following **RED** items as you can!

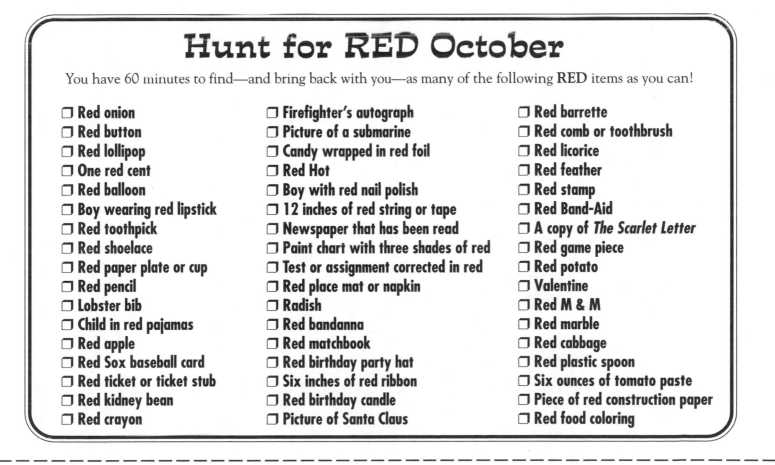

- ❐ **Red onion**
- ❐ **Red button**
- ❐ **Red lollipop**
- ❐ **One red cent**
- ❐ **Red balloon**
- ❐ **Boy wearing red lipstick**
- ❐ **Red toothpick**
- ❐ **Red shoelace**
- ❐ **Red paper plate or cup**
- ❐ **Red pencil**
- ❐ **Lobster bib**
- ❐ **Child in red pajamas**
- ❐ **Red apple**
- ❐ **Red Sox baseball card**
- ❐ **Red ticket or ticket stub**
- ❐ **Red kidney bean**
- ❐ **Red crayon**
- ❐ **Firefighter's autograph**
- ❐ **Picture of a submarine**
- ❐ **Candy wrapped in red foil**
- ❐ **Red Hot**
- ❐ **Boy with red nail polish**
- ❐ **12 inches of red string or tape**
- ❐ **Newspaper that has been read**
- ❐ **Paint chart with three shades of red**
- ❐ **Test or assignment corrected in red**
- ❐ **Red place mat or napkin**
- ❐ **Radish**
- ❐ **Red bandanna**
- ❐ **Red matchbook**
- ❐ **Red birthday party hat**
- ❐ **Six inches of red ribbon**
- ❐ **Red birthday candle**
- ❐ **Picture of Santa Claus**
- ❐ **Red barrette**
- ❐ **Red comb or toothbrush**
- ❐ **Red licorice**
- ❐ **Red feather**
- ❐ **Red stamp**
- ❐ **Red Band-Aid**
- ❐ **A copy of *The Scarlet Letter***
- ❐ **Red game piece**
- ❐ **Red potato**
- ❐ **Valentine**
- ❐ **Red M & M**
- ❐ **Red marble**
- ❐ **Red cabbage**
- ❐ **Red plastic spoon**
- ❐ **Six ounces of tomato paste**
- ❐ **Piece of red construction paper**
- ❐ **Red food coloring**

Know Your Church Scavenger Hunt

Find and bring with you—

- ❐ An item used during worship
- ❐ Something that's alive
- ❐ An item you could give to a church visitor to tell them more about us
- ❐ The autograph of a church volunteer
- ❐ A picture of a Bible character
- ❐ A toy
- ❐ A pastor's middle name
- ❐ The last letter or number on the big sign outside
- ❐ The second box that can be checked on the prayer-request card
- ❐ The first three words of hymn 123
- ❐ Something edible
- ❐ The book, chapter, and verse naming a famous couple in the Bible
- ❐ ______________________
- ❐ ______________________
- ❐ ______________________

Know Your Church Scavenger Hunt

Find and bring with you—

- ❐ An item used during worship
- ❐ Something that's alive
- ❐ An item you could give to a church visitor to tell them more about us
- ❐ The autograph of a church volunteer
- ❐ A picture of a Bible character
- ❐ A toy
- ❐ A pastor's middle name
- ❐ The last letter or number on the big sign outside
- ❐ The second box that can be checked on the prayer-request card
- ❐ The first three words of hymn 123
- ❐ Something edible
- ❐ The book, chapter, and verse naming a famous couple in the Bible
- ❐ ______________________
- ❐ ______________________
- ❐ ______________________

meditation, for example.) Compare answers in a following youth meeting. *Todd Wilson*

MANHUNT

This is a scavenger hunt for people, not objects. Give each team a list that describes different types of people (grandfather, mother, teen, etc.). Teams go door to door in search of people in the neighborhood who fit these descriptions. Kids try to convince those people to come along with them on their search and later return to the meeting place with them. Each person who returns with the team and fits a description is worth 100 points. Here are more sample descriptions that you can include on the lists:

- Varsity or junior varsity football player (or other athlete)
- Police officer
- Someone who speaks Spanish fluently
- Tuba player (with tuba)
- Cheerleader
- A couple who is engaged to be married
- Someone wearing pajamas
- Teacher
- Someone who owns a Jeep
- Someone who has more than 10 letters in his or her last name
- Someone with red hair
- An A student
- Someone who owns a guinea pig
- Someone over six feet tall
- Someone who plays a banjo

So what do you do with all the people who are brought back to the meeting? First, thank them for participating and for being good sports. Then provide refreshments and encourage teams to get to know their guests. Make sure that all guests are safely escorted home later.

INDOOR SCAVENGER HUNT

Divide the group into teams and send each team to a different corner or section of the playing area. Make sure team members have their purses or wallets with them. You stand in the middle of all the teams. Each team appoints a runner to deliver items from their wallets, purses, or pockets to you. Call for items such as those listed here. The first team to produce the named item wins 100 points, and after 20 or so items, the team with the most points wins. Make sure that all runners are running approximately the same distance.

Church Service Scavenger Hunt

Fill out this sheet during the service, then bring it with you to our next meeting.

1. The greeters:
2. Last one into the sanctuary:
3. One Bible person (other than Jesus) mentioned in today's Bible reading:
4. What the pastor is wearing:
5. The most encouraging answer to prayer you heard at church today:
6. Someone *really* into the service:
7. Someone *really* dressed up:
8. Someone in jeans:
9. Someone wearing green:
10. Number of children who went forward today for the children's message:
11. Length of sermon:
12. Largest family present:
13. Someone missing from church today:
14. The church season we're in now:
15. Number of youth group members in church:

Call for items like these:

Comb	**Hat**
Red sock	**Turquoise ring or bracelet**
A 1994 penny	**The smelliest sock**
Student identification card	**(judge determines the winner)**
Mascara	**Theater ticket**
White T-shirt	**Picture of your mother**
Shoestring (without the shoe)	**Blue sweater**
Four belts tied together	**Toenail clippers**
Sunglasses	**Book of matches**
Picture of a celebrity	**Cowboy boot**
A $20 bill	**Forty-six cents, exactly**
Gum	**Handkerchief**
Denture adhesive	**Wristwatch**

You might also try this variation:

• **Intellectual Scavenger Hunt.** Instead of simply asking for a common item, ask for it in such a way that they first need to figure out what you want:

• A cylindrical object that releases a blue medium used to communicate *(a pen that writes in blue ink)*

• A many-pronged object used by the vain to rearrange their mane *(a comb)*

• A soft item which when exhaled into expands into a flimsy round ball *(a balloon)*

• A slip of paper valued at a net worth of 20 thousand pennies *(a $20 bill)*

• A permanent impression of a comrade often entombed in an album, wallet, or frame *(a photo of a friend)*

• A clean soft piece of recycled paper used to wipe mucus from one's nostrils *(a tissue)*

Don Shenk

CHALLENGE HUNT

Divide your group into teams. Provide enough cars for each team to travel in and make sure each team is accompanied by one adult leader, who will monitor the team's activities. Give each team this set of instructions:

You must follow these instructions and complete as many missions as possible within _____ hours (set a time limit). Follow these instructions in order. (Vary the order of activities for each team.) Follow the instructions without explaining them to people outside of the group that you come in contact with until your mission has been accomplished. For example, you can't say, "Will you help us? We are a church youth group that has been assigned to do such and such . . ."

Include missions like these with the instructions:

• Convince another teen who you don't know to come with you to help accomplish the other missions.

• Get a signed statement from a doctor saying that you do not have the bubonic plague.

• Hop around on one foot at *(location)* for two minutes.

• Find a tennis court where people are playing and each of you take a turn at hitting the ball over the net.

• Go to a girl's dormitory at the local college and serenade the girls with *"We wish you a Merry Christmas."*

• Get everyone in the group on radio or TV, and bring back proof.

• Talk a taxi driver into driving the entire group around the block for only one dollar.

Jerry Summers

PIZZA SCAVENGER HUNT

Divide the kids into groups of four to six. Supply each team with a large premade pizza crust (like Boboli) or have them make their own crust. Send each team on foot, by bike, or by car on a search for pizza toppings—but with no money. They can only go to homes (no grocery stores).

There's no reason to make this hunt a race. Rather make it a contest of creativity. Give them sufficient time to complete the collection, realizing that this is a great community-building and fellowship exercise.

At a predetermined time teams return with their toppings and build their pizzas (or you can have 'finding someone's oven to bake the pizza in' another item on the hunt.) Once the pizzas are baked, teams can share their pizzas with each other or each team can indulge in the pizza they've created.

Be sure to provide plenty of fruit, cookies, garlic bread, and drinks. *Dave Mahoney and Harry Heintz*

PICTIONARY SCAVENGER HUNT

Like most scavenger hunts, your kids are given a list of objects they must return with in a specified time.

But here's the twist—they cannot speak to anyone to obtain the objects on the list, teammate or otherwise. They must take turns drawing, according to Pictionary rules (which prohibit, among other things, writing letters or numbers), what they want from a person: a picture of the U.S. president, a penny, a tea bag, moldy cheese, a toothpick, etc.

They may wear a sign that says

I AM ON A SCAVENGER HUNT AND I CANNOT TALK. I CAN ONLY DRAW THE OBJECT I NEED—SO PLEASE GUESS! *Nancy Graves*

POLAROID BIBLE CLUE SCAVENGER HUNT

The object here is not to bring back the most pictures but the most points (see reproducible sheet on page 59. To score five *bonus* points, satisfy two clues with one picture—though this will mean some extra planning by the teams. And award five *more* bonus points for every photo that includes *every* member of a team. *Carol Romeiser*

POLAROID PEOPLE PICTURES

Have the kids meet on a Saturday morning around nine or ten o'clock. Divide the group into teams and give each a Polaroid camera and two rolls of film. Each team is also given a list of subjects to be shot which involve people. No one from the group can be in the picture. Only total strangers can be used. Each team must work in the same general vicinity, like the zoo, the park, downtown, etc. People must be asked to pose for the pictures.

A sample list:

- **Someone disappointed**
- **Someone showing compassion**
- **Someone showing anger**
- **Someone asleep on a bench**
- **An elderly man and a young child**
- **A police officer doing his or her job**
- **Someone showing courtesy**
- **A dog**
- **A child with a balloon**

The group is given a time limit and the pictures are judged to select the winning team. The pictures can also be mounted for display or be used for discussion as well. *Vicky Allen*

POLAROID SCAVENGER HUNT

In this classic hunt, teams of five or six kids—-each equipped with a Polaroid camera, two packages of film (eight exposures each), an hour or two of daylight, and a list of pictures to be taken—-go out in cars and must take at least 15 pictures chosen from the list (see page 60) within the time limit. The pictures are given point values rated according to difficulty, and the team accumulating the most points wins. The following list of rules and directions should be given to each team:

The rules:

- This is a contest between teams to see which team can accumulate the greatest number of points. Points are earned by taking pictures, as described below, of everyone on the team. The point values of each picture are indicated by the number in parenthesis at the end of each picture description.
- All teams will leave the church parking lot at the same time equipped with a Polaroid camera, a team photographer, and an impartial adult supervisor-driver.
- Each team must pick a team name and a team captain. The team captain will determine where the team is to go to take the pictures.
- All arrangements for all pictures are to be made by the team members–not by the adult supervisor.

POLAROID BIBLE CLUE SCAVENGER HUNT

5 pts. Spread it on the water; sprinkle it for a trail;
Take a picture of it, and this clue you can't fail.
(Mark 14:1)

5 pts. Teachers are tough on even the best,
But this is the hottest to use as a test.
(1 Corinthians 3:13)

5 pts. We dance by its light,
When it's full, dim, or bright.
(Colossians 2:16)

6 pts. Paul and Silas went there without a care;
Take a picture of you in one—if you dare.
(Acts 16:23)

7 pts. Line them all up for one camera shot.
If you find them all, it's a lot you have got!
(Matthew 25:1)

8 pts. Rub a dub dub,
Picture her in a tub.
(Matthew 1:20)

8 pts. Change the *A* to an *O* and drop the *E*
And capture the vehicle of this sky jockey.
(Matthew 27:13)

10 pts. Two items you'll need, so be on your toes;
Set one in the other for this camera pose.
(Matthew 17:27)

POLAROID BIBLE CLUE SCAVENGER HUNT

5 pts. Spread it on the water; sprinkle it for a trail;
Take a picture of it, and this clue you can't fail.
(Mark 14:1)

5 pts. Teachers are tough on even the best,
But this is the hottest to use as a test.
(1 Corinthians 3:13)

5 pts. We dance by its light,
When it's full, dim, or bright.
(Colossians 2:16)

6 pts. Paul and Silas went there without a care;
Take a picture of you in one—if you dare.
(Acts 16:23)

7 pts. Line them all up for one camera shot.
If you find them all, it's a lot you have got!
(Matthew 25:1)

8 pts. Rub a dub dub,
Picture her in a tub.
(Matthew 1:20)

8 pts. Change the *A* to an *O* and drop the *E*
And capture the vehicle of this sky jockey.
(Matthew 27:13)

10 pts. Two items you'll need, so be on your toes;
Set one in the other for this camera pose.
(Matthew 17:27)

Polaroid Scavenger Hunt

Directions:

Take as many of the following pictures as possible within the time limit. They are rated point-wise according to difficulty, so you will want to consider that as you decide which ones to take. The maximum you can take is 15 pictures. Good luck!

- **Hanging by knees from a tree (10 points)**
- **In a storefront window on a main street, blowing bubble gum (5 points)**
- **Inside a police car with a police officer (15 points)**
- **In a private airplane (10 points)**
- **In a bathtub (10 points)**
- **Under a lighted building at ____ p.m. (15 points)**
- **Around a grave (5 points)**
- **Three members of your team in laundromat dryers (10 points)**
- **Standing on the roof of a service station with the attendant (15 points)**
- **Making french fries in the kitchen of a restaurant with the cook (15 points)**
- **In a boat on the water (10 points)**
- **Sitting around someone's dinner table at supper—the family may not be that of a team member, nor are they to be from our church (10 points)**
- **All members trying on a pair of new white tennis shoes in a department store (15 points)**
- **In a wagon (5 points)**
- **Fishing on a pier with a borrowed fishing pole (10 points)**
- **Washing a car in a car wash (10 points)**
- **TP'ing a car—not the one you're in (10 points)**
- **Collecting candy at a home where your team is trick-or-treating (10 points)**

Polaroid Scavenger Hunt

Directions:

Take as many of the following pictures as possible within the time limit. They are rated point-wise according to difficulty, so you will want to consider that as you decide which ones to take. The maximum you can take is 15 pictures. Good luck!

- **Hanging by knees from a tree (10 points)**
- **In a storefront window on a main street, blowing bubble gum (5 points)**
- **Inside a police car with a police officer (15 points)**
- **In a private airplane (10 points)**
- **In a bathtub (10 points)**
- **Under a lighted building at ____ p.m. (15 points)**
- **Around a grave (5 points)**
- **Three members of your team in laundromat dryers (10 points)**
- **Standing on the roof of a service station with the attendant (15 points)**
- **Making french fries in the kitchen of a restaurant with the cook (15 points)**
- **In a boat on the water (10 points)**
- **Sitting around someone's dinner table at supper—the family may not be that of a team member, nor are they to be from our church (10 points)**
- **All members trying on a pair of new white tennis shoes in a department store (15 points)**
- **In a wagon (5 points)**
- **Fishing on a pier with a borrowed fishing pole (10 points)**
- **Washing a car in a car wash (10 points)**
- **TP'ing a car—not the one you're in (10 points)**
- **Collecting candy at a home where your team is trick-or-treating (10 points)**

The job of the supervisor is to take the team where it wants to go and take pictures when necessary. (Each supervisor is to use his own discretion with regard to bailing his team out of jail.)

• At least five team members must be visible and

identifiable in each picture, unless otherwise designated.

• **Video Scavenger Hunt.** It's like the Polaroid Scavenger Hunt but with video cameras! Send your scavenger-hunt groups out with video cameras, lights (if done at night), and a list of scenes they must shoot and bring back for viewing by all. The group with the most scenes successfully shot wins the hunt.

The advantage of using video is obvious; you can include both sound and action in the list of assignments to be videotaped. For instance, your entire group dancing on the courthouse steps or everyone in your group going down the slide in Central Park yelling 'Geronimo!'

You might want to do it this way: Borrow as many video cameras as you need for small groups of your teens to cruise the community and record on tape the funniest thing they can find. Place a 60-second time limit on tape footage. All the teams return at a predetermined time to view and judge which team's entry is funniest.

Round two is played in the same way, except that each team has 30 minutes to hunt, and they must find something funnier than the winning footage from round one. Play as many rounds as you want. *Robin Maxson, Brad Strawn, Rick Bell, and Jerry Meadows*

POLAROID PANDEMONIUM

Head to the mall with cameras and clues to play this scavenger hunt.

Before the event prepare 21 Bible verse clues: 10 clues for one team, 10 different clues for the other, and one bonus question both teams have in common. The clues (see sample below) are simply Bible verses that contain clues to stores or sites in your local mall.

Polaroid Pandemonium

1. **In the beginning,** God created the heavens and the earth (Genesis 1:1).
2. Behold, he is coming with clouds, and every **eye will see** him, and they also who pierced him. And all the tribes of the earth will mourn because of him. Even so, Amen (Revelation 1:7).
3. Then the **churches** throughout all Judea, Galilee, and Samaria had peace and were edified. And **walking** in the fear of the Lord and in the comfort of the Holy Spirit, they were multiplied (Acts 9:31).
4. Now the Angel of the Lord found her by a **spring of water** in the wilderness, by the spring on the way to Shur (Genesis 16:7).
5. And when he had called the people to him, with his disciples also, he said to them, "Whoever desires to come after Me, let him deny himself, and take up his **cross**, and follow me" (**Mark** 8:34).
6. If we live in the Spirit, let us also **walk in the Spirit** (Galatians 5:25).
7. Then the rest of the **trees of his forest** will be so few in number that a child may write them (Isaiah 10:19).
8. And you shall **spend that money** for whatever your heart desires; for oxen or sheep, for wine or similar drink, for whatever your heart desires; you shall eat there before the Lord your God, and you shall rejoice, you and your household (Deuteronomy 14:26).
9. He maketh the barren woman to keep house, and to be a joyful **mother of children**. Praise ye the Lord (Psalm 113:9).
10. The cow and the **bear** shall graze; their young ones shall lie down together; and the lion shall eat straw like the ox (Isaiah 11:7).
11. Then God said, "Let the earth bring forth grass, the herb that yields seed, and the **fruit tree that yields fruit** according to its kind, whose seed is in itself, on the earth...and it was so" (Genesis 1:11).
12. Then he took his staff in his hand; and he chose for himself five smooth **stones from the brook**, and put them in a shepherd's bag, in a pouch which he had, and his sling was in his hand. And he drew near to the Philistine (1 Samuel 17:40).
13. More to be desired are they than gold, yea than much fine gold; **sweeter also than honey** and the honeycomb (Psalm 19:10).
14. When the cloud was taken up from above the tabernacle, the children of Israel went onward in all their **journeys** (Exodus 40:36).

Choose Bible verses that match stores in your mall. As you can see, the key words are in boldface. To raise the level of difficulty, simply don't use boldface.

Award 10 points for each correctly solved clue, proven by a picture taken in front of the location with all the team members in it. They'll have to ask shoppers or clerks to take the picture. Give 20 points for solving the bonus question, and reward kids' creativity generously with extra points if their answers fit—even though they may not be the ones you had in mind).

If you play Polaroid Pandemonium with lists of 10 questions plus a bonus, it will take anywhere from 30 to 90 minutes to play, depending on the size of the mall and the creativity of the clues you write up for your students.

Here are the answers for the clues in the sample:

1. Creation, Origins, First Issue
2. L.A. Eye Works
3. Church's English Shoes
4. The mall fountain
5. Mark Cross Men's Clothing Store
6. Easy Spirit Shoes
7. Timberland
8. Foreign money exchanges, ATM machines
9. Mother's Works Maternity Shop
10. Bear statue outside FAO Schwarz Toy Company
11. Banana Republic, Crabtree & Evelyn
12. Brookstone
13. See's Candy, Ghiradelli's Chocolate, Häagen-Dazs
14. Journeys Shoe Store)

Kimberly Shaver

VIDEO HIT SQUAD

This camcorder scavenger hunt can be played by any number of groups. Each group needs a camcorder with a fresh battery and a blank tape, 20 quarters, and an adult chaperon to drive each carload of teenagers to various locations (and to ensure fair play).

Use the Godfather's Hit List and Scoresheet (page 64) or create a similar one of your own. *Students should not see this list.* (A note about the hits on this list: if you compile your own, separate those that could be easily recorded back to back, at the same location, like a sign that displays the time and a sign that displays the temperature. Make as many copies as there will be teams (mobs), and give them to the Godfather, who sits by the phone at home base.

On the day of the event, divide your kids into mobs and let them choose a mob name. Each mob designates a Hit Man who operates the camcorder and a Liaison who calls the Godfather from the various phone booths. Or mob members can rotate these duties among themselves. Explain that the Godfather has 10 targets (or however many you've chosen) for them to hit with their camcorder, but he will reveal those targets only one at a time. For their first target they can drive to any pay phone. If you want, stipulate how far they must drive before using a pay phone.

Guidelines each mob should follow:

- No speeding. Obey all traffic laws.
- All members of a mob must stay together at all times.
- Be sure you know your home-base phone number.
- No one in your mob may appear in your own video.
- Make all Godfather calls from a pay phone using only the quarters that were issued to you.
- Return to the church at the designated time, whether or not you've hit all the possible targets.

Then let them go. In their first call the Godfather asks them what number hit they want first (1-17). The mob chooses, then the Godfather tells them what that hit is, plus any bonus. After they hang up the mob hits its target, calls the Godfather to report a successful hit, then gets its next target. A typical exchange might go like this:

Mob's Liaison: Godfather? This is the Capone mob. We're at Joe's Pizza Palace on the corner of Main Street and Davis Drive. We just hit number five, a vehicle filling up with gas. We got the bonus, too—it was a motorcycle.

Godfather: (jotting down on the scoresheet the time of call, location the mob is calling from, and the points earned) Nice job, Capone. Your next target is someone washing a car for 500 points.

Mob's Liaison: Got it. 'Bye.

Because of the time limit you've given them, the mobs will quickly figure out that the bonuses may or may not be worth the minutes they eat up waiting for the bonus scenarios (or setting them up). Should they use their time quickly hitting a dozen targets at 500 point each, or should they hit only six or seven targets but accumulate some 1,000-point bonuses along the way?

Mobs return to church when they've hit all 10 targets or by the deadline, even if they haven't hit all 10. Record each mob's arrival time back at the base. An earlier arrival time might break a tie in point scores. To the mobs that return to church before the deadline, having hit all 10 targets, award a bonus of 2,000 points. Penalize mobs 500 points for each minute over the deadline they're tardy. Have the Godfather on hand to tally the points and determine which mob rules the city.

After the big mob fight, serve candy kisses so that mobs can kiss and make up while the entire group views the videos to confirm each mob's claims. You may want an objective judge on hand to settle disputes. *Brett Wilson*

SCAVENGER HUNT SWITCH

First break up the group into an even number of small groups. The number of people within each group does not have to be the same as long as you have an even number of small groups. Each small group is then told to write down 10 of the hardest items (within reason) they can think of for a scavenger hunt because they are going to give their list to another group. No impossible items allowed.

After each group has compiled their list of 10 difficult items, they exchange their list with another group. Allow the groups some time to moan over their new list and then pull the switch. Tell each group to take back their original list because each group actually has to find the items on their own list. *Cyndi Thompson and Wendy Roener*

RAINBOW SCAVENGER HUNT

Go to your local paint store and pick up a few paint color charts. Divide into teams and give each team one of the charts. The object is to go out and find items that match the colors on the chart. Any item will do, but the color has to match exactly. Judges can disqualify any item that is questionable. Set a time limit. The team with the most matched items wins. Extra points can be given for items that have only the matched color on it, the most of that particular color, and so on. Paint and art stores are off limits. Nothing can be purchased. *Dan Brandell*

SCAVENGER HUNT TEAMS...

Next time you do a scavenger hunt with teams, try this. Link the teams together, either inside a hula-hoop or by safely tying them together with a rope or string (not around their necks). This will add some excitement to the scavenger hunt, and it forces the team to stick together. It can be funny as well as frustrating when the team members want to go in several different directions at once. It forces them to reach some kind of agreement. *David Rasmussen*

VIDEO HIT SQUAD

Godfather's Hit List and Scoresheet for __________ Mob

MOB NAME

Hit (with point value)	Score	Time of call (following this hit)	Calling from— (location)
1. Someone buying a paper (500) Bonus: the paper is a *USA Today* (1,000)			
2. A couple walking holding hands or arms around each other (500) Bonus: they kiss (1,000)			
3. A taxi cab (500) Bonus: there's an illuminated light on top (1,000) Double bonus: a passenger is getting in or out of the cab (1,000)			
4. A sign that displays the current time (500)			
5. Someone filling up their vehicle with gasoline (500) Bonus: it's a truck or a motorcycle (1,000)			
6. Someone washing an automobile (500)			
7. A transaction at a drive-thru (500) Bonus: the transaction is *not* food-related (1,000)			
8. Someone with a two-liter soft drink (500) Bonus: the drink is orange flavored (1,000)			
9. Someone using an automatic teller machine (500) Bonus: it's a walk-up ATM (1,000) Double bonus: it's a drive-up ATM, and the vehicle is a van (1,000) Triple bonus: the van drives *backwards* through the ATM (1,000)			
10. Someone eating pizza (500) Bonus: the eater is eating standing up (1,000)			
11. Someone washing their windshield (500) Bonus: at a gas station (1,000) Double bonus: the gas station attendant is washing the window (1,000)			
12. A sign that displays the current temperature (500) Bonus: the sign displays in degrees Celsius (1,000)			
13. A sign containing a person's name (500) Bonus: the name is a biblical name (1,000)			
14. Someone buying a can of soda from a vending machine (500) Bonus: the person buys two cans (1,000) Double bonus: the two cans are both Diet Cokes (1,000)			
15. A railroad car (500) Bonus: the railroad car is moving (1,000) Double bonus: the engine pulling the railroad car sounds its horn (1,000)			
16. Someone using the telephone (500) Bonus: the person is in a phone booth (1,000)			
17. An American flag hung on a flag pole (500) Bonus: the flag is extended by the wind (1,000)			
TOTAL			
ARRIVAL BONUS			
ARRIVAL PENALTY			
GRAND TOTAL			

Organic Scavenger Hunt

The scavenger hunt list on page 66 might come in handy the next time your group is near a river, lake, in the woods, at a picnic area, or at a camp or retreat. *Rodney Coleman*

Zoo-Fari

Here's an event that can make an ordinary trip to the zoo a lot more exciting. Divide the group into teams of roughly equal numbers. It doesn't matter how many teams there are. Each team is given a list

Zoo-Fari

- Make up a song about your youth pastor, an elephant, and a monkey (50 points)
- Bring back some animal food (15 points, 50 points if it is alive)
- Which zoo animal is named Sam? (10 points)
- Signature of a male zoo keeper (15 points)
- What is the youngest animal in the zoo? (5 points)
- What is the oldest animal in the zoo? (5 points)
- What is an Oxyrinchus Pichanosis? (15 points)
- Find the Australian Grodfog (50 points)
- Find the great Mau-Mau (50 points)
- Walk through the aviary singing "Bird Drops Keep Falling on My Head" (30 points)
- Pet every animal in the petting zoo (35 points)
- Bring back a dead fish (45 points)
- Sing "Happy Birthday to You" to a hippo (20 points)
- Talk to a gorilla for five minutes without stopping (40 points)
- Find the smelliest animal in the zoo (40 points)

(see sample) of things to do or find inside the zoo and is given a time limit to complete the list. Throw in a few tricky finds. An Austrailian Grodfog can be a lady sitting on a bench near the kangaroos, dressed strangely and wearing a fake mustache—you plant an accomplice. They do not have to do each assignment in order.

At the end of the time limit, gather at some point within the zoo, (most have picnic areas that work great) and add up the points. They must be able to display any items that were to be brought back. The winning team members should all receive a prize—maybe something from the zoo's souvenir stand. *Tim Jack*

Shopping Mall Derby

Have all the students in your group meet in a specified location in the mall. Divide up into teams of three or four on a team and give each team a list similar to the one below with pencils if they need them. Give the group one hour or so to try and figure out the answer to each item on the list. The team that completes the most correctly within the time limit is the winner. If there is a fast-food restaurant in the mall, meet there for refreshments and awards afterward.

Be sure and clear this with the shopping mall management in advance, and emphasize to the kids that they must not be rude or disruptive in the various shops. No running is allowed, and if it is necessary to talk to a store clerk, they must wait in line if they have to, and be polite. Obviously, you (or someone) will need to go to the mall before the actual event to prepare the list. Make sure that you

Shopping Mall Derby

- What store is using a Hawaiian theme with leis to sell clothes?
- What is the number on the No Fear transfer at Sunshine Shirts?
- What is the maximum occupancy of the Score Family Fun Center?
- Where can you get free ear piercing with a $9.00 purchase?
- How much is a swirl pop at Hickory Farms?
- How many mirrors are there hanging from the ceiling at T.G. &Y.?
- What color is the courtesy gift box ribbon that has two bows on it at Walker's?
- What are Farrell's hours on Sunday?
- What is the address of Beth's Hallmark cards?
- How much is a skein of macrame cord at Accents?
- What is in a Sunshine Supreme at the Old Times Deli?
- How much is a Realistic LAB-500 direct drive turntable at Radio Shack?
- On the Mall directory, what number is Dr. Kenneth Clarke, Optometrist?
- What store has a buffalo head in it?
- About what TV personality is there a featured book at Books Unlimited?
- What is the title of pop hit No. 10 at Sam Goody's?
- How much is Teriaki Sirloin on the dinner menu at Chuck's Steak House?
- What store has an inflatable Zepplin hanging from the ceiling?
- What type of merchandise is on page 1142 of the Sears Spring/Summer catalogue?
- What are the first names of the counter attendants at Orange Julius?
- How much is Luster Teri per yard at House of Fabrics?
- What is the fee for the Easter Workshop advertised at Golden State Fabrics?
- What is the name of the only furniture store in the mall?
- What store has a stained glass parrot in the window?
- How much is Head to Head Football at Walker's Stationery?

don't list things that will not be there when you have the event. Usually it is best to prepare the list no earlier than the day before. *Bob Mentze*

Organic Scavenger Hunt

Some of these items belong outdoors, some do not. Which of these items can you find?

- The words of John 15:13
- A small rock
- A flea
- A yellow wildflower
- A pre-1975 penny
- A snail
- A three-inch twig
- A four-leaf clover
- A paper clip
- A pine needle
- Five different soda caps
- A feather
- A mosquito
- An acorn
- A root-beer can
- An old sock
- A piece of rope
- A baby diaper
- A golf tee
- A box of matches
- A toothpick
- A double pinecone
- Bubble gum
- A live grasshopper
- A ticket stub
- An apple core
- Three live ants
- A red shoestring
- A cotton ball
- A corncob
- A dandelion
- A magazine
- A brick
- A cactus needle
- A live fly
- A mushroom
- A piece of ribbon
- A button
- A clean tissue
- A red leaf
- A strip of cassette tape
- A red handkerchief
- A pencil that isn't yellow
- A new piece of charcoal
- A rubber band
- A walking stick
- An out-of-town newspaper
- A crayon
- Some moss
- A plastic six-pack holder
- A straw
- A Popsicle stick
- A bug
- A canceled stamp
- A live frog
- A bun with sesame seeds
- A 1989 calendar

SHOPSCOTCH

Divide the entire group into small groups of five or six each. Each group then gets an envelope with $10 in cash and a list of items which they must purchase. The groups are then turned loose in a shopping center and have 45 minutes to obtain all the items. The group with the most items and the most money

left over wins. Receipts must be brought back with everything, including items obtained for free. Shoplifting is a big no-no. The leader should go to the shopping center ahead of time to make sure that items on the list can be obtained. A sample list:

- One paint card sample
- Pocket-size Kleenex
- Empty pop bottle
- A toy
- Six peanuts in shells
- Can of fruit juice
- An apple
- A peashooter
- A travel brochure to the Bahamas
- One kernel of popcorn—popped
- Three inches of chain
- One oz. of blue cheese
- One piece of candy
- 12 inches of ribbon
- A bar of soap
- A bookmark
- 12 oz. bag of pretzels
- Toothpaste

Nancy A. Thompson

SOUND SCAVENGER HUNT

Divide groups into teams. Give each team a cassette recorder and a blank cassette. Make a list of sounds for the teams to find, record, and bring back, in order, within a given time limit. Some sample sounds:

- Dog barking
- Siren on a police car
- Roller coaster at an amusement park
- Somebody playing a tune on a violin
- Someone over 65 explaining what macho means
- A tap dance
- A cash register
- A bursting balloon
- Your entire team singing all of "Somewhere Over the Rainbow"

Have each team play their recording for the entire group. Judge winner after listening to the tapes.

SUPERHERO SCAVENGER HUNT

Tell your students you are about to embark on a quest. Your mission is to create a superhero by obtaining particular superhero items, creating a superhero with them, and fulfilling particular superhero tasks. Only one item can be obtained at any one location. All members of your team must be present to complete each step, and the successful execution of each task will be documented by your accompanying adult sponsor. You are not limited to these items or tasks. Your team will be judged by successful completion of each step and creative development of a superhero character. Your only limitation is your creativity.

Find these items: mask, cape, costume, damsel (who must return to the church with the team), energy source, toys/gadgets/secret weapons, and favorite superhero food.

Then invent a name for your superhero, compose and practice a theme song, and perform one super-hero feat documented by an unrelated bystander. *Jerry Hendrix*

SERVICE SCAVENGER HUNT

Throw tradition into reverse for this scavenger hunt. Instead of collecting a list of items as in a regular scavenger hunt, this one allows the kids to give! Each team of scavengers is given an identical list of service projects to do (mow one lawn, sweep three driveways, wash two cars, etc.). The first team to complete the list wins. You'll be surprised at the different feelings your kids will have when they're finished. The neighborhood may feel pretty good about your group too. *Steve Illum*

Telephone Scavenger Hunt

Divide your group into teams. Since each of these will be traveling together, group sizes will be determined by your vehicle capacities. Each group begins with an equal amount of change (such as 20 dimes) and a card with the church telephone number on it. After the designated start all teams depart to find the first available pay telephone. They are to call the church and choose a number from one to 20. They will then be given the information question bearing the number chosen from a list of questions you have collected. Examples of these might be:

- **What is the name of the manager at the Tyrone Square McDonald's?**
- **What is the price of a Biff Burger?**
- **What is the number of the manhole cover at the corner of Center and 34th St.?**

The groups are to find the answer to their question, find a second phone booth, and call in their answer. If correct they can request another question. If incorrect they must call again with the right answer before receiving another.

You can play for as long as you like, but you should designate a certain time after which no more questions will be given out. Winners are determined by the team who successfully answers the most questions. In case of a tie, the group who returns the most of their original phone money will win.

Dick Gibson

Touch-Tone Scavenger Hunt

You can add this idea to any out-in-the-neighborhood scavenger hunt. At the bottom of the list of objects to find, add a mystery phrase with as many numbered blanks for letters as there are objects to find. When a team finds the fourth object on the list, for example, they call you at the church (from a resident's phone with their permission or from a pay phone) and ask for the letter that goes in the corresponding blank in the mystery phrase. The first team to fill in the phrase and get back to church wins. *David Landis*

Cobbler Gobbler

This is a baking contest combined with a scavenger hunt. Divide the group into teams of five, with boys and girls on each team. Each team is given a list of ingredients that they must find (sugar, flour, fruit, etc.). When the team collects all its ingredients, it reports back to the church (or wherever you have the use of large ovens), and a recipe for fruit cobbler is given to the team. Each team gets the same recipe (there may be a different fruit in each). After the cobbler is prepared, it goes into the oven. (While the cobbler is cooking, table games can be played by the team members.) After all the cobblers are done, have judges taste each one and award points for the best tasting, first finished, neatest job, etc. The team with the best score gets ice cream to eat with its cobbler. Everybody else gets whipped cream.

Roger Disque

Fast Food Frenzy

Here's a new twist on an old scavenger hunt idea. Divide your group into teams, one team per vehicle. Each team begins with $15.00 (or any amount you choose) and a list of instructions. Their objective is to spend some money at ten fast-food locations of your choosing, returning with the least possible amount of change. You might select locations like these:

• Pizza Hut	• Taco Bell
• Wendys	• Baskin Robbins
• 7-Eleven	• Arby's
• Dunkin' Donuts	• McDonald's
• Kentucky Fried Chicken	• Burger King

Groups are not allowed to add to, subtract from, or exchange money from their original $15.00 or the change they receive from their purchases. They may stop at each location only one time and purchase only one item at each stop. They must obtain receipts to verify their purchases. They do not have to follow the order listed above and may stop at any store location throughout your area.

Make sure kids understand that speed is not a factor in this event (to avoid hurried driving). In case of a tie, tell teens that the group with the lowest total mileage will be declared the winner.

Dick Gibson

Snack Search

This simple scavenger-hunt-type party can be used with a small or large group, divided into two or more teams (four to eight on each team is best). The object is for each team to take the lunch provided trade items, one at a time, attempting to bring back the most improved lunch in the allotted time. The one preparing the "search" will need to provide a duplicate sack lunch for each team. Small items are suggested (10-12), such as an onion, a lemon, a jar of baby food, a can of dog food and one of cat food, a can of evaporated milk, a small box of cold cereal, a small jar of hot sauce, Kool-aid or iced tea mix, gelatin mix, soup mix, bird seed, a package of radish seeds. Avoid good lunch items like bananas, potato chips, cookies, etc. These will probably come back in a traded lunch. You might even be surprised when a team brings a watermelon or hot cherry pie back. List three simple rules:

1. No purchases allowed.
2. No trading at the homes of any of the team's members.
3. Only one item can be traded at any one location.

It would be permissible for a team to trade two of their items for one other item, but that could cut down on their total lunch. When all teams return, the lunches should be displayed and judged. After adding some punch and cookies, the winning team should be allowed to have first choice of all the refreshments, which includes the lunches.

Harold Antrim

TREASURE HUNTS

TREASURE HUNTS

Aye matey, here ye shall find the most seaworthy treasure hunts ever to sail the oceans of youth. Landlubbers who don't enjoy decipherin' devilish clues to find a hidden treasure should be keelhauled! Ye shall find more treasure-huntin' ideas in these pages than ye can shake a bottle of rum at. Aarrrgh!

Memorization Treasure Hunt

A city park works best for this hunt. Before the group arrives, hide verses of Scripture around the park in various places by taping them to objects—under a park bench, on the bottom of a swing seat, on the back of a sign, etc. Then prepare riddle-type clues giving as little information about the locations as possible. "Something mothers spend much time on," could be a clue for under a park bench. The group is divided into small groups of three or four and each small group is given their first clue. They are then instructed to find the Scripture, memorize it, and come back and recite it, without removing it from the object. Upon successfully doing this they receive their next clue. Everyone should receive the same clues but in a different order. The first group to recite the last verse wins the hunt. *Kent Bloomquist*

House-to-House Puzzle Hunt

This treasure hunt requires a lot of preparation, but the results are well worth the effort. Here's how it works.

First, you will need to line up a number of homes of church members where the people are willing to stay home the night of this event and help out. The number of homes that you need will vary, but you will probably need at least five or six. Eight or nine is ideal.

On the night of the event, you divide the group into car loads (each team traveling together), or you can do this event on bicycles (or on foot) if all the houses are within close walking distance. When the groups leave the starting point, they are each given one piece to a children's puzzle that has eight or nine pieces to it. On the back of the puzzle is the name of a family in the church. They must go to that family's house where they will be given an instruction. They must then do whatever the instruction tells them to do, and then they will be given another puzzle piece. This puzzle piece will tell them where they are to go next. At the next house they do the same thing. The group that arrives back at the starting place with all their puzzle pieces and successfully puts their puzzle together first is the winner.

Obviously, the number of homes must be the same as the number of puzzle pieces you have.

Each team should have a different route so that everyone isn't going to the same house at the same time. You can also give each group a different puzzle so long as the number of pieces is the same. This will involve some advance preparation in which you assign each group a number. When they arrive at each house they receive the puzzle piece with the appropriate number on it. You can set it up so that each group is taking the houses in a different order.

At each house there is a different instruction which the group must do before they are given their puzzle piece. The instructions can be things like:

- Tell three jokes to the family who lives at this house.
- Form a pyramid and sing a Christmas carol while in that position.
- Run three laps around the house.
- Everyone chew a wad of bubble gum and blow a bubble together at the same time.
- Together, recite John 3:16.
- Eat a peanut butter and jelly sandwich (provided there) and have a glass of punch.

The last piece of the puzzle for each group should instruct them to head back to the starting location. Award prizes to the winners, serve refreshments, share experiences, and have a good time of fellowship. It's a lot of fun. *Syd Schnaars*

MONEY HUNT AND AUCTION

Invite kids to an old-fashioned auction where the bidding is done with play money. Ask them to bring the items to be auctioned—old appliances that still work, fishing poles, not-quite-antique dishes or jewelry boxes. The items should have some appeal to potential bidders.

Before the activity begins hide envelopes containing play money and write out clues to help the kids find the money. The search can cover territory as broad as the neighborhood (using cars the teams search telephone booths, grocery stores, various landmarks, etc.), or as confined as your church grounds.

Start the event by forming teams and handing out the clues to each team. Give a time limit for the treasure hunt. When they return, teams divide the money found among the team members. Then start the bidding. *Mike Kwok*

CONCENTRATION CLUES

At your next treasure hunt, try your hand at making up clues using letters and symbols similar to those used on the old television show "Concentration."

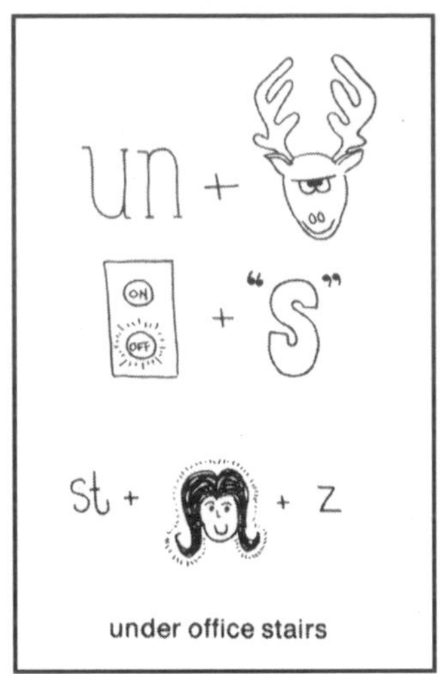

under office stairs

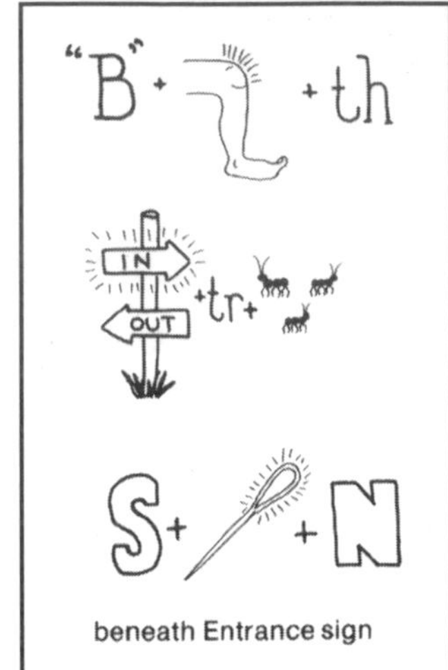

beneath Entrance sign

Almost any clue or location can be written this way. Kids really enjoy trying to solve them. Here are some examples. *Stephen K. Weaver*

INDOOR TREASURE HUNT

This is a good indoor game for junior highers. Place 25 objects in plain sight in various places around the room or rooms available. If in a home, use several rooms. Attached to each object is a number. Each person is given a list like the one below. The idea is to find the objects on the list, write in the numbers attached, and be the first one to do so. No one can move or touch an object when it is found. Simply record the number attached to it. A sample list:

Match	**Ring**
Stocking	**Bobby pin**
Needle and thread	**Postage stamp**
Thimble	**Paper reinforcement**
Straight pin	**Paper fastener (brad)**
Glass button	**Ribbon**
Paper clip	**Toothpick**
White string	**Safety pin**
Penny	**Door key**
Dime	**Rubber band**
Dollar bill	**Stick of gum—don't chew it!**
Bracelet	**Earring**

Bill Flanagan

MOVIE TREASURE HUNTS

Use movie themes to give a wacky facelift to good ol' treasure hunts. For each game create 10 or so clues and give copies to each team—but mix up the order so the teams aren't running into each other. At each location leave packets of clues, color-coded for each team. Award each team a predetermined number of points for each clue uncovered. Inside each clue envelope include an emergency-clue envelope which a team may open if necessary—but they'll forfeit 10 points if they open it.

Here are some ideas to get you going:

• **Back to the Future.** All the clues in this hunt relate to the era or year of graduation of the clue holders—individuals in your church who will play along with your group's hunt.

Tell teams this:

Marty McFly is stuck in 1955. Your team must go back in time, find Marty, and return with him to the present and to this location.

The first team back with Marty wins.

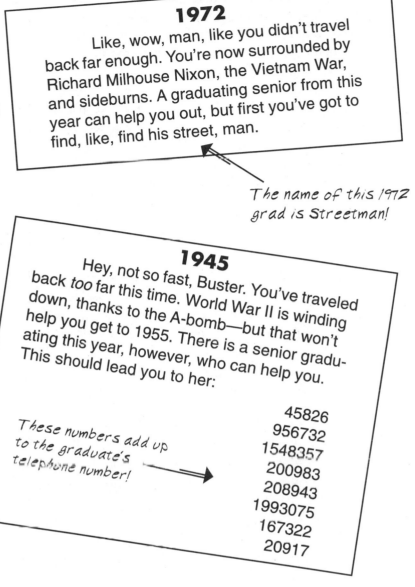

1972

Like, wow, man, like you didn't travel back far enough. You're now surrounded by Richard Milhouse Nixon, the Vietnam War, and sideburns. A graduating senior from this year can help you out, but first you've got to find, like, find his street, man.

The name of this 1972 grad is Streetman!

1945

Hey, not so fast, Buster. You've traveled back *too* far this time. World War II is winding down, thanks to the A-bomb—but that won't help you get to 1955. There is a senior graduating this year, however, who can help you. This should lead you to her:

These numbers add up to the graduate's telephone number!

45826
956732
1548357
200983
208943
1993075
167322
20917

• **The Hunt for Fred October.** Divide your group into Americans and Soviets. Both teams are pursuing poor Fred.

Tell the Americans this:

CIA operatives have found out that the Soviet Union has a new secret weapon, a submarine sandwich. Reports indicate it is incredibly delectable. The KGB hopes to unleash the sub in America, the goal being that Americans will be so taken by this sandwich that they'll abandon McDonald's, Burger King, and Wendy's, thus causing the collapse of the American economy as we know it.

It is believed that Fred October, a Soviet mole planted deep in the U.S. fast-food industry, will bring over the prototype sub sandwich and introduce it into a Cleveland deli, from where news of it will spread like wildfire.

Your mission is to find Fred October, seize the submarine sandwich, and bring it safely back to headquarters.

Tell the Soviets this:

Comrades, our culinary experts are ready to unveil our ultimate secret weapon, a submarine sandwich. We are convinced that unsuspecting Western capitalists will so love this sandwich that they will eat nothing else. As the decadent pigs become enslaved to this submarine sandwich, they will abandon McDonald's, Burger King, and Wendy's, thus precipitating the fall of Western capitalism and democracy itself

Our plans to infiltrate the American fast-food industry with this sandwich have been temporarily halted because one of our own, Fred October, has defected to the U.S. with the prototype sub, the only one. Your mission, comrades, is to capture Fred October and return the sandwich to us.

The teams follow typical treasure-hunt clues that lead them to the last house, where they find a submarine sandwich—a really horrible one, in fact, that you made just for the occasion: pickles, peanut butter, mayonnaise, a little dog food, raisins, etc. When the winners bring it back to headquarters, offer extra points to *whichever* team eats it.

• **The Silence of the Yams.** Police are trying to stop a huge jewel-smuggling operation. Their only clue is that the gem traffickers are smuggling diamonds in sweet potatoes. The police have recruited a supposedly reformed criminal to help in the search—Hannibal Lecter, who, unfortunately, has taken literally the slogan Help Take a Bite Out of Crime.

The teams' mission is to catch the jewel smugglers—and before Hannibal Lecter has them for lunch. The first team to return with the sweet potato containing the missing diamond wins.

Teams follow clues from location to location. Clues are taped to the dismembered body parts of a mannequin. The final location has a sweet potato with a dime-store ring inside.

• **Raiders of the Lost Bark.** Send out teams to find a lost dog. Clues lead to a house, wherein is the dog—if you can arrange it, a large, smelly, friendly canine that they must transport back to home base. The smaller the cars and the more kids in them, the more fun the return trip is.

• **Monastic Park.** A millionaire obsessed with Francis of Assisi creates a sanctuary for gentle animals. He creates the gentle animals, too, by importing experts in hypertech cloning who soon fill the park with gentle lions, gentle scorpions, gentle Tasmanian devils, gentle pit vipers, gentle pit bulls. However, when the brains behind the venture disappears (a kidnapping is suspected), the system begins reverting. Moles become man-eaters, deer turn carnivorous and stalk humans. (And you thought the killer rabbit in *Search for the Holy Grail* was vicious.)

Teams must find the chief techie, led on by clues dealing with the myriad of animal-named products that surround us: cars (Cougar, Pinto, Rabbit, etc.), food and candy (Gummy bears, animal crackers, Turtle Wax, Eagle snacks), people (Mother Goose, River Phoenix). Clues lead teams to homes of people who own the appropriate cars, who have in their cupboards the appropriate food or candy, who own books or videos of the appropriate people. The clues are hidden, of course, in or near the objects, and lead ultimately to the techie, who is bidding his time in captivity playing video games.

• **The Stinkstones.** A Neolithic skunk family that lives in Fred and Wilma's attic tire of his bombast and decide to get even. They steal his bowling ball. Teams must get it back with the help of powerfully odorific clues. The clues can be *about* strong-smelling substances, or they can reek themselves of cheap perfume, ammonia, fertilizer, cod liver oil, etc.

Lynn H. Pryor

Vehicular Sardines

This game is an adaptation of the game Sardines, in which two people hide, and everyone who finds them must hide with them until eventually everyone has found them. Vehicular Sardines adds the fun of a hunt on wheels to the original game.

Divide your students into groups of four or five, depending on the size and type of vehicles available. Assign one adult to each group to ensure safety. Select one group and send them to a destination you have chosen, such as a park, tennis court, mall, etc. Give the hiding car a 10- or 15-minute lead, and give them these reminders:

• They must get out of their vehicle when they reach the destination.
• They must leave the vehicle in plain view at the destination. The car is a legitimate clue for seeking teams.
• They must hide together, not as individuals, and may not change hiding places after they have hidden.

When the hiding group has left, hand out to all the seeking groups a map with cryptic clues to the destination. Set a time—45 minutes or an hour—by which they should return to the church whether or not they've found the hiding group.

For even more fun, send a camcorder along with the hiding group to videotape the other groups finding them—and themselves squishing together trying to make room for each other. Finish the evening back at church with food and a premier showing of the video. *Paul Coleman*

SAFECRACKING SAFARI

The object of the hunt is to find a prize that's locked up in a safe which can be opened only with the correct combination of three numbers. The correct combination is discovered through the process of elimination.

The group is divided into teams and given instruction sheets to help them eliminate numbers on the combination lock. If there are 36 numbers on the lock, the instruction sheet helps them eliminate all but the three numbers in the correct combination. The order of the numbers, however, needs to discovered by trial and error on the lock itself.

The first team to arrive at the safe with the three numbers gets first crack at the safe. If they fail, the second team gets a try, and so on until the safe is opened.

Safecrackin' Safari
• Eliminate the square root of 3,249.
• Eliminate the number of sightless roden
in a popular nursery rhyme.
• Directly behind the Firestone building an
beside the train tracks is a used car dealers
There is a white sign in the yard advertising
this business. There are two phone number
on the sign. Look at the bottom one. Elimina
all one-digit numbers in this phone number.
• What time does Valley Wash House close
Eliminate this number.
• The Yellow Pages' listing for Harvey's On
Hour Cleaners is on page ______. Eliminate
this number.
• Eliminate the number of lanes at the alle
• How old was Abraham when God change
of calories in Tab.
• The last ball you want to put in the pocket
wears this number. Eliminate it.
• Go to Crossroads Mall on the side facing
Airport Road. There is a fire hydrant on the
mall sidewalk at the end of the mall nearest
Terrace Theatre. Walk a *straight line* between
this hydrant and the one at the end of the mall
by Penney's. Counting the two cracks at the
very ends, how many cracks are there?
Eliminate this number. (Count only man-made
cracks. Do not count cracks caused by the
weather or by settling.)
• How much is the cabbage per pound at
Jay's Produce? Eliminate this number.
• Eliminate the number of the day in April
when the Kiwanis will hold their Travelogue.
(Hint: They'll hold it near a McDonalds.)
?
APE
54

Instruction sheets send teams to a variety of locations around town within a limited area and include a variety of ways to eliminate numbers. On page 77 are some sample instructions. *Byron Harvey*

SCRIPTURE CLUES

In this treasure hunt use verses in the Bible that pertain to specific places or events that the youth can relate to their own church property or community. Follow the format of giving out the first clue, which is a Bible verse. The group has a person who looks up the verse and reads it to the entire group. They then relate it to some area and go there to find the next clue. Divide the group into two or more groups and compete to find the treasure. It can be almost anything. Place the treasure in a familiar area but hide it somewhere unusual, like in a tree. It is best to use about five or six clues for each group and to position a clue giver at each location. Try to space the clues the same distance for each group so that traveling times will be equal. Here are some verses that could be used:

- Proverbs 26:14 (a door)
- John 4:6 (a well)
- Isaiah 2:5 (light)
- Exodus 12:38 (death...cemetery)
- Psalms 23:2 (water)
- Psalms 23:5 (table)
- Matthew 13:44 (reward or treasure)

Find places for clues in your church and start digging for verses in the Bible. Your Bible Concordance will be of great help. *Ted Seago*

SUBMARINE RACES

This idea is a fun treasure hunt with an intriguing name and an unusual ending. Like other treasure hunts, you divide up into teams and follow clues from one location to the next.

At the last location each team receives a toy model submarine, unassembled, which they must bring back to the church or meeting place and put together. The hunt is not over until the submarine is completed with decals in their proper places. The entire team must participate in the assembly.

TREASURE HUNT BASICS...

Inject new life into the old treasure hunt theme with these creative ideas:

Name the hunt after the object to be hunted, such as Wild Goose Chase. Or, if you've built a snowman and hidden it somewhere in the vicinity, call the game Search for the Abominable Snowman. One group obtained a live hippopotamus and had a Hippo Hunt. All the kids wore safari hats and followed the clues to the hippo, which was tied up in the middle of the city's largest shopping center. This is where your own creativity becomes important. The possibilities are endless. Just don't rely on the same old thing over and over again.

Place clues in different locations to help the searchers in their hunt. Clues should lead to one another and finally to the treasure itself. The first clue should be handed to the leader of each team to get the game going. Make sure each team receives clues in a different order, or receives a different set of clues, so that teams can't simply follow each other. No clue can be skipped or you are penalized. All clues that have been found must be brought back to the original site at the end of the game. Make sure a leader is at clue site handing out the clues to arriving teams.

Here are sample clues from an actual treasure hunt in San Diego, California:

- An envelope contained an egg yoke and a piece of ham. (Yoke plus ham equals yokahama—a landmark in San Diego called the Yokahama Bell.)
- A piece of paper with scrambled letters which, when unscrambled, spelled out the name of a park in San Diego.
- A list of numbers. When added up, the sum was a seven digit number which was a phone number. Kids used money in the packet to make a phone call to locate the next location.
- A group of sounds were written down: LLL DUH SEE WHR. Teams unscrambled the sounds to discover that the next location was Sea World.

Each team should receive a clue packet that contains items like these:

1. The hunt map (an ordinary road map). The map is marked with numbers and arrows pointing to certain locations. ONLY the locations marked are possible clue locations.
2. List of rules.

The submarines can be found at any toy or hobby store for a few dollars. It's best to buy the same one for everyone. You will also need to provide model cement. After the race serve, what else? Submarine sandwiches. *Rodney Robertson*

White Treasure Elephant Hunt Auction

This idea combines a treasure hunt, a white elephant sale, and an auction. The treasure consists ofpoker chips which are placed in caches, perhaps 100 locations, in an area around the church property. If the group is large and there is enough time and transportation, the area can be much larger. Each cache may consist of from one to 10 chips.

A map is made showing the location of the treasures with an X. The map may be posted in a prominent location where all can see it before the hunt begins. If there are many people involved or if the area is large, make copies of the map for each team.

The treasure hunters should work in teams of three to six persons. At night flashlights are required.

At the start the hunters rush out to the nearest locations, with some crafty ones going to the farther locations to avoid the crowd. A return time should be set, within one to three hours, depending on distances. A penalty of five white chips per minute late can be assessed.

Upon return the teams can look over the white elephant gifts and other items, which each person brought beforehand. The team members can decide what they wish to bid on, knowing only what the total value of all the chips are. The whites are one, the reds are five and the blues are ten.

Then the auction begins! By offering small items first and interspersing them with the more valuable gifts, the excitement can really grow. Having more than one auctioneer is a good idea, too. The auction should last between fifteen and thirty minutes. This can be done by offering more than one gift at a time, if necessary. *Robert C. Hockaday*

3. A general clue sheet containing clue phrases that may or may not be important to the clues. If a group is having a difficult time with a certain clue, players should check the general clue sheet to see if it will help. Example phrases: a) The first two letters are all you need; b) Shamu lives there; c) Blue is a pretty color.
4. General clue items. These are odds and ends that may or may not be of help in solving some or all of the clues. Items could be coins, a bandage, etc.
5. Emergency clues, if a group is unable to figure out a clue. However, each team is penalized 15 minutes for each emergency clue used. The emergency clues are numbered and sealed in envelopes just like the regular clues and must be turned in at the treasure location. If any clues are opened, players must wait out their penalty time before claiming the treasure. If another group arrives during that penalty time with no emergency clues opened, they win.

You should also keep these ideas in mind:

If the treasure is not found, the winner is determined by who got the farthest using the least amount of emergency clues. Plan enough time so that everyone can get to the treasure.

If the treasure itself is not something that the kids can keep, then have some appropriate prizes to give to the winning group. Have a presentation of the hunt trophy to the team captain and make a big deal out of it.

Use a variety of creative clues and make clue locations unusual, such as the top of a church tower, a boat in the middle of a lake, up in a tree, buried in a cemetery, at a tourist attraction, etc.

Make sure speed and traffic laws are obeyed. Team drivers should be carefully screened to avoid problems in this area. Make sure drivers have necessary permissions from parents if they are kids, insurance, and a driver's license. One group put a sponsor in each vehicle who held a spoon with an egg raw in it out the window. If the vehicle went too fast, bounced, swerved, etc., the egg would drop and break. Each vehicle starts with a dozen eggs and is penalized for each egg broken during the hunt.

It is usually a good idea to have the last location somewhere suitable for a meeting. After all the kids are back from the hunt, they can share experiences, you can award prizes, perhaps have some singing, crowd breakers, or a speaker, and some refreshments.

FOTO-MAP

This variation works just like the normal treasure hunt. The players all leave at the same time and go from clue to clue in search of the treasure. The group that gets to the treasure first wins.

Foto-Map is played similarly except that the clues are photographs. At the starting place each group or team receives a photograph. The photo is a picture of the first clue location and the group must identify that location by looking at the picture. Obviously, you can make these photos either easy to recognize or almost impossible to recognize. Groups should be traveling by car (or bikes, etc.) and they might have to just drive around until they spotsomething that looks like their picture. When they figure it out, they go to the location pictured, and there they are given the next photo. A good game can consist of anywhere from five to 10 clue locations, depending on their difficulty. The group that arrives at the final destination first is the winner. You might give each group a sealed envelope revealing the final destination in case they haven't reached it before a specified time. Before that time each group must turn in that sealed envelope in order to win. *David L. McClary*

OTHER HUNTS

OTHER HUNTS

Yes, there are still <u>more</u> hunts that your kids are bound to enjoy. Some of them require a public setting, while others can be conducted close to home.

MURDER MADNESS

This is part murder mystery dinner and part Clue (the classic board game). The difference is you use your whole city, neighborhood, church, camp, or wherever you choose to locate the event.

The object of the game:

A murder has been committed by one of 10 suspects. It is known that the murderer used one of 10 weapons and committed the crime in one of 10 rooms in the victim's house on one of seven days of the week. It is also known that his motive for killing the victim was one of 10 reasons.

Each person will attempt to determine the suspect, the weapon, the motive, the room, and the day of the murder. To do this each person must use a process of elimination to cut down the number of possibilities to be considered. This is done two ways: (1) By asking the suspects simple yes or no questions, and (2) by accumulating clue card quarters. When properly matched four clue card quarters will form an entire clue which will eliminate one of the possibilities.

About clue quarters: For each of the 10 suspects, weapons, motives, etc., you need to make a clue card. It can be any size, though the bigger and thicker they are, the better they'll stand up to the rigors of the road.

Then cut each card into four parts. On each of the four quarters write the same suspect's name (or weapon, motive, etc.) and an arbitrary number. Just plan it so the four numbers add up to an *odd* number—*unless* the suspect, weapon, motive, etc., is the guilty one, in which case that clue's quarters add up to an *even* sum.

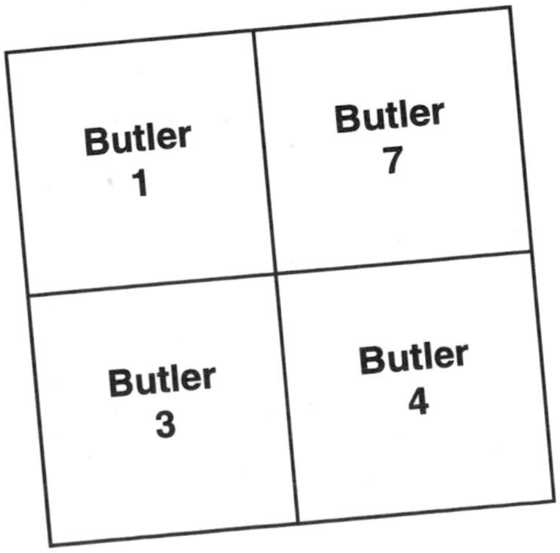

Butler 1	Butler 7
Butler 3	Butler 4

The suspects are located in houses or buildings all over the city. The players in the game must travel to these locations as they question the suspects. If you confine the game to a camp, the suspects can be located in different cabins; if you use one large building, such as a church, then the suspects can be located in different rooms. The suspects can be adult sponsors, staff, or complete strangers to the group. There can be more than one suspect at each location.

Each player receives the following:

- A clue sheet (see page 86) listing all the suspects, weapons, motives, rooms, and days to choose from. This will be used as a worksheet as information is gathered.
- A map showing the location of each suspect. (This point is irrelevant to the game but adds a fun touch.)
- Four clue quarters from four different clues. Additional clue quarters are received at each location. The first four are given out at the start of the game.
- An accusation slip (see page 85) and an envelope. When a person is ready to make a final guess at solving the mystery, the accusation slip is filled out, signed, sealed in the envelope, and handed to any one of the suspects. The time is recorded (to the second) on the outside of the envelope, and the first correct guess is the winner. All the envelopes will be opened at the Mad Hatter's Tea Party following the game. Once a person guesses, he is out of the game and goes directly to the site of the tea party.

All players are on their own. If players travel in carloads, they should not give information to each other freely. Information can be traded, however, to any person's best advantage. Players should be encouraged to come up with a strategy for information swapping, otherwise they may wind up hurting their own cause.

Each of the 10 suspects only has information about one of the five items to be determined. That means that two suspects will know who did it, two will know the weapon, etc. Players may ask each suspect two yes or no questions, such as, "Was the murder weapon a knife?" If the suspect knows, he will answer yes or no. If he does not know, he will answer "I don't know." No suspect may be questioned a second time until all the suspects have been questioned once. Each person should be allowed to question suspects alone. If this is a problem, the players should write their questions down and give them to each suspect.

At each location players will receive a new clue card quarter. When players collect all four quarters of a clue card, they fit them together and add the numbers (see page 83, "About clue quarters").

The winner is the first to correctly identify each of the five parts of the mystery. At the grand opening of the accusations, the envelopes with the earliest time written on the envelope are opened first.

The key to the game is asking the right questions to the right suspects. Some questions will be lucky guesses, but by determining who knows what, a player can be much more precise in his questioning process.

A time limit should be set at which time everyone must make a guess at the five items. The accusation slips are filled out, turned in, and the winners revealed. For accusation slips see page 85.

Award everyone who guessed all five correctly a consolation prize of some kind for a job well done.

If you do use houses all over town for the locations of the suspects, you might want to consider setting up a shuttle service, with cars going from one location to another, making stops at each one. After a player asks a suspect his questions, he then waits for the next available shuttle to the next location.

End the event with a party, refreshments, fellowship, or whatever else might be appropriate.

Bob Griffin

BIGGER AND BETTER HUNT

Create teams of four or five people and give each team a penny. Teams go door to door to try to trade the penny for something bigger and better. Owners must be willing to give the items away. After the penny is traded, teams try to acquire bigger and better items than the last, keeping all of the items for use later in the game. Teams are not allowed to trade for cash other than the one penny.

After an hour teams meet at a central location to display their acquisitions. The group that

Accusation Slip

The suspect who committed the crime is ____________________

The weapon used was a ____________________

The motive for the murder was ____________________

The room of the house was ____________________

The day of the week was ____________________

Accusation Slip

The suspect who committed the crime is ____________________

The weapon used was a ____________________

The motive for the murder was ____________________

The room of the house was ____________________

The day of the week was ____________________

Accusation Slip

The suspect who committed the crime is ____________________

The weapon used was a ____________________

The motive for the murder was ____________________

The room of the house was ____________________

The day of the week was ____________________

Accusation Slip

The suspect who committed the crime is ____________________

The weapon used was a ____________________

The motive for the murder was ____________________

The room of the house was ____________________

The day of the week was ____________________

Murder Madness

Suspects	Weapons	Motives	Rooms	Days
Maid	Knife	Money	Hall	Sunday
Chauffeur	Candlestick	Passion	Lounge	Monday
Surfer	Gun	Jealousy	Dining Room	Tuesday
Gardener	Rope	Power	Kitchen	Wednesday
Movie Star	Lead Pipe	Amusement	Ballroom	Thursday
Old Lady	Wrench	Accident	Closet	Friday
Farmer	Meat Cleaver	Greed	Library	Saturday
Butler	Hatchet	Hatred	Bathroom	
Singer	Poison	Fear	Parlor	
Magician	Shovel	Insanity	Garage	

Murder Madness

Suspects	Weapons	Motives	Rooms	Days
Maid	Knife	Money	Hall	Sunday
Chauffeur	Candlestick	Passion	Lounge	Monday
Surfer	Gun	Jealousy	Dining Room	Tuesday
Gardener	Rope	Power	Kitchen	Wednesday
Movie Star	Lead Pipe	Amusement	Ballroom	Thursday
Old Lady	Wrench	Accident	Closet	Friday
Farmer	Meat Cleaver	Greed	Library	Saturday
Butler	Hatchet	Hatred	Bathroom	
Singer	Poison	Fear	Parlor	
Magician	Shovel	Insanity	Garage	

brings back the biggest and best item is the winner. Teams have acquired things such as washing machines, watermelons, electric toasters, and all kinds of very usable stuff. The items can be sold later in a church rummage sale or can be donated to a local service organization. *Jerry Summers*

Blue Gnu

Recruit five or six people who are strangers to your group. Assign each a name such as the Blue Gnu, the Pink Panda, the Yellow Yak, the Green Goose, the Purple Parakeet, the Red Rhino, etc. Have each of these people wear an item of clothing that is the same color as the color in their assigned name and then go to a shopping center and mix in the crowd of shoppers. Then the kids in your youth group are sent out in pairs to the shopping center to find these animals. They must go up to strangers and, depending on what color they are wearing, ask them questions like, "Are you the Blue Gnu?" If they are right they get the person's real name and return to the meeting place. The kids who get the most right win. The pair that gets them all first is the grand prize winner. Set a time limit. *Vicente Trujillo*

Bounty Hunt

Want to get together with another youth group for an afternoon of fun? Play Bounty Hunt! Here are the rules:

• Each youth group's members are forewarned to bring a few bucks (for pizza afterwards) and a recent, clear picture of themselves with their first and last names written on the back with a space between them reserved for a middle name. Each group meets at its own church or at opposite ends of a mall—in which this event takes place.

• Get permission from the mall management before scheduling this event.

• Each group establishes its base at its own end of the mall. Both youth pastors collect their kids' photos, then meet each other in the middle in order to exchange them.

• When both youth pastors return to their home bases, they immediately distribute one enemy photo to each of their kids. The students must then track down the enemy whose photo they're holding, say, "Hi, ________. What's your middle name?" The captor fills in the middle name on the back of the photo, then returns to base to get a new photo and repeat the process.

• At a prearranged time the game ends. Both groups return to their bases, drive to a nearby pizza place, and compare scores. The group with the most middle names wins.

• You may have to emphasize a few rules: no running, no leaving the mall, the parking lot is off-limits, kids must surrender their middle names when greeted as above (you may need to design a penalty for refusing to give one's middle name when asked for it), players may take only one photo at a time, and the losing group buys pizza for the winning group.

Bruce Lininger and Ed Dorworth

Grocery Store Car Rally

Divide your group into cars. Each carload gets 10 one-dollar bills. Instruct them to buy 10 items costing a dollar from 10 different grocery stores and bring back a receipt for each dollar spent. Prizes are awarded on the basis of speed and variety. *Ralph Moore*

Picture Perfect

Before the event tour your city during the same approximate time of day that your group will play Picture Perfect and take Polaroid shots of fairly familiar landmarks—the statue in front of the library, the railroad trestle—from unusual perspectives.

On the day of the event, divide your group into teams, then lay out your photos for their inspection but not for their note-taking because a good memory is part of the game. Their assignment: to find the site of each photograph and to recreate as accurately as possible from memory your photographs—same angles, same lighting, same perspectives.

An hour and a half should be long enough for this event. Penalize teams a few points for every minute a team is late. Teams write their team name or number on the back of their photos, then turn them in to the judges who decide which team best matched each of the master photos.

Pictures can be worth different point values (kept secret until the judging) to reflect the relative difficulty of duplicating some shots. *Brett C. Wilson*

Columbo Sleuth Night

The Briefing:

Lt. Columbo, a hideous crime has been committed right here in our city under our very noses. I called you in because I know that you are the only person who could solve such a complex and baffling case. You see, Columbo, in this case, not only do we not know who the murderer is, but we don't know the weapon, the place, the time, the day, the accomplice, the get-away method, or even the identity of the victim! In fact, all we have is this senseless batch of clues which nobody can decipher. I'm counting on you to solve this case as quickly as possible. And, by the way, Columbo, could you comb your hair once in a while?

The Clues:

- The Dane with this name was known to brood.
The place with his name serves burgers for food.
Leave off the first word and write down the name
Of the culprit we know whom Shakespeare brought fame.
The murderer Hamlet *(Hamburger Hamlet, a restaurant)*
- A giant eye will greet you there
Upon a wall beyond compare.
Above the eye, a yellow ad
Bears the name the victim had.
The victim Alice *(Alice's Restaurant)*
- There is a store that bears the name
Of a man of great wealth and fame.
Three paces from its door you'll see
The murder weapons surrounding a tree.
Murder Weapon Bricks *(at Hughes Stationers)*
- Where Indian food is next to Chinese,
There is a place that's sure to please.
For it is right across the street,
Where our poor victim met defeat.
Place of Murder Foyer de France
- Now you need to go real high
To a steak house with health club nearby.
The first hour on Sunday you get fed,
Is when the victim was made dead.
Time of Murder 5:00 *(Opening time for the steak house)*
- The name of our church you'll find on this store
Full of bright-colored objects which Mom Nature bore.
The address upon it tells the month, day, and year,
When blood on our victim began to appear.
Date of Murder 10-9-32 *(Florist shop address)*
- On a chromium sign is written the name
Of the beast that you need to help bring you fame.
He's close to some pants, some jewels, and a bank.
For helping with murder, he'll be thrown in the tank.
Accomplice Hungry Tiger *(Restaurant)*
- This place never closes, no matter the hour.
On a corner of Wilshire you'll find its sign tower.
The name on the sign is all you need know,
Of the way the murderer decided to go.
Get-Away Method Ships *(Restaurant)*

The Rules:

Solve the clues in any order, go to the location and fill in the corresponding blank. When you have solved all eight parts, return to the designated starting place as quickly as possible. If you are not finished by 8:15, go there anyway, because the game is over. Good luck, and may you always get your man!

Columbo Sleuth Night

This is a type of treasure hunt named after the old TV detective series "Columbo" starring Peter Falk. Kids can come dressed up Falk-style, with wrinkled raincoats, messed up hair, etc. The rules are the same no matter who the game is named after.

Each team or carload of kids gets an instruction sheet which includes a briefing, the clues, and the rules. The first team to fill in all the blanks correctly is the winner. The clues below were used by one youth group, and they are shown here to give you an idea of how to design your own. You will need to come up with clues and answers to the clues that fit your own particular situation. *Jim Berkley*

Progressive Pandemonium Party

This event is similar to a treasure hunt in that the object is to reach a final destination by following certain clues in a certain order. The difference is that the Progressive Pandemonium Party uses a map and complicated instructions instead of clues.

Print up a map for each team similar in style to the sample below. The map should be of actual streets, buildings, and landmarks in your area. The map should be to scale.

The map is accompanied by a list of instructions which pinpoint the various locations where each team must go. For example, the following list was used for the sample map:

1. Extend the east wall of building 8 straight north to the edge of map. Draw a line from the S.E. corner of building 1 to the N.W. corner of building 5. Meet where the two lines intersect.

2. Draw a radius of three inches from the S.E. corner of 7. From the center of 5 draw a four-inch radius. Then from the N.E. corner of 4, draw a line to the tip of the N marker arrow. Meet where the three lines intersect.

3. From the N.W. corner of 4 draw a line to the S.W. corner of 2. Draw a line from the northern most grave marker to the S.W. corner of the map. Then draw a line from the west side of WT to the extreme S.W. corner of 8. Meet where the triangle is formed.

4. From the N.W. corner of 1, draw a line to the center point of the northern edge of the map. From the S.W. corner of 1, draw a line to the N.W. corner of 9. Then from the S.W. corner of 5, draw a line to the western tip of the second PL dash line west of the northern most road. Then from the N.E. corner of 5, draw a line to intersect the first line drawn for this stop. Meet where these four lines form a square.

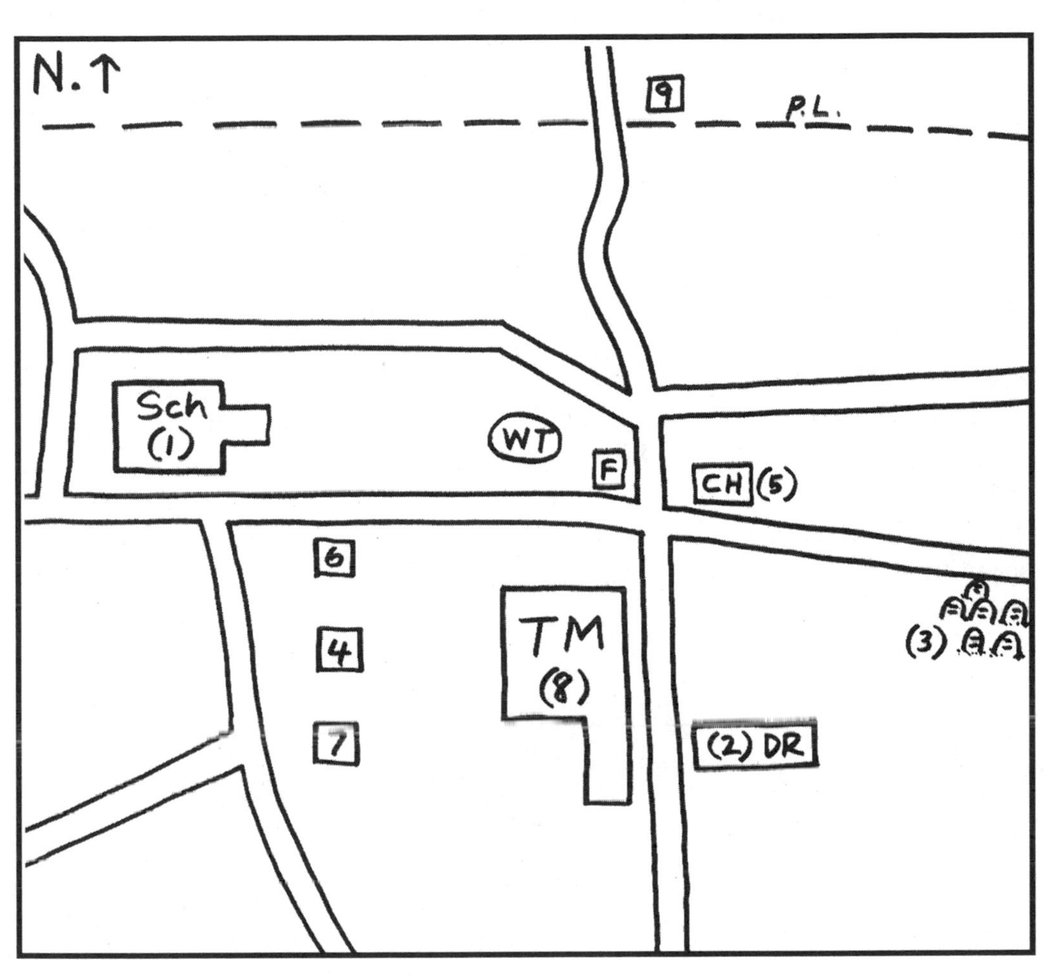

Each team should receive the same list of instructions but in a different order. With a little imagination you can create your own instructions, making them as easy or as difficult as you wish.

To add to the fun, this can be combined with a type of scavenger hunt. At each location the team must find a certain item which may be hidden, buried, or otherwise concealed. Before the team may continue, the specified item must be found. You may also hand out the next instruction at each location rather than passing them out all at once.

This event can also be combined with a progressive dinner by serving each course of the meal at the various locations designated by the map. The first team to finish all the courses of the meal and end with dessert is the winner. *Terry Ketchum*

MISSING PERSONS PARTY

This event can be done on foot or by using cars. It takes place in a shopping center or business district on a late shopping night when the stores are open. Select ten to twenty volunteers to be missing in the shopping area. The victims have pictures of them taken in normal dress that are given to the groups looking for them.

The people who are going to be missing meet together ahead of time and make up riddles or clues as to the location they'll be in. They also select a disguise appropriate to themselves and the surroundings they'll be in. For example volunteers can disguise themselves as bus drivers, cab drivers, old men, blind men, nuns, pregnant young wives, a man in a wheelchair, repairmen, store clerk, or anything that they think they can pull off.

The rest of the group are the hunters. They meet at some central location in the shopping area and divide up into groups of from six to ten per group. Each group gets pictures of the victims and the set of riddles and clues in numerical order. Each group is to stick together for the duration of the hunt. When a hunter thinks he has spotted a victim, he approaches the suspected person and says some sort of password like, *"Beep! Beep!"* If the person is a victim, then he must admit that he has been found. He then tells whether or not there is another missing person with him. If there is another the hunter informs his group and they continue the hunt. If not, the group goes on after the next victim. The first group to find all its missing people wins.

This game works best when you can go in with another youth group and have one group be the victims and one group be the hunters. That way the kids don't know each other very well which means they will be harder to find. Also it gives you more people to participate in the hunt, which makes it more fun. If you have, say, thirty missing people and thirty hunters, then give each hunting group (of six per group) six missing people to find. Each group hunts for a different bunch of victims. That way you only need one picture of each victim rather than several (one for each hunting group.) Preparation is an obvious requirement of this game. Pictures and disguises must be taken care of well in advance.

You can add another twist to this game by having the hunters kill the victims rather than just find them. At the same time the victims can kill the hunters. The killing is done by getting a sticker or piece of tape off the back of the other person. If the victims can kill off more than half the hunting and group, the group has to call off its hunt and is out of the game. However, the hunters have the advantage, so they must kill all their victims.

This basic idea can be changed or adapted to meet your own local requirements. It can be called a Manhunt or any other name that you choose. After the event, meet together to share experiences, have some refreshments and a time for fellowship. *Neil Graham*

WHERE'S WALDO?

Rumor has it he may still be lingering a mall near you. So don't look in a book—take your group to the mall to look for a real, live Waldo.

To play this version of Where's Waldo? have a youth worker or parent dress like Waldo, or at least wear something—a tie, stocking cap, conspicuous socks, etc.—that bears the trademark red-and-white Waldo look. In addition to Waldo himself, plant 10 Carriers of Waldo's Possessions in the mall, too, each one carrying or wearing one these:

Scroll	**Message in a bottle**
Flag	**Skates**
Deck of cards	**Bird's nest**
Baseball bat	**Football player**
Duck	**A cane**

With your volunteers planted at the mall, and after the kids have arrived at church, explain the game. Divide into teams of three or four, and give each team a Where's Waldo? sheet. Before you release them to the mall (or other area you've chosen), give them a Waldoesque pep talk—something like this:

> **Continue on your journey and never rest until you have found Waldo and all his possessions. For in finding them, you will help Waldo understand the purpose of his journey—and then he will perceive the truth about himself. Let the search begin!**

Kids should meet back at the church (or a designated location) as soon as they find Waldo and all of his items, or when the time expires, whichever comes first. *Tommy Baker*

Waldo ??? Where's Waldo ??? Where's Waldo ??? Where's

Where's Waldo?

Item	Verifying signature	Points
1. Waldo's scroll	______________	7,000 points
2. Waldo's message in a bottle	______________	8,000 points
3. Waldo's flag	______________	2,000 points
4. Waldo's skates	______________	3,000 points
5. Waldo's deck of cards	______________	6,000 points
6. Waldo's duck	______________	4,000 points
7. Waldo's bird nest	______________	2,000 points
8. Waldo's baseball bat	______________	2,000 points
9. Waldo's football player	______________	5,000 points
10. Waldo's cane	______________	8,000 points
11. Waldo himself	______________	1,000 points

Rules of the Game

1. Be kind, courteous, and polite at all times. Avoid being rude and obnoxious.
2. When approaching someone ask, "Are you Waldo?" or "Is that Waldo's —?"
3. The first team to find Waldo and all of his items and get to the designated location—or the team with the most points—is the winner.
4. We will meet at ______________ (PLACE) at ____________ (TIME).
5. When you find Waldo or his belongings, ask the person you found to sign your game sheet for verification.

So onward, ever upward, O noble friends of Waldo!
Join your hero on his fantastic journey. Let the Great Waldo Search begin!

Waldo ??? Where's Waldo ??? Where's Waldo ??? Where's

Where's Waldo ??? Where's Waldo ??? Where's Waldo ??? Where's

Where's Waldo ??? Where's Waldo ??? Where's Waldo ??? Where's

Crash-the-Party Party

This is part guessing game, part kidnapping party. Here's the gist of this party: There's a group of 10 forewarned individuals from your church who are supposedly a clique, and it's each team's objective to crash the clique's party.

Select 10 people from your congregation. Include people from several age groups. Make sure they'll be home the night of the party.

Prepare a clue sheet with creative yet vague descriptions of the 10 (a deacon, has the initials A.M., was listed in last Sunday's bulletin). The clues should be clear enough so that the teams won't get discouraged, yet ambiguous enough to keep them guessing.

Divide players up into teams, one per carload. Give each team 10 pieces of string or yarn, one for each potential arrest victim. Each team car has its own team color of string. Teams will identify their captured party members by tying the strings around their victims' wrists.

When groups are set, read the following instructions:

You have been called here this evening because of a group of 10 people in our church who have formed a clique. They call themselves "The Party." It is your job to arrest these 10 people and thereby crash the party.

Our decoders have been working for days to identify these 10 people, but what you read on your clue sheet is as close as they can get. Your job is to find the 10 people who fit these descriptions and to arrest them. An arrest is made by tying one of your team's strings around the person's wrist. Remember this, though—members of this clique are deceptive. They may act as if they have no idea what you're talking about. They may even resist arrest, so feel free to take them by force if need be.

[This makes things interesting, especially if they suspect and attempt to arrest the wrong people.]

Once you make an arrest, you must either bring your captives back here in your car or try to persuade them to drive here themselves. If they don't want to leave their homes by themselves, they may bring along family members. But only Party members with strings around their wrists will be considered arrests.

All captives and carloads must be back here in 70 minutes. You must obey all traffic laws. A team receives 10,000 points for each correct arrest and looses 2000 for every incorrect arrest. You will be penalized 100 points for every minute you're late.

Then turn them loose. As the arrested people and car teams start trickling back in, it may be a good idea to have table games and food to keep them occupied. Don't reveal how accurate any of the arrests are until the full 70 minutes are up and everyone is together. Award prizes. *Merle Moser, Jr.*

Picture Search

Borrow a 35mm camera or a photographer with a 35mm camera. Then stroll around inside your church building, photographing both familiar and not-so-familiar objects from unusual angles. Close-up and wide-angle lenses are helpful. How many people know what the back of the pulpit looks like? How about the inside of the janitor's closet?

When the photos are printed, post them on a bulletin board with identifying numbers. Then give each of the kids a simplified copy of the floor plans of the church building. Instruct them to figure out where in the church each photo was taken, then to write the photo's number in the corresponding area of the floor plans. The student with the most correct locations wins.

Be careful—common objects can be the most difficult to identify ("Now which exit sign had the yellow paint spattered on the bottom?"). And you can make the game more challenging by using black and white film instead of color. *Howard B. Chapman*

Weenie Hunt and Roast

For this crazy version of hide and seek, recruit parents or adult volunteers to be the weenies who hide. Kids are the hunters. Play where there are lots of places to hide, though within designated boundaries. If you play this at night, use flashlights.

Ask each of the weenies to choose a name for himself or herself. Use the names on the list on page 93 or let them make up their own. Weenies wear costumes that give subtle clues to their identity. Hunters divide into groups and choose team names. Give each team a score sheet.

Gather all players at a designated headquarters. At a signal the hunters close their eyes while the weenies hide. At a second signal the hunters

Weenie Hunt and Roast

NAMES	POINTS	CAUGHT
Polka-Dotted Pottie Chaser	400	☐
Bearded Boom Fang	200	☐
Violent Violet Sissy Killer	700	☐
Purple Pitter Spitter	400	☐
Stripped Broom Stomper	300	☐
Blue Moon Growl	200	☐
Brown Ground Cobbler	500	☐
Black Jack Shalack	10000	☐
Lemon-Lime Lip Pucker	800	☐
Gold Mold Sucker	600	☐
Orange Ganu	400	☐
White No-Hair Sal	300	☐
Red Curly Pop	200	☐
Green Meenie	700	☐
Yellow Yippie	400	☐
Gray Granite Geek	500	☐
Slick Silver Quick	300	☐
Plain Padded Pansy	700	☐
Pink Puddle Plopper	400	☐
Terrible Tan Terror	900	☐

begin searching for the weenies. Teams need not stay together to hunt. When hunters capture weenies by finding them, they bring them to headquarters and, judging from their captives' clothing, attempt to guess their names. Hunters who guess correctly win points for their team (see page 93 for suggested point values), and the identified weenie is out of the game. If players guess incorrectly, the weenies are allowed to hide again. Until they hide they are immune from capture. The team with the most points at the end of the time limit wins.

Then have a weenie roast—with hot dogs, that is. *Mike Martinelli*

THEME EVENTS

It takes serious planning in advance to pull off one of these, for you've got to build the publicity, games, food, etc., all around a common theme. The good news, though, is that planning a theme event is usually as much fun as the event itself. (See Holiday Ideas in the Ideas Library for activities and events built around holiday themes in particular.)

Anti-Prom Night

The annual high school prom is still a big deal on a lot of campuses. Unfortunately many kids are excluded because of their social status or because of the expense. Here's a tongue-in-cheek alternative to the prom that will probably go over great with your kids. Even though it is called Anti-Prom Night, it should not be seen as a negative response to the prom but a positive one. The key is to make it as ridiculous as possible and to emphasize the idea of having a great time without spending a lot of money for it. The theme can be Poverty with Style. No dates are allowed and no formal clothing is allowed unless it's all done as tacky as possible.

The planning and the program can be patterned after the typical prom, only worse—or better, as the case may be. For example, decorations can come from the church supply closet with toilet paper streamers, paper place mats, table centerpieces with weeds or donated funeral flowers, etc.

Some activity suggestions:

• A banquet of fast food chicken, fries, and other junk food
• The crowning of someone's dog as the Anti-Prom Queen
• An Anti-Prom Mad Lib (see page 98)
• A special 7 1/2-minute anti-prom dance to the latest country and western hit or some silly song
• A celebration that includes blowing soap bubbles

Trudy Moody, Lori Schneider and Wendy Rosene have an informal bubble blowing contest during "Anti-Prom Night" activities Thursday evening at the United Methodist Church. About 50 Storm Lake High School students attended.

'Anti-prom night' attracts 50 teenagers

By LORI GUNTHER
Staff Writer

Tables arranged under a canopy of streamers. Tall decorative centerpieces, place mats and dinnerware in position. Happy guests, dressed for the gala event, parade in. The queen is crowned and the banquet begins. Music fills the room throughout the meal.

The scene brings to mind the most exciting and colorful event of the high school year — prom night.

For this particular occasion, the canopy of streamers was made of toilet paper. Fluffy pink Kleenex and toothpicks stuck in paper cups made creative centerpieces, placemats were various color book pages, and the dinnerware included paper plates, Coke cups, and plastic forks—not quite the image of an elegant and elaborately decorated prom.

Obviously this was not prom, but rather "Anti-Prom Night." The event, sponsored by the United Methodist Youth Fellowship (UMYF), was designed to give the students a "cheap alternative to prom", according to UMYF Director Michael Bell.

"Poverty With Style", theme for the evening, included the rules: No dates or couples allowed; No expensive prom dresses or tuxedos allowed; Weird clothes are encouraged; No monetary expense will be tolerated.

"We wanted to prove that you can have fun without all the pomp, the pressure and expenditure," explained Bell.

Nearly 30 Storm Lake high schoolers gathered in the Fireside Room of the Methodist Church Thursday night to prove that they could indeed have a good time without the sophisticated dress and five-course meal that makes a Prom.

The attire, as they paraded into the decorated room, included sweats, jeans, peddle-pushers and black lights. There were students wearing cat glasses, purple glasses, paper corsages, headbands, baseball caps—the guest dog even had a bow in her hair.

The satire of prom was carried to the fullest as Bell crowned his dog, Jagger, Anti-Prom Queen 1982.

A prayer thanking the fact "that we can be fun and crazy" opened the banquet, consisting of chicken, chocolate milk, and chocolate cake.

There was even an alternative to the traditional after-prom party. Singing, blowing soap bubbles, and reading the ridiculous story of "Prom Night in Warm Cake, Iowa" entertained the students attending the after-anti-prom party.

Although named "anti-prom", the event wasn't meant as an insult to prom, said senior UMYF member, Tatiana Dierwechter. "Prom is a good memory, but it leaves a lot of people out. It's getting real expensive, too. People need a chance to be themselves and act the way they want to without so much pressure."

Many students in attendance agreed that prom offers pressure from various angles — pressure to find a date, pressure to spend money

Mike Bell and 'Jaggar'

Prom

Continued on back page

You can add all kinds of crazy things to make this event a success. Play some games, put on some skits, show some great films—whatever it takes to make sure the kids have a good time. Be sure to advertise it well on campus and in the local paper, and be prepared for lots of true anti-prom sentiment that can be channeled into an appreciation of Christ's acceptance of everyone. *Michael Bell*

Anti-Prom Mad Lib

Have kids come up with a name, word, or phrase for each of the following statements. Then place those words or phrases next to the numbered spaces in the mad lib, Prom Night in Gomer, Iowa.

1. Name a guy in the group.
2. Name a girl in the group.
3. Name something that you would hate to drink.
4. Name something that a girl wouldn't be caught dead wearing.
5. Name something a guy would hate to wear.
6. Name a guy in the group.
7. Name a girl in the group.
8. Name the last place here in town that you would want to go.
9. Name of someone in the group.
10. Name something to eat.
11. Name something bizarre that you wouldn't eat.
12. Give the title of one of the worst current songs you can think of.
13. Name what you had for lunch today.
14. Name a guy in the group.
15. What would you really like to say to your mother when she asks you to clean your room?

Prom Night in Gomer, Iowa

Once upon a time in that beautiful city we all dream of going to called Gomer, Iowa, there were two lovely people who were extremely, incredibly, madly, passionately, and ridiculously in love. These two were, of course, ____________(1) and ____________(2).

One day while they were sitting around after school picking fleas off ____________'s (2) dog and watching reruns of Leave it to Beaver on T.V., they began to discuss what they would be doing on the night of Gomer High's Prom. Well, ____________(2) got so excited that she had to go get a glass of ____________(3) and ____________(1) got so excited that he had to go to the bathroom. The prom was a big deal for these folks. Upon returning they began to discuss what they were going to wear to the prom. ____________(2) said she was going to wear ____________(4) along with her mother's purple garter belt and large pink triangle earrings. ____________(1) said he was going to wear ____________(5) along with his dad's fishing cap, wading boots, and gold chain necklace.

While they were talking, two other Gomer High School students appeared at the door. They wanted to watch "Leave it to Beaver" too. These two were infamous for doing weird things together like sitting and reading *The Adventures of Heroic Cows* or gazing into each others eyes while listening to old Barry Manilow records. These two were, of course, ____________(6) and ____________(7). They said that after the prom that they would be going to ____________(8) where they would kiss each other twice on the cheek. Then they would be off to ____________'s (9) house where they would play Chinese Checkers and drink hot grapefruit juice. After these exciting events they would finally go to their respective homes at around 11:30 P.M.

Well, here is what happened at the Gomer High prom later that week. First, there was a banquet at which was served ____________(10) and ____________(11). After that they all had their pictures taken in their lovely outfits. ____________(1) and ____________'s (2) were the most outstanding. Their prom theme was ____________(12). To top things off they all danced to the music of that famous band, ____________(13).

And so goes another exciting adventure of the Gomer High School prom. Join us next year when we will report on how ____________(14) talks Sharon Stone into going to the prom with him.

So long and ____________(15)!

Alphabet Fellowships

Plan a Sunday evening get together using a letter of the alphabet as your theme. Try one of the following ideas or make up your own. *Greg Price*

Food: Desserts
Activities: Decorating contest (teams decorate a cake or package or cookie), Decathlon (10 quick events like dominoes, Delaware trivia quiz, dog-breed bingo, etc.)
Devotional: from Deuteronomy

Food: Tacos and trifle
Activities: Talent show and T-shirt auction
Devotional: Truth (John 8:32)

Food: Hoagies, Heath Bars, Hawaiian Sunrise punch
Activities: Homemade hats (prize for most original), Humor (joke-telling contest)
Devotional: Hebrews heroes

Food: Cookies, cakes, and candies
Activities: Card games, Christmas carol singing
Devotional: from Corinthians

Back-to-School Night

For this high school end-of-the-summer event, decorate your party area with school-related items. Penalize tardy party goers. Kids should bring a lunch box or sack lunch to really make it seem like school. Before the event begins the kids can gather in the school yard and play hopscotch, foursquare, and other playground games. Get a buzzer or school bell to start the action.

During orientation the principal explains what is going to happen. Then she places kids in classes (teams) for competition. Each class will be graded (A, B, C, D, or F). At the end the grade point average is figured out to determine the winning class. Here are some game ideas:

- **Homeroom.** Play any animal-oriented game.
- **English Class.** Kids act out "what I did during the summer." Each class presents a skit or charade while other classes try to guess the activity. The leaders (teachers) judge for the best job and assign grades.
- **Speech Class.** Any game that involves speaking, like the old Gossip game.
- **Science Class.** Run a scavenger hunt.
- **Study Hall.** Play a word game of some kind, such as Hangman. Each group can be given a word to guess.
- **Gym Class.** Any game that involves physical activity.
- **Lunch.** Any game that involves food, such as an egg toss.
- **Biology Class.** Have teams dissect an avocado. Give each team a plastic knife, spoon, avocado, needle, and thread. Instruct them to remove the pit and sew up the avocado. The first team to complete the task is the winner.
- **Between Classes.** No school day is complete without a trip or two to the locker. For this event make a number of lockers out of hanging clothes bags. Inside each of the bags put a stack of books, magazines, a soda can, a tennis racket, and a pair of gym shorts. Each member of a team must open the locker (unzip the bag), remove the contents, and hold them while putting on the gym shorts. They then must close the locker, run to a specific point, and return to the locker and repeat everything they have done in reverse (open the locker, take off their shorts, replace the contents, close the locker), then run and tag a teammate who then does the same thing.
- **Pep Rally.** Some singing; any rowdy activity that gets everybody yelling and cheering.

Fred Coates and Dan Craig

BACKWARD NIGHT

This is a fun activity in which everything is done in reverse. Invitations and posters should be printed backward (even from bottom to top) and oral announcements should be made with your back to the audience.

As the kids arrive they should use the back door of the church or meeting place. Appropriate signs, spelled backward, could be placed at the regular entrance directing them to the rear. Each person should come to this event with their clothes on backward and inside-out.

Kids should be greeted at the door with "Goodbye! Hope you had a good time," and other such salutations. The program should be run in reverse. Begin with a devotional if you usually have one at the conclusion. As the kids leave, put name tags on them, welcome them, and introduce visitors. If paper plates are used for refreshments, use them upside down, and make everyone eat left-handed if they are right-handed and right-handed if they are left-handed.

Divide the group into at least four teams for the following games. Subtract points for the winner rather than awarding points. Have each team begin with 10,000 points, then they lose points as they win. The team names can be barnyard animals, and the team members must make the noise of their animal during the games. The sounds can be in reverse. For example, a donkey would go haw-hee, a dog would go wow-bow, and a cow would go ooooom.

Here are a few suggested games:

- **Backward Charades.** This game is just like regular Charades, except the titles must be acted out in reverse. For example, instead of *The Sound of Music*, the player must act out *Music of Sound The*. The team must guess correctly the backward title.
- **Backward Letter Scramble.** Prepare ahead of time four sets of cards (one set for each team) with the letters B-A-C-K-W-A-R-D on them. In other words each team gets eight cards, each with one of those eight letters written on them. The cards are passed out to the various team members. You then call out certain words that can be spelled using those letters, and the first team to get in line spelling the word backward is the winner. Words to use include *backward, drab, rack, ward, raw, ark, back, crab, bark,* etc. If you called out the word *drab*, for example, the kids with those four letters must quickly line up facing you so that the cards spelled it b-a-r-d.
- **Relay Games.** Run any relay you like, only do it backwards.
- **Behind-the-Back Pass.** Teams line up shoulder to shoulder. Several objects are then passed down the line from player to player, behind their backs. The first team to pass a certain number of these objects all the way down the line is the winner. For fun, try using cups of water. Spilling is a penalty and points will be added to the score.

Ed Bender

BALLOON RODEO

Form two teams and let them choose a name for themselves. Allow each team to select contestants for the following events. Each event is worth 25 points to the winner and 20 points to the loser.

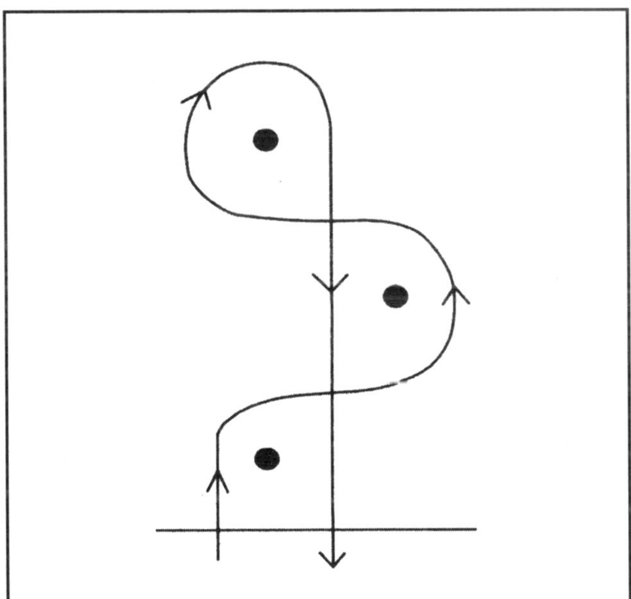

- **Barrel Racing.** Place three barrels (or plastic cones or stacks of books) on the floor in a triangle shape (see diagram). Each team enters three racers. Blindfold both starting racers. At a signal each one kicks an inflated balloon in a pattern around the barrels by following their team's shouted instructions. Each team adds up its three times. The lowest total wins.
- **Bucking Balloon Riding.** Mark off starting and ending lines about 15 feet apart. Riders each place four balloons between their legs. Then with one

hand in the air, the rider hops toward the finish line. Every rider who makes it all the way without losing a balloon gets credited with a full ride. Each team enters six riders. The team with the most full rides wins.

• **Balloon Lassoing.** Tie a large washer on a long string and wrap double-sided tape around both sides of the washer. This is the lasso. Give it to the lassoer, who stands in the middle of the room. Place 35 or so balloons at one end of the room. The lassoer's opposing team attempts to herd the balloons to the other end of the room while the lassoer tries to lasso as many balloons as possible. Each team enters two lassoers. The team with the most lassoed balloons wins.

• **Stompede.** Now you don't want to pick up all those balloons on the floor yourself, do you? So send both teams to one side of the room and gather the balloons on the other side. When you say go, both teams rush the balloons and begin stomping them and picking up the pieces. The team that collects the most balloon knots wins.

Doug Partin

BOOB TUBE BASH

This special event is for Halloween or any time of the year. Have teens dress up as their favorite TV characters, past or present. Award prizes for the most original costume, the character associated with oldest TV show, best look-alike, and so on. You can have everyone vote on these and then announce the winners.

Activities can include takeoffs on TV game shows or skits that parody sitcoms and soap operas.

Serve TV dinners or hot dogs and, finally, play a video of a favorite TV show. If you have a camcorder, you can videotape the entire event and then play it back at the conclusion of the evening.

John Erwin

BLOW DRYER BLOWOUT

Have the kids bring their blow dryers to this theme party and play games like these (and invent a few of your own):

• **Blow-Dryer Relay.** Have the kids divide into relay teams with equal numbers of guys and girls. Players run one at a time to a large bucket filled with water, dunk their heads in, and soak their hair. They run back to their teams, where two teammates with blow-dryers dry their hair as quickly as possible. A leader can judge when the hair is dry enough for the next person to go. First team finished wins.

• **Ping-Pong Ball Relay.** You'll need extension cords for this one. Kids try to blow a Ping-Pong ball around a goal and back, relay style, using blow-dryers.

• **Blow-Dryer Steal the Bacon.** Play the old game

Steal the Bacon with a lightweight ball (like a Nerf Ball) and blow dryers. When a number is called out, the two players with that number from each team run to the center where the ball is, grab their team's blow dryer, and try to blow the ball across the other team's goal line. Blow dryers may not touch the ball.

• **Blow Out the Candle.** Have a contest to determine the most powerful blow dryer. Set up candles at various distances: six inches, 12 inches, 18 inches, and so on. At each distance contestants try to blow out the candle with their blow dryers. Whoever stays in the game the longest (has the strongest blow dryer or the best aim) wins.

Jerry Meadows

BLOWOUT

Invite the big wheels in your group to come in their grubby clothes and play tire games. For these events teams can name themselves after tiremakers, such as the Uniroyals, the Goodyears, and so on.

• **Tire Scavenger Hunt.** Divide into teams and have the kids go out and find one tire (no rim or wheel) for each person in the group. The first team to return is the winner. Set a time limit. Teams are not allowed to go to tire stores or service stations, nor are they allowed to swipe tires without asking permission. If you think teams will have a hard time finding enough tires, have extras on hand so that everybody can have one.

• **Roll the Tires.** Each team rolls a tire with a teammate inside it. Race relay style.

• **Pack the Tires.** See how many kids each team can fit inside a large tractor tire (around kids' waists) within the time limit.

• **Find the Tires.** Teams compete to collect the most old tires or inner tubes.

• **Change the Tires.** Teams race to be the first to rotate all four tires on a car.

• **Dive Through the Tires.** Hang a large tire from a solid tree limb. Teams compete to have all team members dive through the tire in the least amount of time. Or set a time limit and have each team try to get as many kids through the tire as possible.

• **Race the Tires.** Teams rolls tires along a complicated slalom course that you have created. Players will find that it's not easy to turn sharp corners with a tire. They'll also have fun bumping their tire into tires from opposing teams.

• **Stack the Tires.** If you have access to a lot of old tires, have teams compete to stack the highest pile of tires, one on top of the other.

• **Eat the Tires.** Bake or buy angel food cakes with holes in the center (to resemble tires). Have one hungry player from each team compete to see who can eat a whole cake first.

• **Capture the Tires.** Place a bunch of tires in the center of the game area and mark off each team's territory around the tires in the shape of spokes on a wheel. At the signal, players try to move as many tires as possible into their team territory. Once a tire is in a team's territory, it cannot be captured by any other team.

Invite the big wheels in your group to come in their grubby clothes and play these tire games:

• **Obstacle Course.** Arrange tires into an obstacle course that the kids must run through. One tire can be set on its end (standing) with someone holding it up (or it could be hung from a rope). Another

set of tires could be set up in a slalom course, and another set laid flat on the ground, side by side, like those a football team uses for exercises.

• **Pit Crew Contest.** You will need a pit crew of at least three people for each volunteer. Have the volunteers stand at a starting line alongside their own piles of tires (eight tires per volunteer). The volunteer's pit crew places eight tires over his head, with him in the center. When all eight tires are stacked, the volunteer moves to the finish line ten feet away, with the help of his pit crew. There the pit crew unstacks the tires one at a time. The first volunteer and pit crew to complete this process wins. Rotate volunteers and pit crews so that everyone has a chance to do both.

• **Indy 500.** In this game tires represent race cars. Give each team one race car and have teams line up single file. Create an oval race track. Mark the curves with sturdy markers. The goal of the game is to be the first team to have each member make one lap around the track by rolling the tire. Add to the excitement by having a referee wear a striped shirt and wave a checkered flag to begin the race.

• **Tire Transfer.** In this timed event teams must transfer a stack of tires from one spot to another. Make sure kids have to move the tires about 30 feet and that they neatly restack the tires.

• **Tire Toss.** Kids compete to see who can throw a tire the farthest distance.

• **Tire Ball Toss.** Place tires at various distances from a line behind which players toss softballs or bean bags. The tires farther away are given higher point values. Each person gets the same number of tosses to try and earn as many points as possible.

A good refreshment would be doughnuts (because they are shaped like tires) and cider (it looks like gasoline). There are also plenty of other races that can be run if time allows. Try a three-person, two-tire race in which one person lies inside the two tires while the others push, tire painting, and lots more. Be creative and your group will never tire of this event. Hal Herwick and Dan Scholten

BLUE JEAN BANQUET

This informal banquet has only one acceptable dress code: blue jeans. The best setting is an old barn or some other rural setting with wooden tables and bales of hay for seats, and so forth. Award prizes for the oldest blue jeans, dirtiest blue jeans, clean jeans, best fitting jeans, best decorated jeans, and other appropriate ideas. You can give away blue jeans for door prizes, and you just might even get a local clothing store to donate them. *Doug Crabb*

BUBBLE BUST

Your kids will enjoy this crazy event. Get some dishwashing soap and make hoops from old wire or buy the commercial stuff, but have enough for everyone. Then try these ideas:

• **Bubble Count.** Form groups of three: one blower, one counter, and one stopper. The blower's job is to make as many bubbles as possible before the first bubble touches the floor. The counter counts the bubbles and the stopper tells the blower when the first bubble hits the floor. Bubbles that pop before the counter can count them don't count (whew!). To add to the challenge, play this game outdoors. To give each person on every team a chance to be the blower, counter, and stopper, you will need to play this game three times. Add up the three scores for the overall team score.

• **Bubble Bounce.** How many times can you bounce one bubble off another bubble that is resting on the hoop? If the bounced bubble is swallowed up by the bubble on the hoop, count that as a bounce and continue. If your hoop bubble breaks, catch another one and continue until time is called. Set a one minute time limit and rotate the team as above. You will need a blower, bouncer, and counter on each team.

• **Bubble Burst.** How many bubbles can you burst with a toothpick in a given time period? Variation: hold toothpick in your mouth.

• **Bubble Nose.** Blow bubbles with your nose. Make sure nobody has a runny nose or you may have more bubbles than you desire.

You may want to make this a part of a bubbles theme for the night by adding bubble gum blowing contest or balloon bubbles. *Richard Moore*

COME-AS-YOU-WERE PARTY

Have everyone come dressed as a baby, and have them bring a picture of themselves when they were one year old or younger. The name of the person should be on the back of the picture and the picture should not have anyone else in it such as parents, brothers, sisters, or other relatives. Place the pictures on a bulletin board and number each picture. Everyone is to number a piece of paper according to the numbers on the board and decide who each baby is. You can also vote on—

• Most beautiful baby
• Most likely to cry
• Most likely to break new toys in one day
• Most likely to get out of training pants first

Then play some of these games and contests:

• **Best-Dressed Baby.** Award prizes for the best baby costumes.

• **Baby Picture Guess.** Display everyone's baby picture and have kids try to guess who each baby is.
• **Baby Burp.** Have someone from each team drink a can of soda and try to burp while a teammate slaps him on the back. Award prizes for the loudest burp, the longest one, etc.
• **Baby Buggy Race.** Run relays with old, discarded baby strollers. A player pushes the stroller while a teammate rides in it. Provide safety helmets for the riders in case of spills or crashes.
• **Baby Bottle Contest.** Give one player from each team a baby bottle full of warm milk. The first player to empty a bottle wins.
• **Diaper Change.** Give each team ripped up bed sheets and masking tape. Half the players from each team must diaper their remaining teammates (over their clothes, of course) in the least amount of time.
• **Baby Food Race.** The first player to feed a teammate a jar of baby food wins. To make it a little harder, make sure you provide jars of unsalted vegetables or meat, not tasty fruits or desserts.
• **Crying Contest.** See who can cry the loudest, the most convincingly, the longest without taking a breath, etc.

Earl Burgess

CRUISE

Bon voyage! Throw this theme social on a single night, or run it for several consecutive nights. Tell your group in advance that your youth room will be leaving port soon and they're invited on the cruise. Drape fishnet from the ceiling, hang portholes on the walls, design passports (especially for your students to pass out to their friends), and dress the crew (your sponsors) as islanders or tourists. Soon after everyone arrives, the youth room departs amid a noisy bon-voyage extravaganza.

Then lock the doors—er, the hatches—and the kids throw themselves into typical cruise activities: limbo contests, pineapple games, on-board movies. When it's time to dock the room again, have a big farewell until the next cruise. *Doreen Rayne*

GOOD OLD DAYS NIGHT

Each kid arrives dressed in costumes from another era—you decide the era. Prizes for costumes should reflect the era. For example, costumes from the 1920s could earn prizes such as an a-oo-gah horn from a Model-T car, etc. Show old-time movies (W. C. Fields, Charlie Chaplin), and then perhaps after the meeting go to an ice-cream parlor, or something similar.

CRAZY ROCK CONCERT

Everyone would like to be on TV, but few really make it. Here is a chance for your whole group to become celebrities.

Have your kids (fans) dress as one of their favorite recording stars and bring one of their CDs. Play one song on the CD while the fan imitates the celebrity.

Fans cannot use real instruments. They must make and bring an instrument (i.e. a tennis racquet instead of a guitar; kitchen pans instead of drums). Fans cannot sing; they must lip-sync. Fans cannot make any noise while playing their instruments along with the music.

Videotape the whole thing for later laughs. *Rodney L. Puryear*

FOOT PARTY

Here's a great party idea to *kick* off your social activities. First divide the group into teams and have them choose a name. It must have something to do with feet, i.e., toe jams, bunions, etc.

The remainder of the evening is spent in foot competition:

- **Foot Painting Contest.** Teams choose an artist to draw pictures with feet. Each group is given newsprint and paper plates with poster paint, and then must paint a mural using their bare feet only on the paper. Best job wins.
- **Foot Awards.** Each group selects the biggest, smallest, and most unusual (or ugliest) foot in the group and prizes are awarded for the winners in each category. Special toe-rings can be made to designate the winning feet
- **Foot Footage.** Have teams line up their feet toe to heel. The team with longest combined length wins.
- **Foot Stack.** Stack feet on top of each other. Group with the highest stack wins.
- **Foot Songs.** Each team can make up a song about feet and perform it for the whole group.

At the end of the evening serve foot-long hot dogs. Award cans of Foot Guard to the winning team. *Richard Boyd and Bobbie B. Yagel*

FROG DAY

Your kids will love Frog Day. It's a perfect St. Patrick's Day event (since, uh, frogs are green).

Decorate with lots of frog cut-outs and brainstorm some games and activities with a frog theme.

Here are a few suggestions:

- **Frog Look-Alikes.** Encourage kids to wear green and to dress up like a frog or a frogman (diver). At the least, everyone should wear swim fins. Award a prize for the best costume. How about a croaking contest?
- **Wart Teams.** Have the kids divide into teams designated by placing a certain number of warts (round stickers or marking-pen dots) on their faces. The number of warts is the number of their team.
- **Fly-Catching Contest.** In this game team members try to toss jelly beans (flies) into a teammate's mouth from a certain distance. Points are awarded for successful catches.
- **Leapfrog Relay.** Teams must leapfrog over each other to a goal and back.

• **Longest-Tongue Contest.** Each team chooses a contestant for this tongue beauty contest.
• **The Long Jump.** Each team member's jump is measured and added together for a team total.
• **Frog Race.** If you have access to genuine frogs, have a frog race or frog-jumping contest.
Carol Potratz

GARBAGE-IN-GARBAGE-OUT PARTY

Hold a party in a garage or some other junky place with lots of old furniture and trash around for decorations. Have the kids dress in their worst clothes. Make punch out of watered-down lemonade with orange peels, lemon peels, apples, peppers, celery, and other garbage floating around in it. Serve it in a (clean) garbage can. Have parents provide real leftovers for snacks.

You can also send kids out in groups on a trash scavenger hunt. Give them a list of stuff that is going to be (or should have been) discarded. A variation of this would be to have a Bigger and Worser hunt in which kids keep trading down at each house for something worse than they had before. Use your imagination to make this the absolute worst event of the year! *Tim Smith*

GOLDEN ERA

This is a great idea for an inter-generational fellowship. Make recordings of old songs popular during the '30s and '40s. Assign songs to appropriate youths and have them pantomime.

The setting and props are the most important segments of this event. You might want to simulate a dinner audience with an orchestra and master of ceremonies and depict the time as being a night on the top floor of the Moulin Rouge with guest performances from the Andrew Sisters, Spike Jones, Tennessee Ernie Ford, and Kate Smith. This can really make senior adults feel a part of your youth program. *Randall Perry*

GREAT AND GLORIOUS GOOFY GOLF GETAWAY

Here's a new twist to a special event featuring an evening of miniature golf. Have the kids meet at the clubhouse (church) wearing their favorite golfing garb. While kids are arriving you can provide putters and golf balls for some putting around on the carpet or lawn. Get some automatic ball returners and putting cups for this.

You can begin your evening of fun with some games at the church featuring golf balls:
• **Spoon and Golf Ball Relay.** Kids hold a spoon in their mouth with a golf ball in it while they run around the flag and back.
• **Down the Drain.** Kids roll marbles from one person to the next using those long plastic tubes that come in golf bags.

Following the games serve some food, featuring the following One-Course Menu:
• Club sandwiches
• Chip shots (potato chips)
• Iced tee
• Golf balls (donut holes)
• Holes-in-one (donuts)

Above the trash can, post a sign that says PUTT TRASH HERE. Perhaps you can think of other golf puns to use throughout the evening.

After the kids have eaten, head for your local miniature golf course and let the kids play a few rounds. Give awards for the best scores, holes-in-one, and other achievements. *John O. Yates*

Hallelujah Hoedown

Depending on which part of the country you're from, your young people may enjoy an event centered around the theme of hillbillies. You could call it a Hallelujah Hoedown and Hayride (if you include a hayride, of course).

Or you might call it Hillbilly Night with the Hills Brothers. Select four sponsors to be the Hills Brothers: Mole Hill, Boot Hill, Aunt Hill, and Bunker Hill. They should dress up hillbilly style, and they can be creatively introduced to the crowd. Use the Hills Brothers' names for the teams, each of which is led by the corresponding sponsor.

Activities can include the following:

- **Hillbilly Fashion Show.** Have the kids come dressed as hillbillies. Award prizes to the best-dressed hillbillies.
- **Hayride.** Check around your area for possibilities. If you can't use a real hay wagon, perhaps you can use trucks, or even a bus filled with hay!
- **Hillbilly Talent Competition.** Have the kids come prepared to compete for prizes. Talent must be authentic hillbilly talent, like banjo-playing, yodeling, cow-chip tossing, hog-calling, singing through the nose, knee slapping, spitting, etc.
- **Outdoor Cookout.** Have a barbecue and serve good ol' country vittles like corn on the cob, black-eyed peas, mashed potatoes and gravy, biscuits and the like. You might even have a few ice cream makers ready to crank up as well.

Decorate with a country motif and have some country or bluegrass music playing in the background. You can close with some country Gospel songs like "Will the Circle Be Unbroken?"

Randy Nichols and Gary Tangeman

International Night

Hold a parent-teen potluck dinner with an international theme. Ask students to bring foods that relate to their families' nationalities. Ask some of your students ahead of time to tell stories about their famous and infamous ancestors.

Chances are, most of the kids don't know much about their family histories more than their parents' generation (and some not even that much), so the assignment encourages conversation with their parents. The occasion brings youths and parents together in dialogue, and the stories they share at the meeting can be very interesting—and maybe scandalous, so be careful! *Laurie D. Calhoun*

Hogwash Contests

If you can't get live pigs for these outdoor contests, buy a large canned ham for each team.

- **Name the Pig.** If you have one pig for each team, let each team name its pig. Judge the best name and give a booby prize to the worst names. Or have teams name their ham.
- **Eat the Pickled Pig's Feet.** Buy pickled pig's feet at a grocery store and have one person from each team race to see who can eat the most feet within a set time limit.
- **Decorate the Pig.** Provide shaving cream, hats, ribbons, clothes, and whatever you have on hand, and let each team decorate its pig. Set a time limit.
- **Hogwash.** Give teams soap, talcum powder, deodorant, etc. so they can try to make their pig as lovely as possible.

- **Tie the Tail.** Put all of the pigs in an enclosed arena so they can't escape. Have one player from each team chase down the team's pig and tie a ribbon on its tail.
- **Decorate Pig Pen.** This game is based on the character Pig Pen from the "Peanuts" comic strip. Each team decorates one of its members using mud, dirt, old rags, charcoal, or whatever. Give awards for the dirtiest Pig Pen, the most creative, etc.
- **Call the Hog.** Separate the pigs from the teams and have teams try to be the first to call their pig by yelling "Su-u-u-u-u-e-e-e-e-e-e!" This should be done one team at a time.
- **Fight in the Mud.** Have teams fight each other in a mud hole during one minute rounds. The cleanest team is the winner.

• **Feed the Pig.** Serve refreshments, such as ice cream sundaes, in a trough lined with tinfoil. Kids must eat without using their hands.

I Don't Think We're in Kansas Anymore, Toto

This *Wizard of Oz* theme party includes games, a devotional, and a snack that all play off lions and tigers and bears (Oh My!). It's perfect for celebrating the start of a new school year, of a new youth group program or season, or of any phase in the life of your students. Publicize the evening with the name of this idea: "I don't think we're in Kansas anymore, Toto."

•**The crowd breaker.** Tape index cards on the backs of the arriving kids. Each card bears the name of a character from *The Wizard of Oz* (Toto, Wizard, munchkin, a girl from the Lullaby League, etc.). The object is to discover who they are by asking only yes-or-no questions of others.

•**The games.** After dividing everyone into teams of four to 10, tell the kids in your most serious voice that there's a time for playing and a time for seriousness, and now's the time to be serious. Instruct them to follow you quietly into another room, which you have earlier set up to resemble the Wizard of Oz's throne room. At the front is a fierce head, off to one side is a hidden microphone for the Wizard, off to another side is a similarly inconspicuous niche where someone else mans the lights. Most church sanctuaries are perfect for this.

As the kids enter, the lights flash and the Wizard booms out, "WHO COMES TO SEE THE MIGHTY OZ?" then asks them what they want. The adult sponsors should be prepared to prompt the forgetful: brains, a heart, courage, and a home. The Wizard then instructs the teams that they must first complete the evening's games before returning to receive their requests.

When the kids leave the Wizard's presence, a leader explains that each game is a race against time. At the conclusion of the games, the teams reenter the Wizard's chamber according to their scores. The team with the fewest accumulated minutes and seconds enters first, etc.

—Crush the Witch. This game parallels the death of the witch under Dorothy's plummeting house. Before the event cut house shapes out of construction paper (a different color for each team), tear the houses into jigsaw-puzzle pieces, then hide the pieces in different places where the kids have to search for them (for example, tape them under pews). After each team finds its entire house and tapes it together, they bring it to a cut-out paper witch (which you earlier showed the kids) and throw the house on the witch. Each team's time for this is recorded.

—Lions and Tigers and Bears—Oh My! In this simple relay game, each team has a dress, a woman's hat, a pair of high-heeled shoes, and jewelry. Players must dress themselves in all the clothing one at a time and run to a marker 100 feet or so away, yelling all the way, "Lions and tigers and bears, oh my!" At the marker they must click their heels three times and say, "There's no place like home." Then they run back yelling, "Lions and tigers and bears, oh my!" Each team's time is recorded.

—Follow the Yellow Brick Road. You could call this Bricks of Fortune—a version of Wheel of Fortune, but without the wheel. Use phrases from *The Wizard of Oz* ("Somewhere over the rainbow," "If I were king of the forest," "There's no place like home," "Surrender, Dorothy"). Write the letters on the backs of pieces of construction paper cut to look like the bricks on the Yellow Brick Road. Instead of points the kids work to reduce their time. Each team starts a new phrase with five minutes added to its time. A team reduces its time by 15 seconds for each letter guessed, and by two minutes for getting the phrase. Vowels can be bought for 45 seconds each. A team's time for any one phrase cannot exceed five minutes or be less than zero minutes. Record each team's time after each phrase.

—**What Do You Want?** For this game of charades, use phrases from the movie. Each team gets one or two phrases to act out, and their time is recorded.

• **The talk.** As the teens enter the Wizard's room, let the Wizard be revealed accidentally as in the movie. He then admits sheepishly that he isn't an actual wizard, nor has he special powers. So the kids want brains, a heart, courage, and a home, huh? Since he has no special powers, he cannot grant these wishes—but he does know One who can. God wants to give us good gifts as the group enters this new season. He wants to give us brains (a knowledge of him and his Word), a heart (a love for God and his people), courage (the courage to take a stand for God), and a home (a place in this group where you can feel comfortable and important). This talk can be adjusted to any length and supplemented with Scripture.

• **The snack.** If you have a Dunkin' Donuts nearby, pick up some Munchkins. Otherwise, any kind of Munchkin munchies will do. *Steve Matson*

IncREDible Red

Start an IncREDible Night—which features the color red—with the You're IncREDible! mixer (page 110). Everybody must wear red to the party, of course. Give a bag of red M&M's candies (Christmas M&M's with the green ones removed) to whoever wears the most red. Include a red-grape toss and whatever other games you can adapt to the evening.

By the way, Red Cloud is from the Sioux Indian tribe. *Wayne Craft*

Indy 500

This is a special event which can be extremely successful when used with a little creativity. The idea is a sort of soap-box derby in which your entire group is divided into teams (two to four) and races cars they build on-the-spot. You provide the wheels (baby carriage wheels, skates, etc.), axles, wood, rope, tools, nails, etc., for each team, and they have an hour to build a car. It is best that each team receives the same amount and types of material to start with. An hour or two in a junkyard will produce plenty of material with which to build four cars.

After each team builds its car, they are brought to the starting line and are first of all judged (best-looking car, best-painted car, etc.). An obstacle course is set up and each team races its car around the course. The cars and drivers are pushed by team members. Pit crews are ready to make repairs when the car falls apart.

After the race, a meeting can be held to present awards, guest speaker, etc. *Bill Flanagan*

Is It Spring Yet?

Speed Spring's arrival with these games and activities:

• **Fly Your Kite Contest.** Kids make their own kites and try to fly them. Give awards for the best kites in categories like these: most unusual, largest, smallest, best flight, and so on.

• **Mow the Lawn Race.** This is done with the chassis of a power lawn mower. You can find them in repair shops with the engines removed. One kid rides on the lawnmower and makes engine noises while the other person pushes.

• **Earthworm/Caterpillar Race.** All players lie facedown, side by side. The first person on one end rolls over everyone and lies facedown at the other end. The next person follows, and soon the earthworm rolls to its destination.

• **Tricycle Race.** Since kids love to get on their bikes in the spring, have various trike races. Make sure the trikes you use don't have to be returned to owners in case they get broken.

• **Pick Your Flowers Race.** See who can scavenge for the most spring wildflowers, dandelions, or whatever.

Center devotions for this event on the newness of life in Christ or the Resurrection.

Dan Van Loon

Live and in Color

Build a huge false-front TV screen out of cardboard

You're IncREDible!

Find these people and have them initial the blank: someone—

1. ______ Wearing a red shirt.
2. ______ With bloodshot eyes.
3. ______ Who drives (or whose family owns) a red car.
4. ______ Who eats ketchup on eggs.
5. ______ Whose first or last name begins with R, E, or D.
6. ______ Who turns red (or blushes) when they're embarrassed.
7. ______ With something red in their pocket or purse.
8. ______ Wearing red pants.
9. ______ Wearing red lipstick.
10. ______ Who can name the current manager of the Cincinnati Reds.
11. ______ Who likes tomatoes.
12. ______ Who initials this space with a red pen or pencil.
13. ______ Who knows the location of Red Square.
14. ______ With red hair.
15. ______ Who owns a red-letter edition of the Bible.

or plywood which has an opening about 7 feet high by 10 feet. A platform is set up behind the opening from which the program is presented. Paint the front, including a trade name (RCA, Zenith, etc.) and affix big dials on the front. The idea is simply to create the illusion of a giant TV set to give programs with a TV theme a more authentic setting.

There are many ways to use your giant TV screen in youth programming. If the props are built durable enough to last, this can be a regular monthly feature of a youth group. Programs used should take on the format of well-known TV shows like "The Tonight Show," game shows, the news, amateur hour, soap operas, and many others. Announcements can be in the form of TV commercials.

Another approach, especially good at camps, is to divide the group into teams named after the major TV networks. All the competition and activities follow a TV theme. Simply rename familiar games with TV titles. Evenings can include teams putting on TV shows for entertainment. Use your imagination and the TV idea can work very well for you. *Ed Childress*

Make It a Date

Promote a fancy banquet to which everyone is required to bring a date—not the girl from third-period English, however, or the captain of the football team. Each date must be handmade from broom sticks, paper bags, basketballs, and any other household items. Award prizes for Best Male Date, Best Female Date, Most Outrageous Date, etc.

Have fun with the food you serve, too. Suck Jell-O through straws, spell words with alphabet soup, build crouton houses. You'll probably want to order pizza for later. *John Fehlen*

Music Video Night

Let the kids create their own music videos.

Before you have your Music Video Night, divide into small groups or bands and allow them a week or so to plan their show and assemble their props. They can put anything they want on their video (within reason, of course). They can perform their music live, or they can lip-sync a record.

On the night of the event, have the groups meet in separate rooms to plan and rehearse their videos. After this let your camera person videotape each group one at a time. Arrange the taping so that each group can perform in isolation without the other groups watching. At the conclusion of the taping, have everyone meet together and show all the videos.

Arrange some snacks and things to do for the kids who are waiting while others are taping. To speed things up tell the groups they only get one take. It's a lot of fun to see what everyone comes up with, and the bloopers are great! *Steve Gladen*

Newspaper Night

To prepare for Newspaper Night get a huge pile of old newspapers. The following games can be played with two or more teams:

- **Newspaper Costume Race.** Teams have five minutes or so to dress kids up with newspaper to look like certain things. For example: Santa and his reindeer, Butch Cassidy and the Sundance Kid, Snow White and the seven Dwarfs, etc. Tape can be provided for each team to help them construct the costumes. Judge for the best job.
- **Newspaper Treasure Hunt.** Put in each team's pile of papers several specially colored pages. The team to find the most in the time limit wins.
- **Newspaper Scavenger Hunt.** Call out certain items from the papers. The first team to find them wins. For example, a Honda ad, a want ad for a 1956 Chevy, a news item about a murder, etc.
- **Wad and Pile.** Teams get ten minutes to wad up all their paper into a big pile. The highest pile wins.
- **Hide and Seek.** Hide as many kids as possible under the pile of wadded-up papers. The team with the most kids out-of-sight wins. Set a time limit.
- **Compact Newspapers.** Teams try to compact the paper on their side into the smallest pile possible.

• **Snow Fight.** Make a line of chairs between the two teams. On a signal the teams throw all their paper on the other teams side. When time is up (two or three minutes), the team with the least amount of paper on their side wins.

• **Disposal Event.** Give each team plastic trash bags. The team to get all of the paper in the bags in the fastest time wins.

Greg Kinloch

A Night in the Tropics

Have a tropical party during the dead of winter doldrums. Pretend you are on a South Pacific island for a night. Decorations should include travel posters from travel agencies, fishnets on the wall, potted green plants and palms, seashells, wicker chairs, tropical fish, and the like. Play Hawaiian music or the Beach Boys in the background.

If possible, it would be fun to simulate a beach scene with sand, suntan lotion, beach chairs, towels, sandals, and lights borrowed from a professional photographer.

On the invitations tell kids to dress in casual island style and let them figure out what it means.

Leaders can wear muu-muus, sandals, beachcomber hats, puka shell necklaces, and so on. Have some extras on hand for kids who can't get any on their own. When kids arrive give them a flower lei and play some appropriate games. Good ones include the limbo (you know, the walking-under-a-stick game), bobbing for bananas, hula dancing contests, and clik-claks (dancing between sticks as they are clicked together and on the floor in rhythm by two people holding the stick ends just above the ground).

Refreshments can include a giant fruit tray, tropical punch bowl, and appropriate goodies such as lemon bars, coconut granola, and fried bananas. You might even want to put on a complete luau, serving barbecued pork, rice, and all the trimmings.

You can conclude the evening with music, skits, or a film that features surfing and water sports. Kids will love it, especially if you do it in January or February. *Steve Burkey*

Noise Night

Use these contests and relays to give kids in your youth group an opportunity to make a lot of noise for a change.

See the Real Screamers fun sheet on page 113 for a mixer you can use early in the party. Award a prize to the first player who successfully acquires the appropriate signatures for the fun sheet.

• **Scream.** Have individuals or teams compete to see who can make the loudest noise. Have contestants stand about 20 feet from the microphone of a sound system that can monitor volume. Then watch the needle jump! Noise can be made with mouths only, not feet or hands.

• **Identify the Noise.** Before the night of the event, record a variety of noises and have kids try to identify them.

• **Yeller Relay.** Teams make noise to try to prevent players on other teams from hearing relay instructions given by teammates. At the same time Player 1 on each team runs to a leader and receives an instruction (run with your hands above your head, for example). He must try to yell that instruction to his teammate, Player 2, who is on the team line 15 feet away (Player 1 can't make any gestures; Player 2 can). Once Player 2 comprehends the instruction, she follows it while running 15 feet to the leader to receive an instruction. Player 2 then tries to communicate that instruction to Player 3 and so on. Opposing teams should try to foil communication on other teams by making as much noise as possible.

• **Night Contest.** Send each team to a private area to create and practice the most obnoxious, disgusting noise possible. Then one by one teams perform their sound for a panel of judges who determine the winner.

• **Skits.** Find a script or write your own, but make sure it motivates the group to make a lot of noise.

• **Cap Smash.** Each player tries to set off the most caps with a hammer in 10 seconds (while the group counts). Hint: This game is even more fun when the contestant is blindfolded.

• **Dessert.** How about some ice scream?

Jim Walton and Tia Booth

On the Ritz

Here's a twist on a dress-up dinner that allows your

Real Screamers!

Directions: Get as many signatures as possible. Have fun making your friends prove it!

Who in this room...

has the biggest Adam's apple? ____________

loves party time? ____________

screams at spiders? ____________

can think of a song with the word *scream* in it? ____________

can play their vocal cords? ____________

has the shortest neck? ____________

uses Shout! detergent? ____________

is in the chorus? ____________

has the roundest mouth? ____________

has the longest scream? ____________

has the loudest scream? ____________

has the thinnest neck? ____________

fears roller coasters? ____________

has the longest tongue? ____________

can hit the highest note? ____________

can throw his voice? ____________

gets chilly thrills from scary films? ____________

can YODEL LE DEHOOO? ____________

loves party time a lot? ____________

can whistle a happy tune? ____________

has a deep belly laugh? ____________

can hit the lowest note? ____________

Real Screamers!

Directions: Get as many signatures as possible. Have fun making your friends prove it!

Who in this room...

has the biggest Adam's apple? ____________

loves party time? ____________

screams at spiders? ____________

can think of a song with the word *scream* in it? ____________

can play their vocal cords? ____________

has the shortest neck? ____________

uses Shout! detergent? ____________

is in the chorus? ____________

has the roundest mouth? ____________

has the longest scream? ____________

has the loudest scream? ____________

has the thinnest neck? ____________

fears roller coasters? ____________

has the longest tongue? ____________

can hit the highest note? ____________

can throw his voice? ____________

gets chilly thrills from scary films? ____________

can YODEL LE DEHOOO? ____________

loves party time a lot? ____________

can whistle a happy tune? ____________

has a deep belly laugh? ____________

can hit the lowest note? ____________

young people to pull out their I've-only-worn-this-to-the-prom-once outfits and get some culture, too—all for the price of a movie!

Getting tickets to the symphony, ballet, or opera is usually easy. To promote the arts, they frequently offer student tickets for a song. Add the allure of a formal dinner (at which parents serve and church musicians play during the meal), and your kids will be begging for the classics. *Frank Riley*

Once in a Blue Moon Party

A blue moon is supposed to occur when two full moons appear in the same month, but you don't have to wait for that rare occasion to throw this party. Just have it on a night with a full moon.

Everyone dresses up in blue, anything from blue pajamas to blue-faced moon creatures. At sunset serve barbecued moondogs (blue mayo and blue cheese optional) and blue punch. As you eat you can watch the horizon for the first hint of the moon's arrival. Cheer as it comes up.

Have a moon trivia game and a moonwalk contest, awarding the winners packs of flat glow-in-the-dark stars and planets (found at toy stores, Wal-Mart, Target, etc.). Show a video of the moon landing (borrowed from your local public library), then go outside to play moonball (blind volleyball with a blue tarpaulin for a net). Wind down with some singing (the blues, of course) and let someone do a solo rendition of "Blue Moon." Use Psalm 8 for a devotional. If you like, set up a telescope or two for better moon viewing. *Evan D. Wise*

Out of School for the Summer Party

Most kids would enjoy a year-end party that celebrates no more school and the beginning of the summer. Games could include:

- **Dunce Relay.** Divide into teams. One player on each team runs to the blackboard and writes TEACHER IS A DUNCE, then returns to his or her seat and tags the next player on the team. The game continues in relay, and the first team to finish wins.
- **Unspelling Bee.** Just like a regular spelling bee, except each word must be misspelled but still recognizable. Give an award for the most creative entry.
- **Unlearning Contest.** Each team comes up with the most creative way to forget anything learned during the school year that they still happen to remember.
- **Excuse List.** Each team tries to write the most excuses for not getting an assignment in on time.
- **Bubblegum Blowing Contest.** The teacher (sponsor) turns his or her back to the class. Each student is given bubble gum and begins blowing bubbles behind the teacher's back. When the teacher turns to face the class, the biggest bubble seen by the teacher wins.
- **Shootout at the O.K. Corral.** This is an historic reenactment of My Final Day in High School. Each member is armed with a squirt gun and is mounted piggyback for a shootout.
- **Class Notes Bonfire.** Have all the kids bring any class notes they don't want to save and send them up in flames.

Dan Van Loon

Peanuts Picnic

This special event is based on the immortal "Peanuts" comic strip characters, created by Charles Schulz, and is a great activity for junior highers. Advertise it as a "Peanuts" Picnic on posters, flyers, mailings.

Refreshments can include peanuts, peanut butter sandwiches, etc. Play the games below, plus any others that you can think of that reflect the theme, and award appropriate prizes to the winning teams. (Many stores carry a wide variety of "Peanuts" toys and gifts.)

- **Charlie Brown's Game.** This is a game of modified softball. Play it on a regular softball diamond, only use a mushball and run the bases in reverse order. The infield players cannot throw the ball, but they can pick it up and run with it to tag the runner or the bases. Three innings are played, with two outs per inning. The points scored are given to the other team, and the team with the most points loses. All other rules are the same as regular softball.
- **Linus's Game.** This one can also be called Steal the Security Blanket. A blanket is placed in the center of a large square. Each team lines up on one side of the square (there should be four teams). Each team should number off 1-2-3-4-etc., so that each player has a number. To begin the game, one or more numbers are called out by the leader, and all the

players on each team with the corresponding numbers run to the center and try to pull the blanket across their team's side of the square. As soon as any part of the blanket crosses their side, a point is scored and the blanket is returned to the center of the square and the players return to their sides. Two connecting sides may receive points at the same time if the blanket crosses connecting teams' lines. Call out new numbers until everyone is sick and tired of playing the game. For best results use a blanket made of tough material, such as canvas.

• **Snoopy's Game.** This is a doghouse pack which requires you to acquire or build a doghouse. Each team simply tries to pack as many players as possible inside and on top of the doghouse within a given time limit. The team that gets the most kids in and on it is the winner.

• **Red Baron versus Snoopy Game.** This game should be played on a large open field. Draw a line of demarcation which separates the Red Baron's territory from Snoopy's territory. Divide the group in half and assign players to their territories. Each player on the Snoopy team has a tail that can be a flag (like those used in flag football) or a piece of tape on the clothing. Before the game begins the Snoopys gather at the end of their territory, as far away from the line of demarcation as possible, and the Red Barons line up on the line. On a signal the Snoopy players try to get into Red Baron territory with their tails on. The Red Baron players try to capture tails before they cross the line. The Snoopy team gets a point for every tail that crosses into Red Baron territory, and the Red Baron team gets a point for each captured tail.

• **Schroeder's Game.** Schroeder is the little boy who loves to play his toy piano, so this game is a musical one. Each team must compose and perform a short team song. A panel of judges selects the winner.

• **Pig Pen's Game.** Each team decorates one teammate to look like the Pig Pen character. Mud, grease, dirt, charcoal, marking pens, torn clothes, etc., may be used to make the kid look as dirty as possible. A panel of judges can select the winner.

• **Lucy's Mouth.** Each team creates the loudest noise possible. Judges award prizes to the winner.

Personal Potato Awards

To honor teens at your next awards event, put together a personal potato trophy for each teen.

Working with staff or volunteers, gather a bag of potatoes and craft supplies: pipe cleaners, craft eyes, Styrofoam cups, tape from an old audio cassette (for hair), straight pins, markers, fabric, ribbon, yarn, Popsicle sticks, buttons. Create Mister and Miss Potato Heads complete with faces, hair, and even clothing and accessories. Present each teen with the trophy after the standard congratulatory remarks. *Dave Mahoney*

Picture Party

Here's a good party idea with a photograph theme. Below are some suggested ideas for the party, but don't limit yourself to them. Any activity that incorporates the use of pictures can be used.

• **Picture Invitations.** For your publicity send a picture of the party location, along with other details.

• **Baby Picture Guess.** Have kids bring their baby picture. Collect and post the pictures on the wall or bulletin board. The first game can then be to identify each baby. You can also give awards (have the kids vote) to the cutest baby, the most unusual baby, and so on.

• **Picture Scavenger Hunt.** Distribute magazines, divide into small scavenger-hunt teams, and give the kids a list of pictures they need to find. Pictures can include such things as a 1990 Toyota, a Timex watch, a family on vacation, someone who looks funny (judge for the funniest), a fish, more than 25 people (whoever can find the most people in one picture wins), someone doing something heroic, and so on.

• **Picture Identification.** Shoot ahead of time some slides or photos of various locations around town and have the kids try to guess what they are. Some can be easy, others can be tough. Award points according to difficulty.

• **Polaroid Scavenger Hunt.** If you have time include this old favorite. Give everyone a Polaroid camera, film, and list of pictures they need to go out and shoot. Examples: your entire group up in a tree, in the back seat of a police car, in someone's bathtub, etc.

• **Group Portrait.** End the event by taking a group picture. Get a professional photographer to take it. Have the group pose for a serious picture as well as a crazy picture. Arrange to have enlargements made that the kids can order for their scrapbooks. Because of this photo alone, you might want to advertise this evening in advance so that everyone is present for the group shots.
Ralph Gustafson

PIRATE NIGHT

Invite youths to the event with posters and treasure maps cut from brown paper bags. Students who come in theme costumes can be admitted free to encourage active participation.

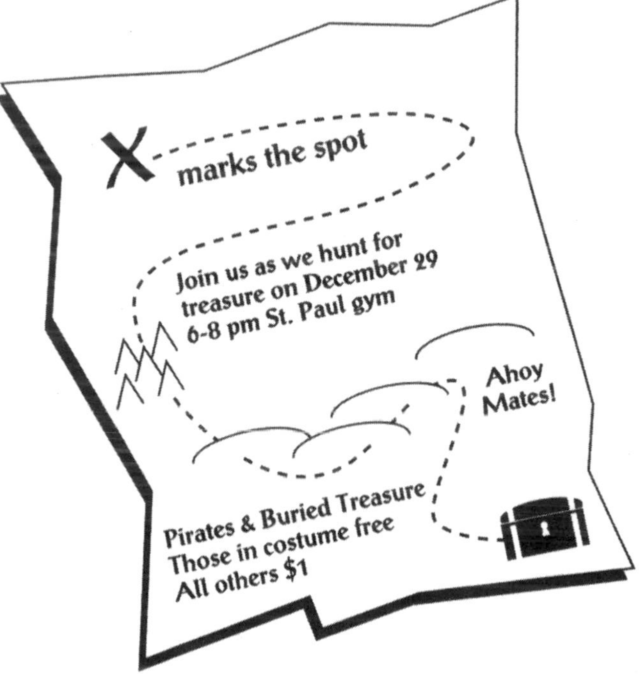

Make a number of treasure chests using the pattern provided. Place chocolate coins from a candy store and a Bible verse pertaining to treasure inside each one. You can use the following verses:

Proverbs 2:1-5	Exodus 19:5
Isaiah 33:6	Malachi 3:17
Matthew 6:21	1 Chronicles 29:3
Matthew 13:44	Proverbs 10:2
Luke 12:33	Matthew 6:19-21

Hide the treasure chests around the meeting location and prepare a list of clues. Be sure plenty of Bibles are available. Decorations can include pirate ships, a large treasure chest, fish netting, and gold coins (poker chips wrapped in foil). For refreshments provide apple juice for ale, submarine sandwiches with flags inserted, and rum (butterscotch) candies.

The first part of the evening is the hunt for treasure. Give all the students a handout with scriptural clues to hidden treasure chests. For a sample handout see the one below. If you make it challenging, the hunt can last about an hour. When all the chests have been found, the teens return to the meeting spot for the lesson. Read and discuss all the Bible verses in the treasure chests.

During the refreshments enjoy a few sea chanteys. You can finish off the evening with a friendly game of Royal *RUM*my. Have fun, mates!
Sue Lilienthal

RECORD-BREAKING EVENT

Since CDs and cassettes have made records obsolete, collect from your neighborhood and congregation a pile of old, discarded records, both 45s and LPs. Then have a record-breaking event! (This is not a bring-your-rock-records-so-we-can-burn-them rally.)

• **Record Hide.** Hide all the records beforehand. When the kids arrive tell them how many records are hidden and give them 10 minutes to find them all. Award a prize to the person or the team who finds the most.

• **Record Wrap.** Give your students wrapping paper, scissors, and tape. Here's the contest: who can gift-wrap a record (not in a jacket) quickest and neatest—with one hand?

• **Bowling Record.** From behind a starting line, have each person in your group roll a record. Award prizes for longest roll and shortest roll.

• **Fetch the Record.** Stack the records at one end of the room. Have players in relay teams race down to bring a record back to their teams. The team with the most records in two minutes wins. Only one record at a time may be carried.

• **Record Sculpture.** With masking tape and records, students must create a sculpture in 10 minutes that resembles a recognizable object. (Hint: by warming records in an oven, you can bend them into shapes.)

• **Frisbee.** Award prizes for Frisbee throwing: farthest throw, most accurate throw (at a target), etc.
Alan Wiersma

PIRATE NIGHT TREASURE CHEST PATTERN

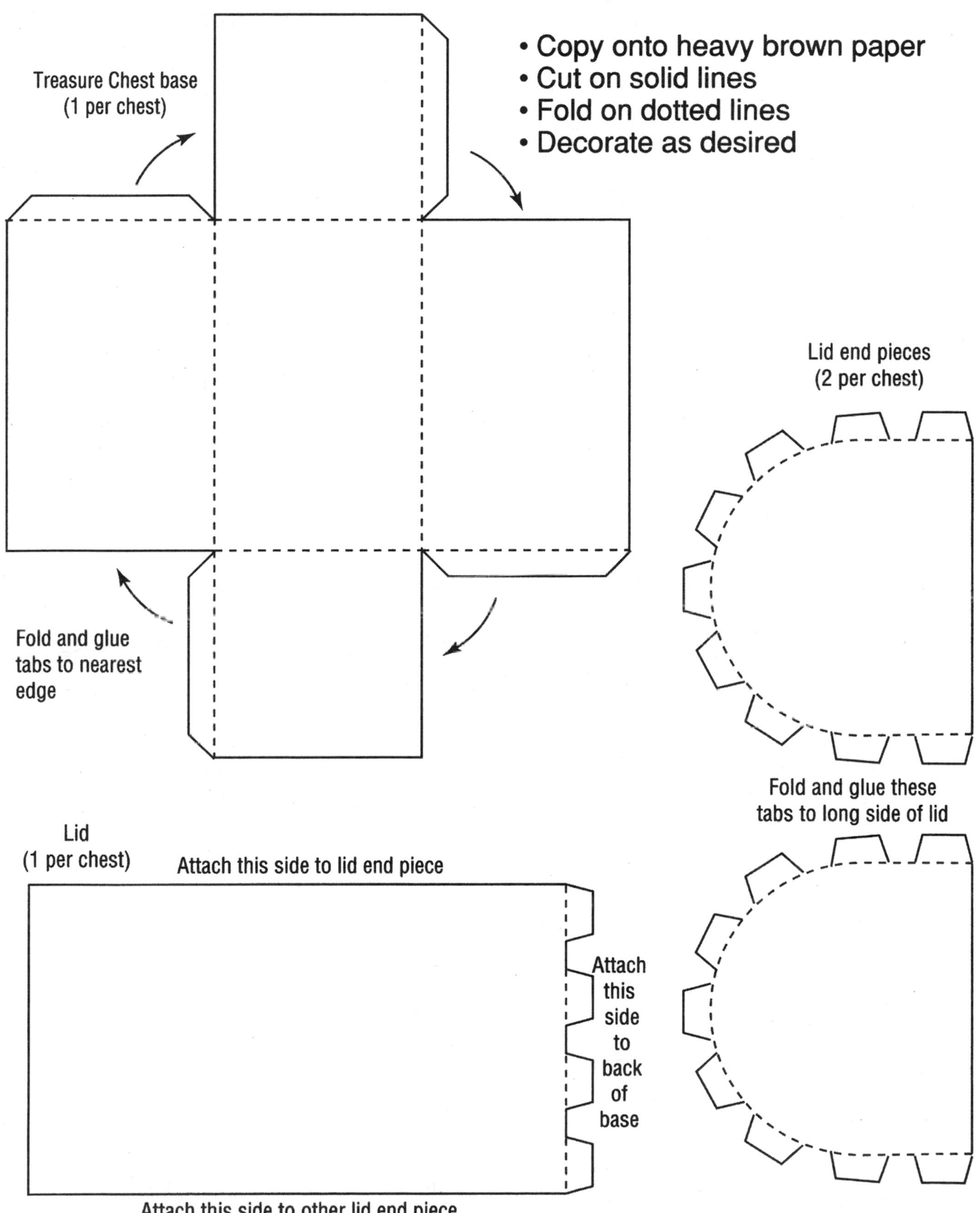
Treasure Chest base
(1 per chest)
• Copy onto heavy brown paper
• Cut on solid lines
• Fold on dotted lines
• Decorate as desired
Lid end pieces
(2 per chest)
Fold and glue
tabs to nearest
edge
Fold and glue these
tabs to long side of lid
Lid
(1 per chest)
Attach this side to lid end piece
Attach
this
side
to
back
of
base
Attach this side to other lid end piece

SUPER BOWL BASH

Celebrate the Super Bowl or any major sporting event with this party plan. When choosing the different homes, take location into consideration so that you won't miss much of the game during travel from place to place.

Teens may wear the colors of the team they are rooting for.

Divide the evening according to periods, quarters, or innings depending on what sport you're watching. Then enlist different parents to host portions of the evening in their homes. For a Progressive Super Bowl Party, for instance, you could use as few as two homes (pregame and first half, and half-time and second half) or as many as six (pregame, first quarter, second quarter, half-time, third quarter, fourth quarter).

Ask each host to supply snacks that fit the event (cookies shaped like footballs, ballpark hot dogs, etc.).

Feature games like these:

- **The Super Bowl Bible Quiz.** Prepare a list of Bible questions ahead of time. The object of the game is to score touchdowns by answering eight questions correctly. Each question is worth 10 yards. Divide into two teams. Teams on offense start on the 20-yard line and have 80 yards to go for a touchdown. You keep the ball as long as your team answers questions correctly. When one team answers incorrectly the ball goes to the other team, and they begin where they left off on their last possession. After each question the team can huddle to discuss the answer to the question and then make their play by answering the question. After a team scores a touchdown, both teams start over on their own 20-yard lines for the next series of downs. Play for as long as you like.
- **Coin Flip Football.** This game is played by two people. Have the kids pair off and give each pair a copy of the gridiron on page 119. Each pair will need one coin and one marker to indicate the location and direction of the football.
- **Super Bowl Bingo.** Distribute bingo games similar to the sample below. Write your own questions in the spaces, incorporating the current Super Bowl teams as much as possible. Then have kids mill about the room asking people to answer the ques-

Super Bowl Bingo

What was the Super Bowl score last year?	What emblem do the Bears have on their helmets?	Which NFL team has had a perfect season?	Who is the 49ers' coach?	What NFL team has the most famous cheerleaders?
Who is in today's Super Bowl?	Who is the 49ers' quarterback?	Which team did Joe Namath win a Super Bowl with?	What city is today's Super Bowl being played in?	What team plays in Indianapolis?
How many games did the 49ers win in their regular season?	How many games did the Dolphins win in their regular season?	FREE	Who is the Dolphins' quarterback?	Put your own name here!
What is Walter Payton's football jersey number?	Who is the Chicago Bears' head coach?	Name a defensive player for Miami.	How much does 1 minute of commercial time cost for this Super Bowl?	Name a defensive player for the 49ers.
Name four other bowl games	Which team is going to win this Super Bowl?	Where was last year's Super Bowl played?	Name three coaches for the Bears.	Where did Joe Montana play college football?

Coin Flip Football

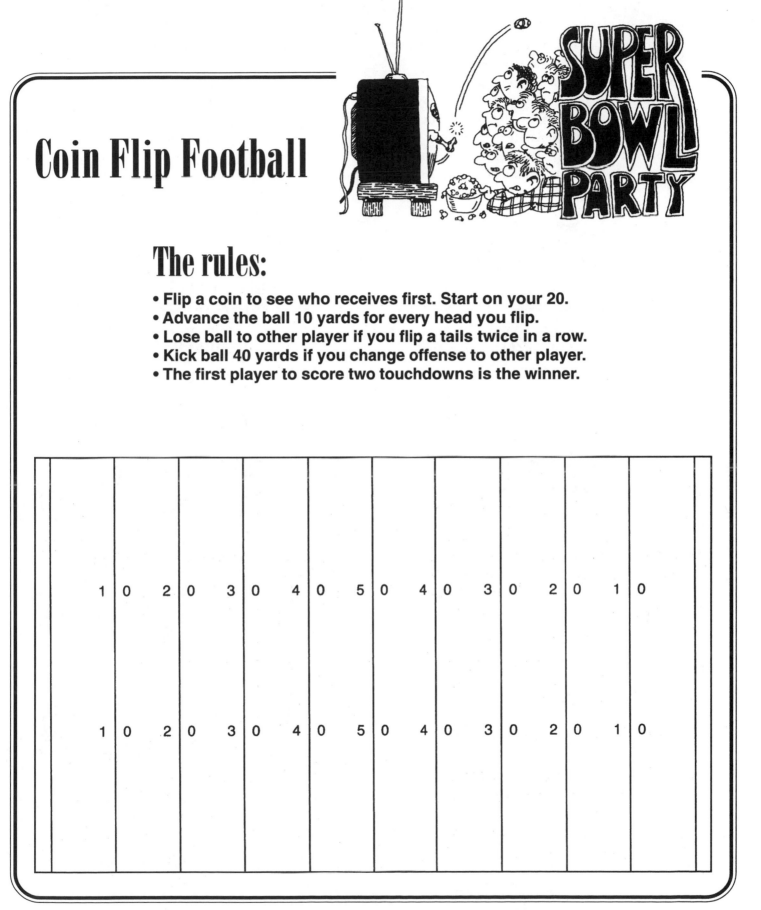

The rules:

- **Flip a coin to see who receives first. Start on your 20.**
- **Advance the ball 10 yards for every head you flip.**
- **Lose ball to other player if you flip a tails twice in a row.**
- **Kick ball 40 yards if you change offense to other player.**
- **The first player to score two touchdowns is the winner.**

10 20 30 40 50 40 30 20 10

10 20 30 40 50 40 30 20 10

tions on their sheets. Whenever someone knows (or thinks they know) the answer, they give that person their answer and sign their name in the space. The first person to get five in a row wins, but they automatically lose if their five people cannot correctly answer the questions they have signed.

Instead of having a Super Bowl party for all the kids, you may want to have the guys in your group sponsor a Super Bowl party for their dads. Meet in a home where two or more TV sets can be arranged so the entire group can see. The kids can provide the snacks for the event.

Use the time to develop father-son relationships and to get to know the dads better. It's an especially good way to get acquainted with non-Christian fathers. *Tim Borgstrom, Tim Gross, and Ed Laremore*

RAIN DANCE

So often our most carefully made plans for an outdoor event are laid to rest by rain or foul weather. So for the fun of it, put a date on your calendar that will be canceled in the event of sunshine! Call it a rain dance or a rain out and plan activities to do in the rain (volleyball, Frisbee, water balloon wars, etc.). Afterward move indoors and have a Bible study on Genesis 7 and 8 (Noah and the flood), listen to appropriate music ("Raindrops Keep Falling On My Head," "Singing in the Rain," "Rainy Day People," "Kentucky Rain,"), and have a feast on—what else?—watermelon! *Rod Klinzing*

SKITZOPHRENIA

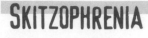

Divide your entire group into four or five teams. Each team must make up, rehearse, and perform a skit to be judged by a panel of experts.

One set of props and costumes is used by all the teams. Show them to the kids before they plan their skits. Each team must use all of the props and costumes provided.

A theme is given to each team and they must create a skit around that theme. Possible themes can be The Old West, Babies and Parents, Man on the Moon, etc.

The teams are given 30 minutes to plan, and then one at a time present their skits. They are judged for the best, funniest, most original, best actor, best use of props, etc.

STUFFED ANIMAL NIGHT

Return your teenagers to their childhood, if only for an evening. Get the word out for them to bring their favorite stuffed animals to a youth group meeting. Pile the menagerie in the middle of the room and play games that help your group think about being kids again.

Adapt games and relays by using stuffed animals instead of the usual items called for.

When you're ready to tone down the evening, have the kids gather into a circle and let them spend some time sharing what makes their stuffed animals so special. You might focus on unconditional love, for instance (both stuffed animals and God love no matter what).

Finish the evening with a story time. Hand out graham crackers and read *The Velveteen Rabbit* while kids sit with their stuffed animals. Mark Jackson

TOURIST TRAP

This activity works especially well with junior high kids. The idea is to have everyone dress up as tourists—shorts, flowered shirts, straw sun hats, sunglasses, cameras, maps, leis, whatever—and then go see as many sights as possible in a designated time. Six hours is average, and maximum time spent at any sight should be half an hour.

Pile everyone into the same bus or van if possible and have the kids bring a sack lunch and some spending money. You'll also need some extra adults to help supervise. Remember, lots of silly pictures posed with one another and with strangers are a must. It's a bit insane, but it's worth the fun. Steve Simpson

WATER DAY

This is an excellent event for a hot, summer day. You'll need a lawn, some hoses, a water tub, water balloons, some volleyball gear, and a few other odds and ends. Kids come in swimsuits or shorts, and the games below are played.

• **Waterlogged Volleyball.** Have sprinklers set up on the net and around the area so that water will be raining down everywhere on the playing area. Then follow regular volleyball rules.

• **Cup Splash Relay.** For this one you will need a large tub filled with water. Each group has one large plastic cup. With the sprinklers running and the volleyball net lowered, the participants have to run from one end of the volleyball court to the other. They must slide under the net, get up, run to the tub, fill their cup with water, run back, slide back under the net, run to the group, and splash the water in the next person's face. Each person follows the same pattern. If the group is small, do the event twice.

• **Water Balloon Race.** With the tub filled with water, put a bunch of water balloons in it. Run it like race 2; each person must run, slide under the net, run to the tub, get a water balloon, run back, slide under the net, and run to the starting line. This time instead of hitting the next person in line with the balloon, teens must break the water balloon over their own head. Then the rest of the group, one at a time, goes through the same process. In both the water balloon race and the cup splash relay, if a person drops her cup of water or pops her balloon, she must go back and get another one.

• **Three-Legged Cup Pour Relay.** This is like a regular track relay with several stations to receive a baton. However this relay is a three-legged race and the baton is a cup of water. Two people pair up at each station with their legs tied together. The first group is given a cup filled with water, the other stations have an empty cup. Group 1 runs to Group 2 and empties its cup of water into Group 2's cup of water. Group 2 runs to Group 3 and repeats the process and so on. The winner is the group that has the most water left in its cup.

For prizes, give the winner Perrier water, second place club soda, and last place dishwater. Serve watermelon for refreshments. Francis Fontana

INFORMAL FORMAL

Instead of having your kids spend money on tuxes and formals, bill your next banquet or other formal

event as an informal formal. What do you wear to an informal formal? The best rule of thumb is this: If it looks good, don't wear it! Of course, the men must wear a tie but not around their necks.

You'll be amazed at the creations your group will display. Pictures are a must, so set up a backdrop and have someone act as a photographer. And don't forget to take a group picture! *Tommy Baker*

Boxer Ball

Bill your next high school or college banquet as a boxer ball. Attire? Coat, tie—and boxer shorts. Footwear is optional. Formal events at camps or retreats are ideal settings for a boxer ball. For decorations, use a variety of types and sizes of boxes. And don't forget your camera! *Tommy Baker*

Dove Awards Party

In April the Dove Awards, the Grammy awards for Christian music, are broadcast. In 1994 the Family Channel ran a three-hour special. Invite your group members to meet at the church or at the home of someone with a big screen TV for a Dove Awards party.

As the kids arrive, give each one a copy of page 123 and a list of the nominees in different categories and ask them to guess who will win. Keep a master list, and as you watch the televised ceremony, keep track of who guessed correctly. Give your own awards for the most correct guesses. Dove candy bars or ice cream bars make a hit. *Brett C. Wilson*

Progressive Sprinkler Party

For this progressive party, have everyone wear bathing suits and bring towels. Play different water games at the various homes you visit. Play sprinkler games at the first house, Slip-n'-Slide at the second house (you can make one with a large plastic sheet), water balloon wars at the next house, water volleyball played under a rainfall created by several sprinklers around the net, and swimming pool games or an open swim time.

You can add any number of attractions along the way if you live near a beach or near one of those giant water slides, etc. The extra dimension that this brings to traditional water events is variety. Kids love it! *Marge Clark.*

Prison Party

This prison-theme event can be a lot of fun by itself or it can be combined with a field trip to a local police headquarters or county jail. Decorate a gym or large room in prison decor. Put simulated bars on the windows and have youth leaders dress like guards. Have a siren handy for crowd control. Everything can look pretty drab, as prisons do.

When the kids arrive, they have to be arrested, of course. To set them up for an arrest, have them retrieve one bill of play money that is hanging from a string on the ceiling in another room. As they return to your room, you can arrest them for possession of stolen money. Being framed is no excuse. You can use handcuffs, take them to an interrogation room, question them under a bright light, confiscate their personal belongings, fingerprint them, etc. The prisoners receive prison clothing or prison hats, an identification number, or whatever.

Now you're all set to play prison games like these:

- **Ball and Chain Stomp.** This is the old balloon stomp game with a new name. Tie balloons around each person's ankles. The object is to stomp and pop other prisoners' balloons while keeping yours from getting stomped. Whoever lasts the longest wins.
- **Tunnel Escape.** This is similar to the old car stuff game Set up a tunnel, made of cardboard boxes, tables, or just about anything, and divide into teams (cell blocks). The idea is to see how many prisoners can escape to freedom through the tunnel within a set time limit. Prisoners crawl one right after the other in the tunnel. When they crawl out of the tunnel, they race back to the line at the start of the tunnel and crawl through again. A warden or guard counts the prisoners and keeps the official time. Teams can go one at a time. That way, you only have to make one tunnel.
- **Murder in Cell Block 5.** Play this game in the dark. One person is secretly chosen to be the murderer. When the lights are turned off, the murderer approaches other players (victims) who are milling about and whispers, "You're dead."

The victim counts to five, screams, and falls to the floor. This continues until someone correctly guesses the identity of the murderer. Incorrect guesses result in the guesser's death. The murderer must try to kill

THE

Who-Will-Win-This-Year Dove Awards

GUESSING FORM

General Awards:

Male vocalist of the year ______

Song of the year ______

Female vocalist of the year ______

Songwriter of the year ______

New artist of the year ______

Group of the year ______

Artist of the year ______

Producer of the year ______

Song of the year - categories:

Rap ______

Metal ______

Rock ______

Contemporary ______

Inspirational ______

Southern Gospel ______

Country ______

Contemporary Black Gospel ______

Traditional Black Gospel ______

Album of the year - categories:

Metal ______

Rock ______

Contemporary ______

Inspirational ______

Southern Gospel ______

Country ______

Contemporary Black Gospel ______

Traditional Black Gospel ______

Video of the year:

Short form ______

Long form ______

as many victims as possible before his identity is discovered.

• **Break Out!** Play this game outside on a starless, moonless night. Set up a guard tower of some kind

that can hold a couple of people. Two kids are chosen to be guards and are given powerful flashlights. Place a bell underneath the guard tower. On a signal, the rest of the kids try to sneak to the guard tower and ring the bell without getting shot with the flashlight. As soon as someone successfully rings the bell without getting hit with light, they may trade places with one of the guards. When you get shot, you must go back to the starting place (back inside the prison, or 100 feet or so away from the tower) and try again. Some sponsors can referee to decide whether or not a prisoner got through successfully. This can also be played with teams. One team can provide the guards while the other team tries to get to the bell.

• **Find the Loot.** Divide into teams with each team choosing a team captain or leader. The object is for each team to find as much loot as possible. The loot can be play money that has been hidden all over the place ahead of time by the sponsors. If you are using a church, the loot can be hidden in classrooms, trees, desks, trash cans, or anywhere else. On a signal the teams take off looking for the loot, but the team captains must stay in a central waiting area. As soon as a team member finds loot, she must run back and tell her team captain where it is. The team captain may then retrieve the loot herself. No one else may touch it. The team captain must return to the waiting area before being allowed to go after more loot. The rules can be adapted or changed as you see fit.

• **Exercise Yard.** Run relays of your choice.

Don't forget to serve refreshments in the mess hall or combine this event with any number of other activities with the same theme. You could put on a mock trial or discuss issues such as justice, freedom, or the prison system. *Dan Craig*

FOOD EVENTS

If there's one thing kids know and appreciate, it's food. You'll find here lots of whacked-out renditions of the good ol' progressive dinner, a few elegant fetes–and, of course, slobfests galore.

Awful Waffle Party

You'll need a few waffle irons and a huge batch of waffle batter. As the waffles come off the irons, have a table ready with various toppings—syrups, ice cream (a must), nuts, jelly, peanut butter, whipped cream, fruit, and the like. You might also want to include some awful toppings—pickles, onions, catsup, beets, spinach, whatever—and dare kids to try them. This is a great refreshment after an afternoon event or a swimming party, or you can do it all by itself! *Dan Gray*

Build Your Own Tacos Night

This is similar to pizza night, but instead of pizza you put out all the fixings for tacos: pre-shaped corn tortillas, several kinds of cheese, sour cream, jalapenos, cooked ground beef, refried beans, tomatoes, lettuce, olives, and mild, medium, and hot sauces. The kids create their own tacos. Delicious—and a good draw as well, especially when combined with another activity. *Rob Moritz*

Bus Banquet

Here's a unique banquet idea. Decorate the inside of your church bus to fit the occasion (Christmas, Valentine's Day, etc.). Then save the back two seats for the food. Have your sponsors act as servers. Serve one dish at a time while driving around town or whatever. This can be a blast and a change of pace from the normal banquet. *Rick Wheeler*

Cake Bake Night

You can't lose whenever you use an idea that involves food. Get a good recipe for flat-pan cakes

and large cookies and spend an evening baking and decorating. Have all sorts of decorating items on hand, such as jelly beans, frosting, sprinkles, and so on. Encourage creative individual designs or challenge kids to decorate everything around a certain theme. If possible, make extras and deliver them to shut-ins or to the pastor's family. *Richard Moore*

DO YOUR OWN DONUT

This idea breaks the cookie-and-Kool-Aid refreshment routine and is a fun activity as well. Start with several tubes of refrigerated baking powder biscuits, available at any supermarket. Form the biscuits into donut shapes and drop them into a skillet filled to one inch with cooking oil heated to 375 degrees. Turn when needed and remove when golden brown.

Have a variety of toppings on hand. Chocolate, vanilla, and peanut butter frostings work well. Sprinkles, coconut, and powdered sugar can be added on top of the frosting base. The secret is to let every person make his or her own donut creation from the ingredients on hand. Serve with hot chocolate in the winter for a pleasant way to warm up after an outdoor event. Be sure to have plenty of biscuit dough on hand because the donuts go fast. Approximately 10 donuts can be made from one tube of dough. *Craig Johnson*

FAST FOOD FOLLIES

For this delicious event, have each kid bring a specific amount of money, just enough to pay for a fast food meal. Divide into teams and travel by car to various fast food locations around town. Give each team a list like this one (adapted to the food available in your area):

- ❒ A double hamburger from Wendys
- ❒ One scoop of chocolate ice cream from Baskin-Robbins
- ❒ One hush puppy from Long John Silver's
- ❒ One apple turnover from Burger Chef
- ❒ One bag of fries from Burger King
- ❒ One hamburger from White Castle
- ❒ One Cheese Coney from Gold Star Chili
- ❒ One taco from Taco Bell
- ❒ One chicken leg from KFC
- ❒ One peanut butter shake from DQ
- ❒ One liver or gizzard from Famous Recipe
- ❒ One root beer float from A&W
- ❒ One roast beef sandwich from Arby's
- ❒ One burrito from Zantigo's
- ❒ One Slurpee from 7-ELEVEN

The team can pool its money and decide which team member eats which item at each location. When that person eats the specified item, he puts his initials on the list next to that item. Set a time limit. The team that completes the list first or has the most items checked off is the winner. Use adult drivers and make sure there's no speeding or rudeness at the various locations, etc. *Doug Newhouse*

BON APPETIT!

Check with the management of your local McDonald's and reserve a special section of the restaurant at a specified time. Send out formal invitations to the group. Have the kids dress up. Divide into table groups (four to a table) and give each group a bag containing a tablecloth, linen napkins, silverware, a centerpiece, and menus. You may even want to provide a musical serenade.

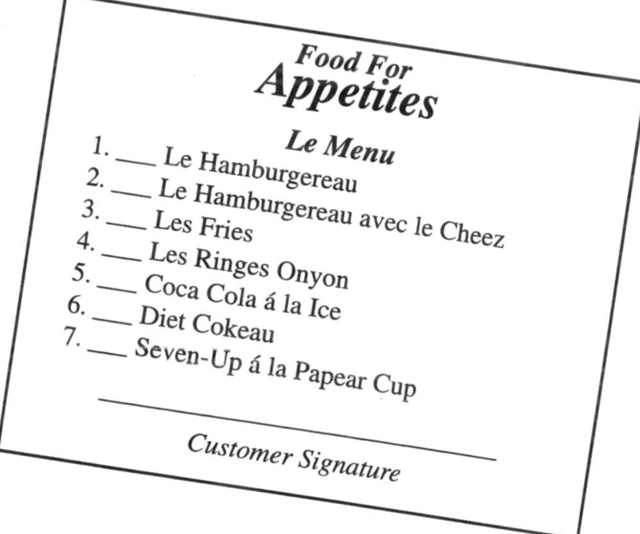

Food For
Appetites

Le Menu

1. ___ Le Hamburgereau
2. ___ Le Hamburgereau avec le Cheez
3. ___ Les Fries
4. ___ Les Ringes Onyon
5. ___ Coca Cola á la Ice
6. ___ Diet Cokeau
7. ___ Seven-Up á la Papear Cup

____
Customer Signature

After the tables are set, a waiter (whom you've provided) can come around to each table and collect the menus. These should be filled out and signed by each patron. The front of the menu can include instructions, including the fact that they are limited to one hamburger, one order of fries or onion rings, and one drink per person. The waiter also serves the food when it's ready. *Tim Smith and Ken Wortley*

FAST FOOD PROGRESSIVE DINNER

This is a great variation on an old favorite activity. Find a street with several fast food restaurants on it and plan a progressive meal accordingly. Start with a salad at one restaurant (salad bar preferable), then move on to "hors d'oeuvres" (french fries, soup, chili, taco chips, etc.), then the main course (Big Macs, tacos, pizza, fish, hamburgers, etc.). Let the kids decide on the route. (You can allow them to split up for the main course depending on their preferences.) The more creative ideas you can come up with and the more places you can visit, the better. *James Midberry*

JUNK FOOD POTLUCK

Since churches are famous for hosting potluck dinners, host a weird version of one for your youth group. Have a junk food potluck and encourage your kids to bring generous amounts of their favorite junk food to share with others. Anything healthy or nutritious should not be accepted. To add to the fun, plan to show a movie along with the dinner. You might find that this would be a good time to encourage everyone to bring along a friend who has never been to a youth meeting. *Philip Popineau*

WORLD'S GREATEST FRENCH FRY

Here's an excellent activity that lets your kids become critics or reviewers of the things they consume. The object is to find the very best french fry in the city. The kids go from one fast-food joint to another, sampling the french fries. Each person rates the fries on qualities such as taste, appearance, amount per serving, price, saltiness, etc. To really add a professional touch, have each member eat a cracker before tasting the fries to wash the palate. The group's ratings and any additional comments can be shared in the church's bulletin.

Other foods can be tasted, such as the best hamburger, or the tastiest vanilla ice cream, etc. You could compile a "Christian Consumers Guide" or something like that. And by notifying the restaurants in advance, you might even get some free food to sample. *Milton Hom*

FLAKE-OFF BAKE-OFF

Divide into small groups of three or four. Have on hand a number of baking pans and other containers of various sizes and shapes plus the following ingredients: sugar, margarine, oil, eggs, milk, salt, cheese, flour, baking powder, baking soda, cans of fruit pie filling, honey, and cinnamon.

Each group must make a dessert using anything available. But none of them will have a recipe. They must create their own. Ask each group to write down its recipe (just for the record) and help them use the ovens in the church kitchen to bake their creations. When they're all finished serve the desserts to the group and present awards according to various categories: best tasting, best looking, most creative, most nauseating, most burnt, hardest to chew, or whatever. *Jim Walton*

FUNNY MONEY BOX SOCIAL

You know how these work. Girls pack box lunches or dinners that the guys bid on without knowing which girl made which lunch, and then they eat with that girl. The girls bid similarly on desserts that the guys made.

The bidding, however, is done with funny money. And everyone acquires it at the beginning of the event, before the bidding starts, according to how they answer trivia questions. For example, you say, "Fifty dollars for each state you've lived in." Then you and a few other sponsors hear the kids' answers and dole out the play bucks accordingly. Award the money generously and frivolously. All the kids should have plenty of money for the bidding and should have a good time "earning" it, too.

Beside answering Bible trivia questions, here are other ways for them to earn money:

- **$50 for each filling in your mouth.**
- **$100 if you brushed your teeth before coming to the party.**
- **$100 if you showered in the last four hours.**
- **$100 for all who are wearing colored underwear.**
- **$50 for each hospital trip your parent made with your injuries.**
- **$50 for every pair of gym shoes you own.**
- **$100 if you're wearing socks.**
- **$100 if you have to cut your fingernails and don't bite them.**
- **$100 for each ring you're wearing.**
- **$100 if you flossed your teeth today.**
- **$500 if you kissed your mom goodbye today.**

Len and Sheryl DiCicco

Get Along, Little Doggie

Some meat markets can special order wieners up to 10 feet long for your use. Barbecue them over a long fire or try to bend them into a circle and cook them. This adds a dimension of fun to any wiener roast, beach party, etc. *Larry Houseman*

Heritage Dinner

In order to help kids get in touch with their own backgrounds and to facilitate communication of this to the other members of the group, try this variation of the old potluck dinner.

Each person is instructed to bring to the event a dish that represents his or her ancestry. Nearly every American has roots in some other nationality, and this could be preceded by a little research into family trees, etc. If a person has many nationalities in his or her background, then one could be chosen. If a person doesn't know of any representative food for his or her ancestry, then more research may be needed.

In addition to the meal, the kids should bring with them a "family treasure" or some relic, photo, or other item of interest that has been passed down through several generations, and be prepared to tell its story. The item need not be valuable except in terms of the story behind it. Another possibility would be to have kids bring baby pictures of themselves that could be posted and have a contest to see who can guess the identity of each picture.

A further extension of this idea would be to have each kid bring or tell about an item that he or she hopes will be passed on to future generations and remembered. You might have each person think of herself as her own grandchild and then talk about "My grandmother..." What kind of a heritage do you hope to leave for your future family? Good discussion and sharing can follow. *Jay McKenzie*

International Progressive Dinner

Find several homes that can accommodate your kids. Decorate each home in accordance with the national decorations of the dish served.

Collect some card tables and turn someone's basement into a French sidewalk cafe. Serve a special chef's salad topped with (what else) French dressing. Turn someone else's living room into an open-air Jewish bread market. Many different breads, rolls, and bagels can be found in the local bakery. Then for your next house, divide the upstairs and downstairs. Upstairs someone can be serving chop suey or another oriental dish, while downstairs the specialty is wieners and sauerkraut.

When you return to the church, you may have waiting a Hawaiian luau scene with crushed Hawaiian pineapple cake for dessert. Skits and devotions can be mingled in each stop, or saved for last. This is a terrific idea for a missions emphasis. *Marty Lewis*

Jell-O Jamboree

Have an evening of Jell-O games such as the ones listed below. With a little imagination, you should be able to create many more.

Here's a recipe for Jell-O Squares—a hardier version for game playing:

3 six-ounce boxes of Jell-O
4 envelopes of Knox unflavored gelatin
4 cups boiling water

Combine all ingredients in a large bowl, pour into oblong cake pan, and refrigerate. Cut into cubes when solid.

- **The Name Game.** To liven up introductions, try this game. Have the first person give her name, a Jell-O flavor to match a color she is wearing, and a food to add to the Jell-O that begins with the same letter as her name. Example: Samantha, lime, strawberries. The second person must do the same and then add the three words said by the first person. The third person does the same, saying the words given by the other two as well, and so on around the room.
- **Jell-O Slurp Relay.** Form two relay teams and line them up. Place one Jell-O square on a paper plate on the floor about 25 feet in front of each team. In turn, team members must run to the plate, eat the Jell-O, and run back, all with their hands behind their back. Have someone at the plates to replace the Jell-O square as it is eaten. First team to have every member complete the course wins.
- **Two Finger Relay.** Form two or more relay teams

and have players pair off within each team. In turn, each pair must pick up a Jell-O square from a paper plate, with each member of the pair using only one finger. Together they must carry the square around a designated point and return to the starting place. Then one of the members must eat the Jell-O before the next pair may begin. If the Jell-O is dropped, they must pick it up again and continue, still using only one finger each. First team to have every member complete the course wins.

• **Tongue Relay.** Form relay teams. Each person must run to the designated point, place a Jell-O square on his or her tongue, and then return to the starting point without dropping it.

• **The Dreaded Jell-O Drop.** Form relay teams. The first person on each team must lie down on the floor about 25 feet from the starting point. At the signal the second person on each team runs down to the head of his or her team member on the floor, takes a Jell-O square, holds it with arm extended straight out at shoulder height, and drops it into a paper cup on the forehead of the person on the floor. If the drop misses the player must pick it up and try again, continuing until he makes a direct hit. When the person on the floor catches the Jell-O, she returns to the starting point. The person who was dropping the Jell-O assumes the position on the floor, and the next person in line becomes the new dropper. The race is over when everyone on the same team has caught the Jell-O and the last person has returned to the starting point.

• **Jell-O Maze.** Stretch a sheet of plastic across the floor and place a number of Jell-O squares on it at random. Have two teams line up along opposite sides of the sheet. The challenge is for team members to walk one at a time from one end of the course to the other as quickly as possible without stepping on any Jell-O. Players must take their socks and shoes off, and the task is made more difficult by having them walk the course blindfolded and with their knees together. Each player is blindfolded, spun around three times, and headed in the right direction. Team members may help players by shouting verbal directions, but the opposing team may also lead them astray with false directions. Players are timed from the second they begin until they cross the finish line. Add a five-second penalty for each Jell-O square stepped on and for stepping off the sheet. Have a chair, wet rag, and towel at the finish line. For extra fun give the opposing team time to rearrange the Jell-O after the player is blindfolded.

• **Jell-O Mosaics.** Divide into groups of three or four people and give each group a knife and a tray with Jell-O squares in a variety of colors. Have each team create a mosaic with the Jell-O pieces using whipped cream for the finishing touch. Give awards to the best masterpieces and eat them all for a snack.

• **Jell-O Ad Relay.** Get hold of several newspapers that are all the same issue, preferably one with plenty of grocery store advertisments in it. Usually one night a week the local papers feature lots of big food ads. Go through the paper ahead of time and try to find all the ads for Jell-O you can. Cut them out and put them on display. Then have the teams line up. A copy of the paper is placed ten to twenty feet away. On "Go!" the team members run one at a time to the paper, find the ad, rip it out of the paper, and return with it. The first team to get them all wins. There should be at least as many Jell-O ads as there are members on a team.

• **Jell-O Pie Race.** Fill pie tins with cubes of Jell-O, cover them with whipped cream, and have a pie-eating race.

• **Nailing Jell-O to a Tree.** Make Jell-O in 8x8 cake pans, about 1/2 inch thick. Let it cool. About a half an hour before it is needed, take the jello out of refrigerator and place in freezer. When you are ready to begin the contest, take the jello out of the freezer and cut it into one-inch squares. Give the teams nails and let them nail up their Jell-O. Use a log for the tree. The team with the most pieces up in a minute wins.

• **Jell-O Feed.** Teams pick two couples for contestants. They are seated in chairs facing each other. Blindfold them and place a towel around their necks. Give each a dish of Jell-O and let them feed each other. The first couple to finish wins.

• **Jell-O Pail Fill.** Line up each team for a relay race. Give the first person a spoon. Place one-inch-square pieces of Jell-O on dishes at one end of the relay course. At the other end of the course, place buckets. The first person on each team has to get her square of Jell-O on the spoon, run down to the team's pail, drop the Jell-O in the pail, return, and give spoon to person next in line. The first team to get all its squares in their pail wins. If Jell-O is dropped, the person must start over again.

• **Jell-O Flash Cards.** Have four sets of alphabet cards. Take out letters not needed. Have each team line up around the room forming a square. When a Jell-O flavor is called out, e.g. Cherry, those on each team with the appropriate letters must run out five feet in front of their teams and spell it out. The first team to do so gets points. After all flavors are spelled out, the team with the most points wins.

• **The Jell-O Gauntlet.** The losing team gets this one. Lay out a sheet of plastic on the floor. The other teams line up on either side forming a path. Losers must be blindfolded and barefooted. They must walk the path with other teams guiding them by shouting directions as to where to step. On the plastic path place spoonfuls of Jell-O in various places. Give a prize to the person who makes it through without stepping in anything.

Roger Disque and Tim Rehling

ICE CREAM SOCIAL ON THE ROLL

This event is a lot of fun and delicious, too! Divide your crew into groups of four or five, and give each group a one-pound and a three-pound metal coffee can with a plastic lids. Provide each group a copy of the recipe on page 133, make all of the ingredients available, and let the fun begin. *Tom Baker*

GIANT SUNDAE NIGHT FELLOWSHIP

As people arrive give them colored name tags that not only tell others their names, but also determines what teams they are on:

- **Brown tags—The Chocolate Chips**
- **Red tags—The Straw Berries**
- **Green tags—The Pistachio Nuts**
- **Orange tags—The Orange Sherbets**
- **Yellow tags—The French Vanillas**

After a few songs or mixers, break the group into teams and have fun with the following games:

• **I Scream, You Scream, We All Scream for Ice Cream.** Each team creates its own team cheer based on its name. Winners should be judged on creativity, originality, humor, and choreography.

• **Cherry Topper Relay.** Each team lines up single file with everyone having one bare foot. Place a chair about 20 away. In front of the chair place a pan of crushed ice and water with maraschino cherries in it and an empty sundae dish beside it. Each contestant runs down, sits in the chair, fishes out a cherry with his bare toes, places it on the sundae dish, races back and tags the next person, who repeats the same activity. The first team to successfully complete the relay wins.

• **Banana Peel.** Get the captain of each team to take off her shoes and socks and sit facing the audience. Give them each a banana which they must peel using only their feet and toes. The first one to get it completely peeled is the winner.

• **Nut Cracker Relay.** Each team member places a peanut between his knees. One at a time, they waddle down to a sundae dish which is on the floor about 10 feet from their line. The object is to stand over the dish and try to make the peanut fall into it. If they miss they simply pick up their peanut and get back in line to try again. If they drop their peanut before reaching the dish they have to go back to the starting line and begin again. The team that gets the most peanuts in is the winner.

• **Ice Cream Cone Carry.** Place a chair about 30 feet from each line. The first player on each team must walk down to the chair, go around it, and come back while balancing an empty ice cream cone on top of

Ice Cream Social on the Roll

1. In the one-pound can, mix together:

1 slightly beaten egg	1/2 cup sugar
1 cup milk	dash of vanilla
1 cup whipping cream	

2. Put the one-pound can's plastic lid on tightly. Place the one-pound can inside the three-pound can. Pack with crushed ice and 3/4 cup rock salt. Put the three-pound can's plastic lid on tightly. Roll the can on the floor for 15 minutes.
3. Drain the water and stir the ice cream. Pack with ice and rock salt. Roll for 5 more minutes.

Add bowls and your favorite toppings, and you'll have some ice cream sundaes that will make a treat hard to beat.

Ice Cream Social on the Roll

1. In the one-pound can, mix together:

1 slightly beaten egg	1/2 cup sugar
1 cup milk	dash of vanilla
1 cup whipping cream	

2. Put the one-pound can's plastic lid on tightly. Place the one-pound can inside the three-pound can. Pack with crushed ice and 3/4 cup rock salt. Put the three-pound can's plastic lid on tightly. Roll the can on the floor for 15 minutes.
3. Drain the water and stir the ice cream. Pack with ice and rock salt. Roll for 5 more minutes.

Add bowls and your favorite toppings, and you'll have some ice cream sundaes that will make a treat hard to beat.

Ice Cream Social on the Roll

1. In the one-pound can, mix together:

1 slightly beaten egg	1/2 cup sugar
1 cup milk	dash of vanilla
1 cup whipping cream	

2. Put the one-pound can's plastic lid on tightly. Place the one-pound can inside the three-pound can. Pack with crushed ice and 3/4 cup rock salt. Put the three-pound can's plastic lid on tightly. Roll the can on the floor for 15 minutes.
3. Drain the water and stir the ice cream. Pack with ice and rock salt. Roll for 5 more minutes.

Add bowls and your favorite toppings, and you'll have some ice cream sundaes that will make a treat hard to beat.

Ice Cream Social on the Roll

1. In the one-pound can, mix together:

1 slightly beaten egg	1/2 cup sugar
1 cup milk	dash of vanilla
1 cup whipping cream	

2. Put the one-pound can's plastic lid on tightly. Place the one-pound can inside the three-pound can. Pack with crushed ice and 3/4 cup rock salt. Put the three-pound can's plastic lid on tightly. Roll the can on the floor for 15 minutes.
3. Drain the water and stir the ice cream. Pack with ice and rock salt. Roll for 5 more minutes.

Add bowls and your favorite toppings, and you'll have some ice cream sundaes that will make a treat hard to beat.

his head. If it falls simply put it back on and keep going (unless it breaks; then get a new one). The first team to have everyone successfully complete the task is the winner.

Refreshments can be handled in one of two ways:

• Give each person a dish of ice cream, then spread out all the different toppings—bananas, whipped cream, nuts, and cherries—on a long table and let them build their own custom sundae

• For something a little bit different, place all the ice cream in one big, clean wash tub. Cover it with all the toppings and accessories that you have, topping it off with a whole can of cherries. Then just give everyone a dish and spoon and let them get their share.

• You can make the "World's Largest Banana Split" if you'd rather. First, you need to get a long section of house guttering. You may have to plug the ends of it to keep it free from leaks. Line the gutter with heavy duty aluminum foil about three times. After this, you're ready to make the banana split. Let as many as possible have a part in making the split. Be sure to obtain enough ice cream, toppings, nuts, whipped cream, etc. Dip out individual servings into plastic containers obtained at a local dairy bar.

Bob Henry and Andy Stimer

VOLCANO SUNDAE NIGHT

Here's a creative mix of geology, sculpture, and, uh, cuisine. First gather these materials:

• One plastic garbage bag per group
• Three gallons ice cream per group
• Toppings (chocolate, butterscotch, strawberry, whipped cream, cherries, nuts, etc.) for each group
• Spoons, napkins—and a camera

Divide your youth group into groups of about eight kids each. Have each group spread out a trash bag on the floor. Distribute the ice cream and toppings. Then instruct the groups to form giant volcanoes with their ice cream and to decorate them with the toppings in volcanic fashion—splatter, cinder cones, lava flow, etc. Judge the finished sculptures on geologic accuracy and aesthetic qualities.

If you want a taste of each volcano, get it now because the groups' next assignment is to devour their volcanoes. First group to finish eating its volcano wins, as long as there are no eruptions by group members! *David Washburn*

LUCKY LUNCHES

For a quick after-church or before-the-event meal, have everyone bring a can of food such as Spaghetti-Os, chili, baked beans, sloppy joe mix, soup, etc. Kids should remove labels so that others don't know what they brought.

Number each can and put corresponding numbers on small slips of paper (one number per paper). Place paper in a bag and have kids draw a number and claim the corresponding can. The fun is in discovering what they'll be having for lunch. Eating it can be a whole different matter!

Provide can openers and extras such as chips, Jell-O, beverages, or salads. Allow kids to trade and share as they wish. If you're near a kitchen, you may want to provide some cooking utensils for those who need them. *Mark Simone*

M.A.E. DAY

It stands for **M**eet **A**nd **E**at. M.A.E. Day involves your kids in cooking, learning to cook, working together, eating, fellowshipping, and cleaning up a Sunday afternoon dinner in the church kitchen or at someone's home.

Once you choose the meal date, meet with the youths to plan the menu, organize the ingredients, and assign (or draw from a hat) the duties of cooking, washing dishes, drying dishes, sweeping floors, clearing tables, putting away dishes, and so on. Everyone should participate, even those who think they can't boil water or fear dishpan hands. Solicit food from parents, others in the church, or even local markets.

A good opportunity for discussion, icebreakers, or games comes during the required cooking time for the main dish or dessert. The subjects brought up then often stir up meal conversation or provide interesting dialogue during cleanup. *Greg Miller*

MARSHMALLOW TOURNAMENT

Here's an event that features the lowly marshmallow. There are all kinds of fun things you can do with them, so why not have a whole evening of marshmallow activities?

• **Marshmallow Creations.** Give people marshmallows and toothpicks and have them create sculptures. Judge for creativity, etc.

• **Accuracy Throw.** Each person gets a marshmallow and tries to toss it into a basket some distance away. When you miss, you're out. Last person to stay in the game wins.

• **Distance Throw.** See who can throw a marshmallow the farthest.

• **Marshmallow Catch.** Couples stand a certain distance apart and toss the marshmallow. If successful, they take a step backward and toss again. Last couple to remain in the game wins.

• **Marshmallow Relay.** Team members line up about 10 feet apart from each other. They toss the marshmallow down the team line from one person to the next. If they drop the marshmallow, they have to start over. Team members cannot move from their original positions.

• **Marshmallow Refreshments.** Roast 'em, or try making S'Mores.

Samuel Hoyt

Mystery Dinner

After everyone arrives, each kid is given an order sheet. The order sheet lists about 20 different items that will be served. The items are so named, however, that none really knows what they are. For example, a piece of chicken could be called "Crunchy Crud," or a scoop of ice cream might be called "White Slop." Or you might translate the descriptions into another language—say Chinese—if you have a bilingual friend.

Everything is named, including the silverware, and is put on the list. To order, each kid must choose when he wants each item. The order sheet has places to assign each item to either "course one," "course two," "course three," or "course four."

After the order is placed, each person's first course is served. It's best to have a team of food servers who take the orders and serve the courses. Not knowing really what he ordered, a person could receive a baked potato, a stick of celery, a scoop of ice cream, a knife, and some jelly for his first course. Before he can get his second course, he must finish his first. The results are usually hilarious. *Tommy Baker*

New-Fashioned Box Social

This is just like the Old-Fashioned Box Social except that in this case the guys pack the box lunches for two, and the girls bid for them. With the right encouragement, some guys will go all out and bring fancy dishes, table cloths, candles, soft music, and so on. The girls can bring canned food (later to be given to a needy organization or family) and bid on the lunches using the cans as money. The cans are worth the prices marked on them. *Jim Berkley*

Personalized Pizza Party

Provide kids with pizza dough and all the goodies that go on top and let them create their own personal pizzas. Each person gets a lump of dough and shapes it into a creative design. The only stipulation is that there must be a lip to the crust so that the sauce won't run off. The pizza can be decorated with olives, mushrooms, cheese, pepperoni, anchovies and the like. While these creations are being baked, other games can be played. When they are ready, judge them and award a prize to the most creative pizza. Then eat up! *Shirley Smithtro*

Pizza Parade

This pizza party is conducted in progressive-dinner fashion. At the first home your group makes the dough. At the second the sauce is prepared. At the third, cheese. At the fourth, toppings (sausage, pepperoni, green pepper, mushrooms, olives, etc.). The last stop must be where you can bake them all together—maybe your church kitchen is large enough—before sitting down and digging in! *Len and Sheryl DiCicco*

Progressive Dessert Party

Have a different dessert at each stop along the progressive dessert circuit. Serve small portions of ice cream, cake, pie, cookies, mousse, cheesecake, cobbler, and the like. Guaranteed to go over with any group of kids! *Jerry Pattengale*

Progressive Picnic

This is a progressive dinner that has been adapted for summer. Hold the dinners in park picnic areas, friends' backyards, forest preserves, etc. Bring paper plates, plastic utensils, napkins, and cups, and serve each course on blankets on the ground or at picnic tables. You might play a different game at each location as well. It's a nice change of pace. *Bruce Humbert*

Progressive Pool Dinner

In the heat of the summer, schedule several families to set up kiddie wading pools in their yards and to prepare one course of an evening meal for the youth group. Invite all the kids to come wearing their swimsuits and towels. At each house see how many kids can get into the wading pool, and then let everyone alternate between eating and cooling off in the pool. Plan so that the last house has a full-size pool. After eating spend the evening swimming. *Harl Pike*

Backward Progressive Dinner

This is a variation on a regular progressive dinner, in which the participants travel from location to location and receive one course of their meal at each stop. The fun with this one is that the menu is served in reverse. It would go something like this:

Stop One: Dessert and a toothpick
Stop Two: Potato chips
Stop Three: Sandwich
Stop Four: Vegetable
Stop Five: Salad
Stop Six: Soup
Stop Seven: Appetizer

Have something to drink at each stop. *Andy Stimer*

Budget Progressive Dinner

Divide the large group into smaller groups of four people each. Each should have access to a car and some kitchen space. Now give each group $7.50 to $10.00 depending on your budget and the size of the group and have them all bring back some part of the meal—appetizer, drink, main dish, fruit, salad, dessert, etc. It is important that the groups do not confer with each other. This restriction will make for an interesting dinner and at the same time promote creativity. *Bruce Coriell*

Heartburn on the Run

Here's how to combine a progressive dinner with a car rally or treasure hunt. First, make sure you have enough cars and drivers. Then choose four homes to visit, one for each course of a meal (soup, salad, main course, and dessert). All of the foods should be as hot and spicy as possible. Require kids to solve clues in order to get from house to house to receive a complete meal. Distribute the first clue at the beginning of the rally. Kids receive a new clue at each home.

Rules for the evening include the following: 1) You must eat all of the food you put on your plate at each house. 2) You can't drink any liquids. 3) your group must be the first to return to the starting point to win.

Provide lots of water and crackers for kids as they arrive back at the starting point at the end of the rally. The prize can be gift certificates to Taco Bell or a local Mexican restaurant. *Stephen May*

Aggressive Dinner

For this variation on the old Progressive Dinner, load up in cars or vans and eat each course of your meal in a different city. For example go to a McDonald's in one town and have french fries, go to a Burger King in another town and have hamburgers, then head for yet another town and have sundaes at Dairy Queen. (Of course you'll need to have other cities within driving distance.) Kids will enjoy the "trip" aspect of this one. *Kay Jorgenson*

Wheels and Progressive Meals

Before students have their driver's licenses, they use bikes, roller blades, skateboards, even wheelchairs to get around. So create a progressive meal, between whose courses kids get around by their own wheels. Of course, it helps if the homes where the courses (appetizer, soup and salad, entree, dessert) are served are fairly close to each other.

Have a lead driver (biker? skater?) and a

chase vehicle to bring up the rear. If you're in a small town, just maybe the police department can spare a motorcycle cop or squad car to escort your hungry parade on wheels. *Duane Steiner*

Reservations Only

If your normal youth group activities suffer from poor attendance on those long holiday weekends like Memorial Day and Labor Day, this idea might help.

Hold a "reservations only" dinner at the church, complete with linen tablecloths, lighted candles, music, and good food. This would be an excellent opportunity to utilize members of your church of different ethnic backgrounds who can cook exotic foods. Afterwards, have dessert and perhaps show a video at someone's house.

Send out invitations in advance (two to three weeks) and give the event a sense of special importance. Make it an R.S.V.P. deal and you'll find that the kids will respond in a very positive way. Some people are just looking for something good to do on the long weekend, and if you make a tradition out of it, you'll find that it will grow in popularity. It's a creative and effective way to let your kids know that their local church remains active during holiday weekends. *James Wilson*

Sack Lunch Sharing

Next time you have an event in which all the kids bring a sack lunch, try this for a change of pace. Stretch out a blanket on the ground and have all the kids dump the contents of their sack lunches onto the blanket. Then have the group gather around the blanket, hold it up by the edges and raise it high as you offer thanks. Then lower it and allow the kids to pick and choose anything they want from the items that are there for lunch.

Tell the kids to keep in mind that everyone needs to eat, so not to be greedy, but instead, to share. The result will be a good experiment in cooperation and community. You might want to follow it with a discussion of the group dynamic that took place. *Arlene Thaete*

Search-and-Scrounge Smorgasbord

Promote your next banquet as an S-and-S Smorgasbord (don't explain). Collect a reasonable fee for the meal.

As the kids arrive, put them on five teams. Collect the meal fees and equally divide the money among the teams. Have each team draw a sheet of paper from a hat or box on which is written a five-course meal that includes the appetizer, salad, main dish, dessert, and beverage. The teams are then instructed to go out and beg, barter, scrounge, search, or buy the necessary ingredients to prepare and deliver their assigned five-course meal within a given time limit (one or two hours). They may not spend any more money than they are given.

After the kids have prepared and eaten their meals, award prizes for the tastiest, the most unusual, most creative, largest quantity, and best-use-of-the-money meals. You will genuinely be surprised at the great meals kids create. *Greg Chantler*

Social Graces

Conduct a banquet that gently teaches social graces to teens in a fun and nonthreatening way. It will help kids feel confident when they find themselves in a formal social setting.

First of all, consult books on etiquette at your local library to make sure you've got the details right and make the books available to your kids since they will help to pull off this banquet. Set up committees. Have them research etiquette, decorate, cook, serve, make introductions, etc.

Appoint hosts to greet kids as they arrive at the banquet. Have guys seat girls properly and do it several times for practice. Before the meal starts, the hosts briefly discuss how to make restaurant reservations, how to enter a restaurant, how to use the napkin, and how to read the menu and order from it.

When the soup is served, have a group quickly explain proper etiquette for eating soup—what to do with crackers, which spoon to use, where to place the spoon, etc. Everyone practices during the course.

Next is salad. Explain how to properly cut lettuce, which fork to use, how to eat a cherry tomato, how to handle olive pits, bread sticks, and so on.

For a main course, try chicken, baked potatoes, rolls, and butter. Groups can explain how to manage the rolls, butter, sauces for the meat, bones, and how to complain gracefully to a waiter if something is wrong. After the main course, there can be a short program, speaker, or entertainment.

Finally, dessert is served and again, practical matters are brought up. Topics include tough pie crust, drips and crumbs, what to do with the napkins, if something falls on the floor, tipping, paying the bill, and how to leave the table.

This activity can be extremely helpful for the kids, parents will love it, and it can become an annual event. *Roger Davis*

SNOWMOBILE SUPPER

If you live in the right part of the country, here's an idea that might be appropriate this winter. Try having a progressive dinner on snowmobiles.

Although this idea bombed in San Diego, it has proven to be a big hit up in Fairbanks. *Betty Horgen*

SOUP-SLOP-SODA-SLURP

Here's an easy way to provide a meal for your group with minimum expense...and it doesn't taste all that bad. Have each person bring one can/bottle of soft drink and one can of their favorite condensed soup. After everyone arrives empty all the cans of soup into one large kettle and add the proper amount of water, then heat. Empty all the soft drinks into one large container and you will be surprised to find how decent the punch and the soup taste—even when you get that one person who likes cream of asparagus. *Wesley C. Leath*

SPAGHETTI SLOBFEST

You can use this idea on a retreat, for a progressive dinner, or for any other meals you want to liven up. You'll need the help of a few volunteer waiters (preferably not kids from the group).

Tell the kids to be seated for a spaghetti dinner. Have nothing on the tables except their glasses filled with whatever drink you choose. The waiters then place in front of each person a paper plate with a plastic disposable bib (you can buy the bibs at a Red Lobster or other seafood restaurant or at a restaurant supply store) and a pair of thin plastic gloves (you can buy these at most hair salons). Make sure none of the servers talk or respond to any questions while they set the tables. Then have them begin bringing out the noodles, sauces, and meatballs, all without serving utensils.

The kids will realize soon enough that there will be no silverware for the meal, and that they must use their hands. To complete the menu, add a dessert like pudding or Jell-O. It's a meal they'll never forget!

As a variation you can set tables with the weirdest dishes and utensils you can find. For example, one person may have to eat out of a vase with a large wooden spoon. Another person eats out of a coffee creamer with an ice-cream scoop. Someone else gets a fruit jar and chopsticks. Each place setting should be as crazy as possible. *Chris Foley and Pat Christmas*

SPAMARAMA

For this Spam event, coordinate the judge and the theme. We'll list the military-theme games that you might play if Spambo or Sgt. Spamko was your judge, though you could adapt the games to fit with an evening hosted by Spammy Davis, Jr. or Uncle Spam. Points are awarded to winners of each competition and then totaled at the end for overall winner.

You may get a reduced rate on the Spam if you contact the Hormel Corporation. Two cases of Spam (48 tins) will be about right for 60 kids. When you write or phone them, ask about Spam T-shirts, Spam blankets, and Spam cookbooks—some of these may be free, and you can give them away as prizes. Throughout the event play the soundtrack to the Rambo movies, Monty Python's Spam song, etc.

- **Spam Team Name and Battle Cry.** Teams create their own names and cheers early in the competition. Get ready for names like the Spaminals or Meatheads.
- **Spam Chow Line.** Who can consume the most Spam in three minutes?
- **Spam Castle Contest.** Build forts with Spam. Supply teams with toothpicks, plastic army men, and other craft items to adorn their forts.
- **Spam Jeep Races.** Construct jeeps from Spam, then race them on a ramp. Supply teams with wheels and axles (available from hobby shops).
- **Spam Grenade Launch.** Throw Spam "grenades" at targets—outdoors, that is.
- **Spam Rifle Range.** Set up pyramids of empty Spam tins and give each team or person three throws to tumble all the tins.
- **Spam Search-and-Rescue Mission.** Prior to Spamarama, hide empty Spam tins around the church. Mark on each one its point value based on the estimated degree of difficulty in finding it. The night of the event, turn out all the church's lights, give each team a flashlight, and turn teams loose for a limited time to find the tins and bring them back to judges for points.

Tom Lytle

WATERMELON OLYMPICS

Here's a good event for the summer. Have a Watermelon Olympics for the whole family. Each family brings one watermelon and a picnic lunch.

- **Watermelon Grab.** Hide all the watermelons (similar to an Easter egg hunt) and then divide into two groups—the grabbers and the taggers. The grabbers go out and try to locate and bring back a

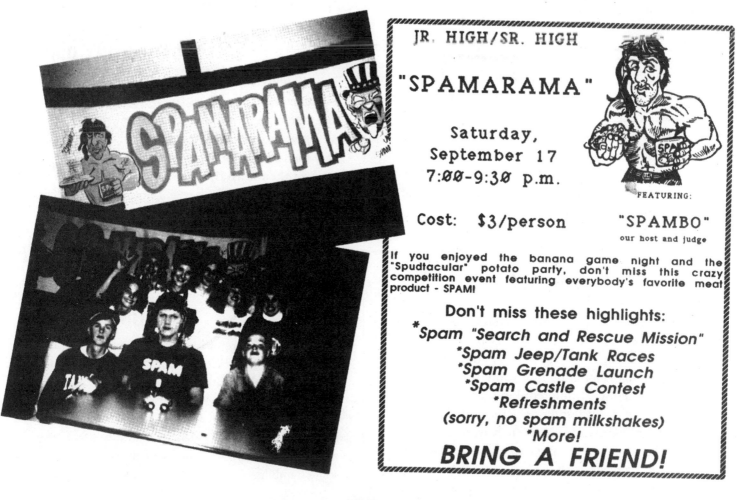

JR. HIGH/SR. HIGH

"SPAMARAMA"

Saturday,
September 17
7:00-9:30 p.m.

FEATURING:

"SPAMBO"
our host and judge

Cost: $3/person

If you enjoyed the banana game night and the "Spudtacular" potato party, don't miss this crazy competition event featuring everybody's favorite meat product - SPAM!

Don't miss these highlights:

*Spam "Search and Rescue Mission"
*Spam Jeep/Tank Races
*Spam Grenade Launch
*Spam Castle Contest
*Refreshments
(sorry, no spam milkshakes)
*More!

BRING A FRIEND!

watermelon to home base without being tagged by the taggers. If they are tagged they must put the watermelon down on the spot where they were tagged and go to jail for three minutes. Grabbers can only be tagged while carrying a watermelon. See how many watermelons can be successfully brought into home base within a given time limit, then switch sides.

• **Watermelon Sack Race.** This is just like a regular sack race except the contestants must carry a watermelon along with them as they hop along with both feet in the sack.

• **Watermelon Balance.** Each team is given a watermelon and a tennis racket. Players must carry the watermelon on the head of the racket to a goal and

back. Players can hold the racket any way they want, but they cannot touch the watermelon with any part of the body.

• **Speed Seed-Eating and Spitting Contest.** Cut the watermelons into wedges and place them on a table. Each team gets a styrofoam cup. On a signal teams start eating watermelon and spitting their seeds into the cup. The team that fills up its cup with seeds first is the winner.

E.J. Nusbaum

31 Ways to Cool Off

Obtain 31 dishes of the different flavors of Baskin-Robbins ice cream in the small servings (or larger if your group is large) for this event. A discount is usually available for church or youth groups.

Place the 31 different kinds of ice cream on a table in a circular fashion, placing a small spoon in each dish of ice cream. Or you may want to place a lot of plastic spoons around each dish, so that each person gets a new spoon. Then give each person in the group a pencil and a list of the different flavors. Usually Baskin-Robbins has this list already printed up and available at no charge. Put a different number on each dish that is found on the corresponding list, and allow the kids to go around the

circle, sampling each dish of ice cream, trying to match the samples with the names on the list.

Many of the names are totally unrelated to how the ice cream tastes, so this can be a lot harder than you think. One thing's for sure: This is one of the most delicious games you'll ever play. *Dave Beckwith*

The Tie That Binds

This dinner idea is built on the theme of unity. If you dine at circular tables tie everyone's left arms together around the table so that they must cooperate to eat. If your tables are rectangular, tie together only the left arms of people along one side. Don't connect them with the arms of the people on the other side of the table. Serve a simple menu such as hoagies and chips. Create a skit or make a brief presentation about the subject of community, cooperation, and mutual dependence. But don't be surprised if no one applauds. *Kathie Taylor*

Winter Picnic

If you live in an area where winters are cold and miserable, have a winter picnic. Decorate a hall or gym so that it looks like an outdoor park in the summertime. Find a way to set up large tree branches in the room. Also set up picnic tables, "Do not litter" signs, trash cans, and so on to add to the atmosphere. Play a few outdoor games, cook up some hamburgers, or serve typical picnic food, and encourage everyone to wear summer clothes. Use your own creativity and this can be a very refreshing change of pace for your group. *Corey Amaro*

WORLD'S LARGEST POPCORN BOWL

This is a very inexpensive attention-getter for your next activity. Announce ahead of time that refreshments at the next activity will include the World's Largest Popcorn Bowl. All you need is a plastic swimming pool (the kind you don't have to inflate)—then fill it with popcorn. *Ben Sharpton*

WORLD'S LARGEST SUBMARINE SANDWICH

Order from a bakery the longest loaf of bread they can make, which is usually from seven to 10 feet long. Have all the kids in your group bring their favorite kinds of lunch meat and cheese. Have on hand plenty of condiments (mayonnaise, mustard, etc.), and then let the kids pack the loaf and whack off as much as they can eat. This is great after a beach trip or some other event that makes kids hungry. *Marty Young*

TATOR NIGHT

These activities all involve fun with potatoes.

• **Tator Contest.** Have a tator-tasting contest using several different brands of potato chips. Put the chips in numbered bowls and have each teen fill out an evaluation form (see page 142) judging the taste. They should keep their answers to themselves. Afterward tally the evaluations and then disclose the brand names from best to worst.

• **The People's Tator.** This skit is like the old TV show "The People's Court." You will need 12 actors for the Tator Family and one person to play Judge Tator. Create some kind of court case to be debated by the defendant, plaintiff, and jurors. Have the judge ask questions to reveal the characters' personalities. Audience members should briefly make a note about each character's personality as it is revealed during the skit. Afterward reveal the Tator names and discuss how people make certain impressions or reveal certain attitudes.

• **Tator Teams.** Have teams choose team names from this list or let them make up their own: Red Potatoes, Russet Potatoes, Sweet Potatoes, Idaho Potatoes, New Potatoes, French Fries, Scalloped Potatoes, Hash Browns, or Potato Skins.

You might want to include the following games:

• **Mr. Potato Head Race.** Everyone is put on a team with the number of teams being equivalent to the number of Mr. Potato Head games you have available. The object of the game is for each team to put together their Mr. Potato Head successfully. They line up single file about 20 feet away from Mr.

The Jury Box

The People's Tator

SPECK TATOR	DICK TATOR	AGI TATOR	HESI TATOR	EMMY TATOR	COGI TATOR
COMMON TATOR	IRRI TATOR	VEGI TATOR	DEVIS TATOR	FACILI TATOR	MEDI TATOR

"TATOR CHIP" CONTEST!

"Choose your Spud, Bud"

"Tator" Night wouldn't be complete without "tator chips." This is your chance to say what **you** think! Rate the chips on a scale of 1–20 considering taste, appearance, texture, etc. Please taste each brand only once, so rate your brand right!

This chip is related to a buffalo chip	**This chip should be in the bag of fame**

1.	1	2	3	4	5	6	7	8	9	10	11	12	13	14	15	16	17	18	19	20
2.	1	2	3	4	5	6	7	8	9	10	11	12	13	14	15	16	17	18	19	20
3.	1	2	3	4	5	6	7	8	9	10	11	12	13	14	15	16	17	18	19	20
4.	1	2	3	4	5	6	7	8	9	10	11	12	13	14	15	16	17	18	19	20
5.	1	2	3	4	5	6	7	8	9	10	11	12	13	14	15	16	17	18	19	20
6.	1	2	3	4	5	6	7	8	9	10	11	12	13	14	15	16	17	18	19	20
7.	1	2	3	4	5	6	7	8	9	10	11	12	13	14	15	16	17	18	19	20
8.	1	2	3	4	5	6	7	8	9	10	11	12	13	14	15	16	17	18	19	20
9.	1	2	3	4	5	6	7	8	9	10	11	12	13	14	15	16	17	18	19	20
10.	1	2	3	4	5	6	7	8	9	10	11	12	13	14	15	16	17	18	19	20
11.	1	2	3	4	5	6	7	8	9	10	11	12	13	14	15	16	17	18	19	20
12.	1	2	3	4	5	6	7	8	9	10	11	12	13	14	15	16	17	18	19	20
13.	1	2	3	4	5	6	7	8	9	10	11	12	13	14	15	16	17	18	19	20

Potato Head, and each person on the team runs to it blindfolded and adds one more part. The first team to finish, or whichever team has the best Mr. Potato Head at the end of the time limit, is the winner.

• **Baked Potato Scramble.** Write on a blackboard or a large piece of butcher paper the words BAKED POTATOES. Have the kids pair off and see which pair can come up with the most words using only the letters in baked potatoes. Each letter can only be used as many times as it appears in these two words.

• **Potato Push.** Have the kids push a potato along the ground in a figure eight course using only their heads (or noses, chins, foreheads). Rather than doing it as a relay, give each person a potato and have them do it all at once in a line.

• **Paul and Penelope Potato's Popularity and Pizza Contest.** Using old catalogs, paper doll clothes, and the kids' own designs, dress potatoes for a beauty contest. Give awards for beauty, poise, charm, and originality.

• **Bowling for Potatoes.** Better than bowling for dollars! Just cut the ends off 10 potatoes to form a flat base on each and stand them up on end in bowling-pin formation. Use a big potato for the ball. Score just like bowling. Want more fun? Use a real bowling ball.

• **Hotter Than a Hot Potato.** Two teams line up and compete to see who can pass the most potatoes from one end of the line to the other before the music stops. Anyone caught not holding at least one potato is eliminated. If you want to get tough, count all the potatoes the team is still holding when the music stops and subtract that number from the team's score.

• **Driving the Potatoes to Market.** For this game you try to drive a potato along a mapped-out course by pushing it with a stick without letting it roll outside the boundaries. The course is timed, and for every time the potato rolls out of line the team has five penalty seconds added to its time.

• **Cecilia's Cellulite Carbohydrate Crunch.** A player from each team is weighed in on a bathroom scale and goes to the other side of the room. Teammates then have one minute to load up his or her clothing with potatoes. When time is called, the contestants must walk over to the scales and weigh in again. Any potatoes that fall out while they're walking don't count. The heaviest contestant wins. Another way to play is to see which team can stuff the greatest number of potatoes into their teammate's clothing, with the highest count winning.

• **Tator King.** See who can build the tallest freestanding tower using potatoes and toothpicks. This can be amazing.

• **Terrible Tommy Tator Toss.** Put instant potatoes into balloons, fill with water, and shake. Then use them to play normal balloon toss but with much messier results.

• **Mr. Potato Head's Neighborhood.** Just like Mister Rogers, the kids design their own children's program using their dressed up tator heads.

• **Icy Potatoes.** Fill a large washtub with chopped potatoes, ice, and one marble. The object of the game is to find the marble and pull it out of the tub with your foot. Better yet, use mashed potatoes.

Other familiar games can be given a fun twist simply by substituting potatoes for the balls. Golf and baseball are two good examples. You can play hopscotch by using potatoes for markers instead of stones, or you can try hunting potatoes instead of eggs at Easter. *Mitch Olson, Bill Williamson, and Mark Ziehr*

OSCAR'S FEAST

This crazy outdoor activity can be adapted for any occasion. We'll explain it here as a Halloween party

idea, appropriate especially for junior highers.

Mailing an invitation creates a mysterious

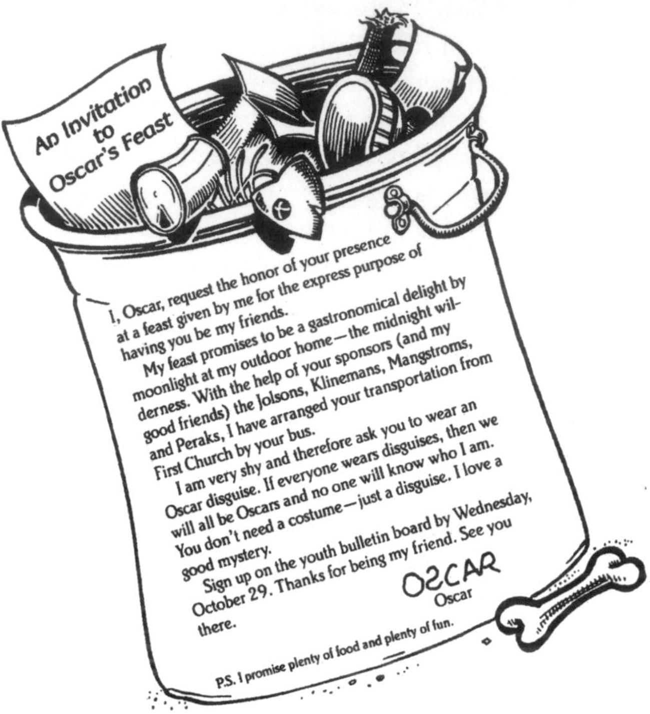

atmosphere and will help motivate kids to sign up. Asking them to disguise themselves adds a creative touch to the event. When they arrive at church, students are greeted by Igor, a two-headed and four-armed mutant gorilla (see why junior highers love this event?), a mad doctor/bus driver, and Schneider—a German spy on Oscar's trail for the last 30 years.

These crackpots (possibly your youth sponsors) accompany the kids on the bus drive to a predetermined place out in the open country. The bus roars off and leaves them alone in the dark wilderness. Schneider, the only one with a lantern or flashlight, now leads them all single-file, stooping every now and then for signs of his quarry. Be sure to arrange a few hidden surprises for the kids as they walk through fields, swamps, and woods.

Finally they all come to a fire over which, on a grate, sits a garbage can, steaming with delicious smells. When the kids inquire what it is, Schneider replies, in his best German accent, "Zat, my dear boy, eez Oscar's Feast." He then lifts the lid to reveal a steamed dinner of polish sausage, hot dogs, potatoes, carrots, onions, and corn on the cob, all steaming together in a garbage can. The recipe is on page 145.

"Oh, gross!" and "That's sick!" will soon change to "This is fantastic!" and "Is there more?" After dinner add games and storytelling to fit your schedule, then walk back to the road at a predetermined time to meet the bus for the return drive. *Doug Bretschneider*

TAFFY PULL

An activity that can be very popular with young people is a good old-fashioned taffy pull. It will keep kids occupied for up to three hours and is a lot of fun. The recipe is on page 146. It's great fun if you last. *Daniel Unrath*

BANANA NIGHT

Here's a party idea that will cause your group to really go bananas. The basic idea behind a Banana Night is to have everyone come dressed in banana colors (yellow, brown, or green) and then play all kinds of games that involve the use of bananas. There are enough ideas here to have Banana Night 2 or Banana Night Strikes Again!

• **Banana Stories.** Give a prize for the best story or poem about bananas.

• **Banana Costumes.** Give a prize for the best banana costume. Have everyone wear yellow and suggest that the kids make good use of those little stickers that come on bunches of bananas.

• **Banana Prizes.** Award banana splits, an inflatable banana, anything yellow, etc.

• **Banana Race.** Each team gets a bunch of bananas with the same number of bananas in each. Teams

line up with their bananas about 50 feet away. Each team member then runs to their team's bananas and

Oscar's Feast Trash-Can Cuisine

• Feeds approximately 20 adults.

• Cook for 3-3½ hours.

• Unnecessary to add water except for the 4 inches (see explanation below).

• The food is steamed and shouldn't fall into the water.

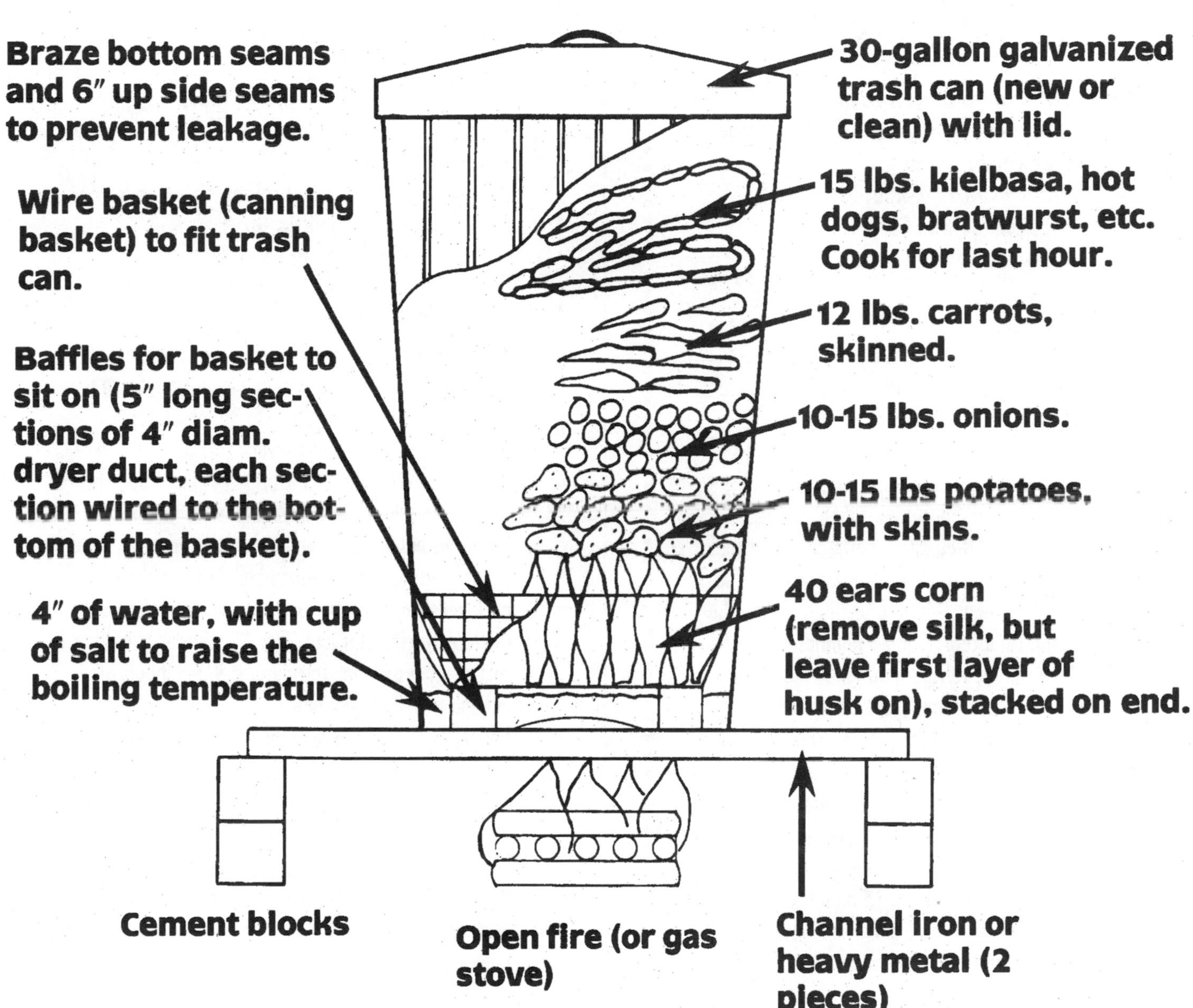

Taffy Pull Taffy

2 lbs white sugar (4 cups)
1 pt white molasses (light corn syrup)
1 pt sweet cream
Paraffin wax, walnut-size chunk
1 T plain gelatin (dry)
1 c warm to hot water

Cut wax paper into 3/4-inch squares for the taffy to be wrapped in. Make sure you have enough. Mix the first four ingredients in a large pan. Bring to a boil. Boiling will take from 20 to 30 minutes. Stir continuously. Add gelatin to water; dissolve; add to boiling mixture. When it begins to boil, turn back heat about a third to a half. Stir it until, when you take a few drops out and let drop into a buttered pan or cold water, it hardens into a round ball. Mixture should be dark yellow and bubbly. Grease a pie tin and pour the mixture into it. Let it cool 15 to 30 minutes outside in cold weather or in the refrigerator. When it gets hard enough to pull, grease hands (take all jewelry off fingers), cut the mixture in the pie tin in half, and have four people begin to tug. It takes 15 to 20 minutes of pulling before it can be cut and wrapped. Pull taffy as if swimming—with alternate strokes hand over hand. Add flavoring to the mixture after you have pulled for about 10 to 15 minutes. Cut taffy as it changes to a lighter color, small sections at a time. Lay this on table and have another individual cut into half-inch strips.

Taffy Pull Taffy

2 lbs white sugar (4 cups)
1 pt white molasses (light corn syrup)
1 pt sweet cream
Paraffin wax, walnut-size chunk
1 T plain gelatin (dry)
1 c warm to hot water

Cut wax paper into 3/4-inch squares for the taffy to be wrapped in. Make sure you have enough. Mix the first four ingredients in a large pan. Bring to a boil. Boiling will take from 20 to 30 minutes. Stir continuously. Add gelatin to water; dissolve; add to boiling mixture. When it begins to boil, turn back heat about a third to a half. Stir it until, when you take a few drops out and let drop into a buttered pan or cold water, it hardens into a round ball. Mixture should be dark yellow and bubbly. Grease a pie tin and pour the mixture into it. Let it cool 15 to 30 minutes outside in cold weather or in the refrigerator. When it gets hard enough to pull, grease hands (take all jewelry off fingers), cut the mixture in the pie tin in half, and have four people begin to tug. It takes 15 to 20 minutes of pulling before it can be cut and wrapped. Pull taffy as if swimming—with alternate strokes hand over hand. Add flavoring to the mixture after you have pulled for about 10 to 15 minutes. Cut taffy as it changes to a lighter color, small sections at a time. Lay this on table and have another individual cut into half-inch strips.

eats one, returns, tags the next player and so on. The team that finishes first wins.

• **Banana Games.** Many other games can be played substituting a banana for a ball, baton, or other equipment.

• **Pass the Banana.** Each team sits in a circle with their feet toward the center. At the signal a banana is passed from person to person cradling the banana with their feet. If the banana is dropped, the person who dropped it becomes the beginning of a new circle so the banana must be passed completely around again. Each team is timed (starting over, of course, if the banana is dropped) and the team with the shortest time wins.

• **Doctor the Banana.** Each team is given a banana, a knife, and several toothpicks. Within an agreed time limit, each team performs open banana surgery. This is done by carefully peeling the banana and slicing it into four equal pieces. These pieces are shown to the judge to verify the cuttings. Then the patients are cured. This is done by putting the banana back together again, peel and all, using toothpicks where necessary. The winning team is the one with the most cured banana.

• **Shootout at the O.K. Banana.** Get two people and stand them about 10 feet apart (give them some real cowboy hats to wear for effect). Then give them their irons—which are bananas. They put them in their holsters (pockets) and at the signal—"Draw!"—they pull their guns out, peel them, and eat them. The first one to finish eating the banana is the winner.

• **Banana Air-Band Contest.** Have the kids lip-sync

records using bananas as instruments. This can also be taped on video.

• **Banana Eating Contest.** Get a number of people situated around a table with their hands tied behind their backs. Then put an unpeeled banana or two in front of them. At the signal, they must peel and eat their bananas without using their hands. Have some towels on hand because it gets messy. The first to finish the banana is the winner. This one can also be done with couples. A couple gets an unpeeled banana, and together they must try to unpeel and eat it without using their hands. It's a riot to watch.

• **The P.B. Banfizz Race.** Select your contestants and then cover their bananas with peanut butter. At the signal they try to eat their bananas and then polish it off with a glass of 7-up or Sprite. The combination usually creates a foamy mess in their mouths. The first to successfully eat their banana and drink their drink wins the race.

• **Barbie Banana Beauty Contest.** All you need are a few naked bananas and some paper doll dress-up clothes. Each person dresses his or her banana to enter the beauty contest. You can use clothing out of magazines and department store catalogs if you don't have paper doll clothes readily available.

BANANA TICKET...

When you put on a Banana Night, have the kids bring a banana as a ticket. It's a great way to generate excitement, build your banana supply, and get things off to a good start. *Winston Hamby*

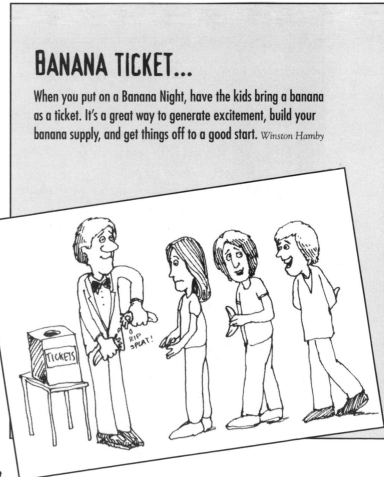

• **All My Bananas Soap Operas.** Have the kids make up their own soap opera using their beauty contest bananas. Limit them to three minutes, and have teams compete for the most gripping dramatic presentation.

• **Custom Banana Hot-Rod Show.** This is a wild one. Give each bunch (team) a model car kit to customize their banana. They then enter the Custom Banana Hot-Rod Show. If their banana car will roll,they can enter the Banana Hot-Rod Grand Prix. Let each team roll their cars down an incline. The champ is the one that reaches the bottom first or goes the farthest.

• **Banana Videos.** Have each group make a video using their bananas as puppets. The bananas can lip-sync their favorite song.

• **Tip Banana Toe.** This game is messy. You need a floor that is easily cleaned, or you can do it outside. Line up chairs so as to create an aisle which you strew with banana peels. Contestants are then blindfolded and must walk down the aisle without stepping on a banana peel. Chances are they won't make it.

• **Banana Power Munching.** See who can eat the most bananas in a certain period of time.

• **Banana Feet Relay.** Kids line up facing one direction, then sit down, lined up. The first person has to pick up the banana with his or her feet and then roll over, straight-backed, and hand off (feet off, that is) the banana to the next person, who takes it from that person's feet using only his or her own feet. The last person in line then has to peel the banana andeat it (yuk!). If done with teams the first to finish is the winner.

• **Banana Rugby.** In a large room that's easy to clean, two teams each try to advance the banana over the opposite goal line. The banana can be advanced only by passing it; players may take only two or three steps before throwing the banana. A team loses possession of the banana if they take more than the acceptable number of steps before throwing or if they throw an incomplete pass.

Have plenty of bananas on hand; they're reduced to mush quickly. And spiking the banana after a score is not recommended. *Harl Pike, Pat Caldwell, Carl Campbell, Mark Ziehr, and Jay Brady*

LIFESAVERS CANDY TOURNAMENT

With a little creativity you can build a successful event around the theme of LifeSavers candies. Have kids bring a roll of their favorite flavor as their ticket to the tournament. Then play games like these:

• **Ring Toss.** Construct two ring toss pegs by nailing a long, thin nail through a small wooden base. Kids then toss LifeSavers candies onto the nail for points. The game can also be played like horseshoes.

• **Distance Roll.** The idea here is to see who can roll a LifeSavers candy along the ground the farthest. The candy may not leave the ground and must roll on its edge.

• **LifeSavers Shuffleboard.** Play a miniature version of shuffleboard by copying the shuffleboard court on page 149 and taping it to a tabletop. Tape together two Popsicle sticks to make shuffleboard cue sticks. Use LifeSavers candies as disks.

• **Guess-the-Flavor Relay.** Put some LifeSavers candies in a bag and have teams line up relay style about 20 feet from the bag. Blindfolded players must crawl to the bag, remove one LifeSavers candy, and try to guess the color by taste. Players get only one guess. If they are wrong they must return to their team and try again. All players on each team must correctly identify a flavor.

• **Broom Hockey.** Play regular indoor broom hockey using a LifeSavers candy as a puck. Brooms are used as hockey sticks. It's really wild.

• **LifeSavers Barnyard.** Give LifeSavers candies to players so that there is an equal number of flavors distributed evenly. Then have players suck on the LifeSavers candy or just place it on their tongue. Without speaking they must gather in teams of the same color by sticking out their tongues. The first team to group completely wins.

Create other games using items that also have holes in the middle such as doughnuts and inner tubes. The possibilities are endless. *Lynn Petrie and Juli Sutton*

M & M'S CANDY NIGHT

Here's a party idea that makes good use of those famous little candy-covered chocolates. Reese's Pieces, Smarties, or similar candies can be used. Have everyone bring a package. Then play games like these (and make up some of your own):

LifeSavers Shuffleboard

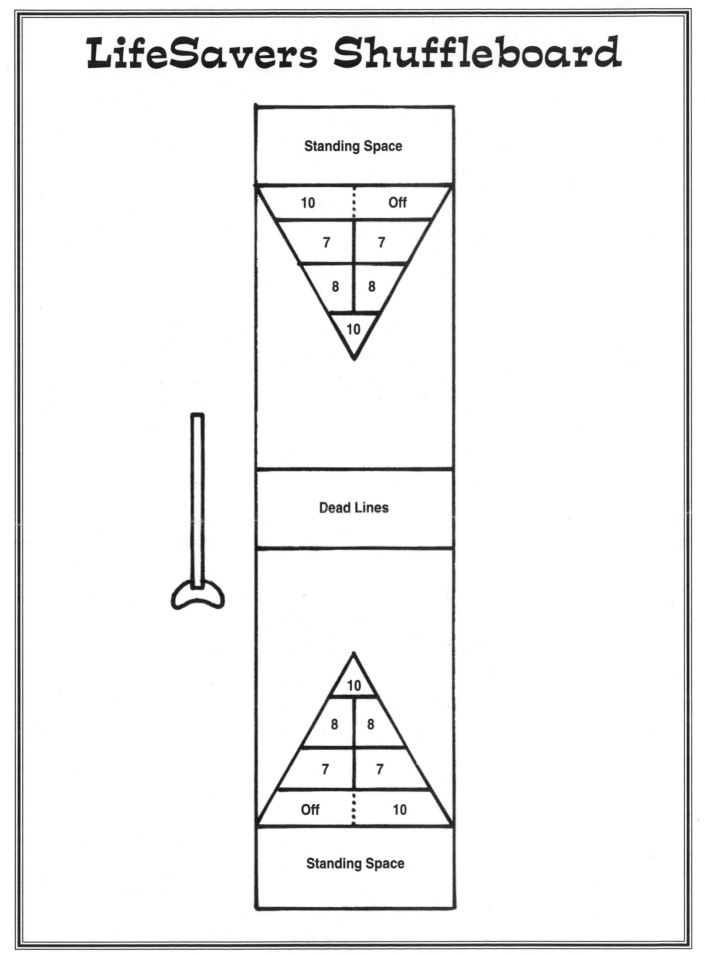

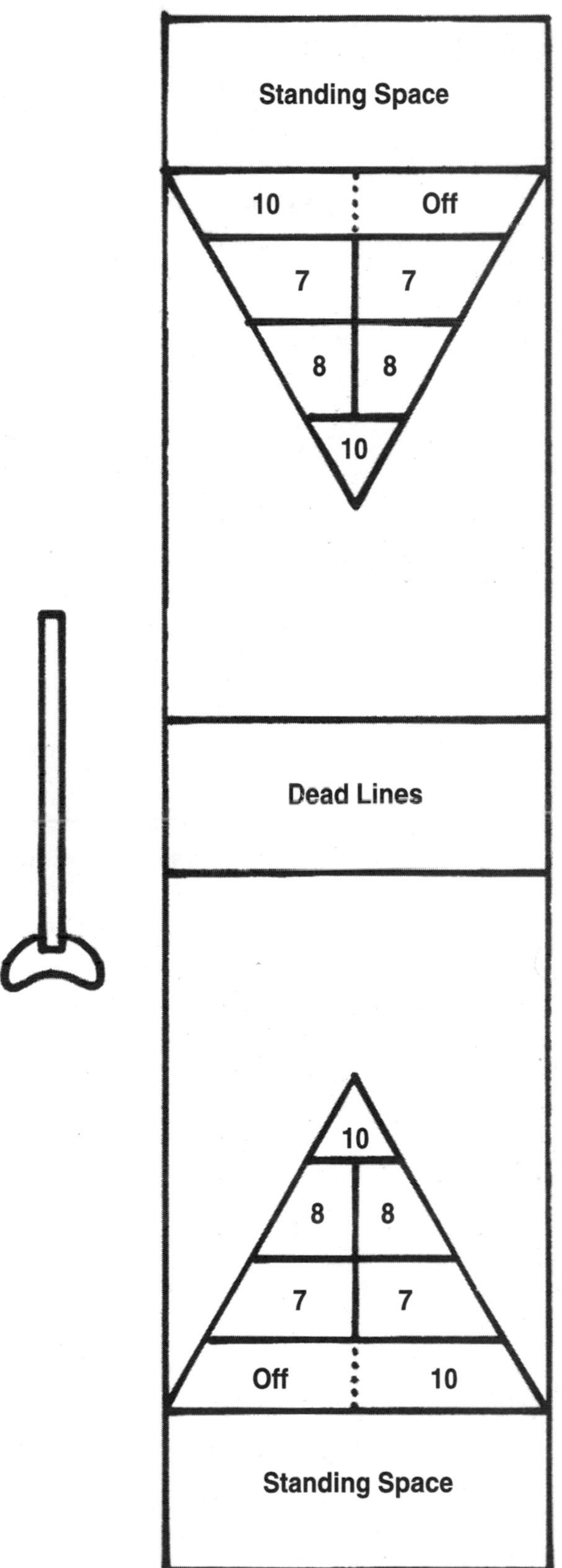

• **M & M Relay.** Team members run to a table where a package of M & M's are poured for them. They must eat the whole package without using their hands.

• **M & M Blowing Contest.** Each team must blow a pile of M & M's from one point to another—ten feet away will do.

• **Find the M & M's.** Have one team hide a package of M & M's around the room, and the other team must find as many of the candies as it can within the time limit. Make some colors worth more points than others.

• **M & M Push.** Have kids push M & M's along a course with their noses, relay style.

• **M & M Trading.** Give each kid a few random M & M's and have them trade among themselves for the colors they like best. After the trading announce which colors are worth the most points. Or have an M & M auction, using M & M's as money.

Donald Douglas

Mr. Pickle Night

You can make a night's event from a couple of gallons of pickles!

• **Pickle-oids.** Make little pickle-men with different kinds of pickles.

• **Pickle Makeover.** One person from each team becomes the model, another the makeup artist. Pickles and pickle relish are the makeup. That's right—they put pickles on their faces!

• **Pickle Tongue Twisters.** Each team must compose a poem that has as many P words as possible and still makes sense. Award points for each P word in poems. The winner is the most creative poem with the most P words.

• **Pickle.** Remember the baseball player caught in a hot box between two bases? Players in this game must run from one base to the other without being tagged. Use a pickle for a baseball.

• **Pickle Shuffleboard.** Use a long serving tray coated with vegetable oil for sliding pickle slices.

• **Chip Flip.** Players lay on floor while partners drop pickles into their mouths. The winner is the one who's caught the most pickles in one minute.

• **Putter Pickle.** Miniature golf with a pickle ball. Stroke your way through a nine-hole course. Least strokes wins.

• **Pickle Shoot.** A shooting gallery. Shoot paper clips from rubber-band guns to knock down pickles.

• **The American Pickle Cup.** Teams construct sailboats from pickles, then race them.

• **We're in a Real Pickle This Time.** Teams write their own TV crime show.

Give points for first, second, and third place in each event, and award something picklish to the overall winner at the night's end. *Mark Ziehr*

Party Passports

Use the theme of an around-the-world cruise for your next progressive dinner. Each of the homes visited could be decorated as a different country and could offer a unique ethnic dish. You could even rig the church bus as a ship and have a brief bon voyage party at the church before leaving.

Create mock passports for each traveler to be stamped at each home. Use one of the passport visa pages as an itinerary that lists all of the stops and gives a brief story about each country (home) to be visited. *R.M. Naron*

SPECIAL EVENTS WITH A POINT

SPECIAL EVENTS WITH A POINT

Sure, fun is fun—but when an event significantly benefits group members or others in the community, the fun can be morally or spiritually substantial. Here are some ideas for activities that are designed to carry long-lasting impact on everyone involved.

CIVIL WAR

This is an idea designed to encourage participation in summer activities of the youth group, but it could be done anytime.

At the beginning of the summer, the entire group is divided into two groups, the Blue Team (representing the Union Army) and the Gray Team (representing the Confederate Army). Each team has a general, a field captain, lieutenants, and soldiers. The soldiers are the kids, the officers are the leaders, teachers, etc. The soldiers earn either Union money or Confederate money (printed up in advance) during the summer by attending Sunday school, bringing visitors, doing certain assignments, attending other activities, memorizing Scripture, participating in service projects, and so on. The different activities can be given military names like basic training, maneuvers, recruitment, etc.

At the end of the summer, have a war. It's all in fun, of course, but it can be either a giant water-balloon war or some other game competition. The kids can buy ammo with the money they have earned during the summer. The more money they have, the more water balloons or other types of ammo they can use in the war. No one is allowed to bring their own ammo. Kids can also use their money to buy hot dogs or other concessions on the day of the war. *David Marks*

SUPER-COURSE

This idea is designed to give in-depth training by professionals in their fields to young people over the course of an academic school year. Tuition is charged each student (to pay the speakers, etc.) and the super-course is held for two or three hours (in one shot) each week (on a Sunday afternoon, perhaps, or a weeknight). The idea is to expose the kids to different thoughts, people, opportunities, methods of self-help, etc., which they would not otherwise receive in typical church curriculum. One group included the following classes:

Role-Playing
Synectics (Problem-Solving)
Simulation Games
Dramatic Expression
Ethics Lab
How to Communicate Effectively

Registration, exams, diplomas issued at the

end of the year, etc., all help to make this a big success.

You may also want to try these variations:

• **Lookin' Good...Inside and Out.** Find out which areas of etiquette and grooming most interest your kids and set up fun interactive workshops titled "Lookin' Good...Inside and Out." Arrange for workshop leaders in such areas as phone etiquette, table etiquette, posture and exercise, hair care, makeup and facial care, and general hygiene.

Try calling local schools, public libraries, hospitals, the phone company, modeling schools, hairdressers, and fitness centers; most will probably be willing to teach the workshop free. Don't forget members of your church who might have expertise in these areas. You can schedule one long day of workshops or several shorter days.

Plan plenty of breaks during the day with refreshments. Don't forget to videotape everything for later use and for those who couldn't come. Make sure you get youth volunteers to help you publicize the event, set up, and clean up. Finally, have participants complete a brief written evaluation to assist you in planning for the next event.

• **Best of All.** Give the young women in your group some special attention with a morning of activities designed especially for them and their friends. You can call it The Best of All, based on the *Living Bible* translation of Proverbs 31:29: "There are many fine women in the world, but you are the best of all."

The day would focus on personal and life skills for contemporary women. Start off with breakfast and a devotional, then allow the youths to choose from among several workshops taught by adults in your church. You could include college and career planning, sewing tips, fashion tips, marriage preparation, computer skills, a fitness program, study tips, whatever you think would be of help. Besides what they learn that morning, they'll gain a deeper acquaintance with adult women in your church that could lead to discipling relationships and long-term guidance. *Quent Peacock, Steve Allen, and Judi Jackson*

MINI-WORKSHOPS

Have a six to eight week mini-workshop for your youths. Sunday nights during the summer is a good time. Have interest groups in drama, art, music, and perhaps a study group. Plans could be made to work toward one theme to be combined for a worship experience at the end of the time, or all groups could go separate ways. Work within the groups could be toward spiritual intent, or fun things that could be shared in a churchwide fellowship. Below are some suggestions:

• **Art Group.** Make banners out of brightly colored felt and burlap, etc., for hanging around the church, or for background for worship themes. Take videos of the sequences that the drama group prepares. Work on collages on various themes for discussion and sharing.

• **Drama Group.** Select and work on a particular play or drama. Try some readers theater. Act out Bible stories.

• **Music Group.**Work on some new types of music not usually heard in their regular worship times. You could have an instrumentalist group (be sure to have instrumentalists in the group). This group could select music for the worship experience that would relate to the theme and readings used.

• **Study Group.** Provide a study group for youths not interested in any of the above areas. Study could be geared to talking about your faith or a topic that they suggest. *Jean Parker*

HOMEWORK NIGHT

Set aside a regular night every week or every other week for your kids to receive help with their homework. Any student is invited to participate as long as they abide by three rules:

- You must bring homework.
- You must keep conversation at a quiet level.
- If you goof off, you go home.

These times can become very special to your group, not just because of the academic assistance, but also because they learn to reach out and help one another. Parents will be especially grateful. *Robin Petura and Keith Clark*

SUNDAY STUDY HALL

At times throughout the school year (mid-term testing, semester finals), young people feel the rigors of academic pressure more acutely. On the Sundays just prior to these stress weeks, your young people may feel the need to decide whether they are going to attend youth group or stay home and hit the books. One way to minister to your students during these times is to set up a study hall at the church. Young people can come for their regular activities (recreation, choir, supper) and then, instead of a program, extend the time for an hour or two and designate it for study. Provide light refreshments and have places available where those who have common classes can review and study together as well as rooms where others can study by themselves.

Vernon Edington

NITE LIFE TOUR

A Nite Life Tour is an intensive, fast-moving, 12-hour (6:00 p.m. to 6:00 a.m.) tour of the night life in your town or city. Take a selected group of senior high students on a tour like the one suggested below. This experience will give your young people some valuable exposure to the "other side" as well as each other.

Suggested schedule:

- **6:00 p.m. Meet at the church. Orientation. Let the people know where they are going, what to look for, questions to think about.**
- **6:30 p.m. Suicide prevention center**
- **7:45 p.m. Movie (secular film at an established theater)**
- **10:30 p.m. City morgue or emergency room at hospital**
- **11:30 p.m. Snack**
- **12:30 a.m. Police department**
- **2:00 a.m. Airport control tower**
- **3:00 a.m. Drug rehabilitation center**
- **4:30 a.m. Breakfast**
- **6:00 a.m. Home**

Some additional suggestions: A TV studio, a church-operated coffeehouse, the telephone company, the local newspaper, interviews with city officials, Salvation Army, Goodwill Industries, a store-front church, a Friday evening or Saturday morning synagogue service, draft counseling service, post office, funeral home, bowling, swimming, a play or musical, a rap session with college students.

Follow up with a discussion of both the good and the bad of what was seen and heard. Obviously it would be best to have the discussion on another day, as the group will be pretty tired after the all-night experience. *Robert Stine*

DEATH WALK

Take a group to a local cemetery. Spend an hour walking around reading what people have had written on their tombstones or plaques. Have each kid take a pencil and small note tablet to copy down

what they find. Come back to the church and discuss what you found. Try to decide the person's philosophy of life from what was written on their grave. Discuss the subject of death as it relates to Christian and non-Christian people. *Paul Sailhamer*

TOUR OF YOUR LIFE

This day-long field trip is great with junior highers, and it gives them an opportunity to view life somewhat more completely and realistically.

Begin by visiting the maternity ward of a local hospital (prearranged, of course) where the kids can see newborns and their parents. Perhaps a doctor can tell about the birth process and give a brief tour of the area. Next take the kids to a local college or university campus and show them around. The next stop should be a factory or shop where people are at work. At this point, the need for work and the types of work available can be discussed. Then proceed to a convalescent home and chat with the residents. Allow the kids to share with them in some way and allow the seniors to also share with the kids in some way. The last stop on the tour should be a mortuary or funeral home. The funeral director may show the kids around, explain what happens to the body when it is brought in, the types of caskets available, and so on.

Close the experience with a meeting or discussion in the funeral chapel. Other places can be added to this tour depending on how much time you have or the types of places available to you. Allow kids to think about their own lives, the kind of life that they want, and how they are going to achieve their goals.

UNDER ARREST

Make arrangements with your city police department or county sheriff's office to lock your young people in jail for an hour. Then, on the basis of Paul's letter to the Philippian Christians, discuss with your young people what real joy was for Paul, even though he was in prison. Relate this to the many ways in which we are imprisoned today, and how it affects our witness as Christians. Other appropriate passages could be used to discuss such topics as freedom, etc. *Wayne Carlson*

INMATE

Arrange for the senior high group to visit a reformatory or penal institution, preferably a small one, and have an official of the institution explain the background and operation of the facility. After this introduction, break up into discussion groups with some of the inmates. It works best if there can be about two inmates and five or six of the kids in one group. The young people will learn a great deal from the experience, especially if the students are prepared with questions ahead of time.

UNDERGROUND CHURCH

To the catacombs! This is part adventure game, part worship and celebration. Your kids' first task in this evening event is to elude the Secret Police of a corrupt, anti-Christian government and locate Safe Houses run by the Christian underground. Then they travel to the Meeting House, a secret, secluded location for celebration and worship, with reminders of what ancient and modern Christians have endured in order to meet and worship together.

Get lots of people from church or the community involved. The evening requires planners, Contacts, Safe House owners, Secret Police, and worship-service organizers. (Delegate!) For practical safety reasons this game must be carried out in a carefully designated area, defined clearly on a map carried by all participants. Choose a neighborhood where traffic is minimal.

The details in the adventure game as explained below can be changed to suit your own community and group. Use more or fewer clues, arm the Secret Police with weapons other than Super Soakers, etc. Make it your event.

• **Background.** The adventure setting is a police state where all Christian gatherings are outlawed. The religious underground has begun a resistance movement, however, to protect and encourage believers. They have organized a clandestine meeting of Christians in their neighborhood.

Thanks to old church membership lists, all believers have been organized into cell groups. For their own protection, they know the identities of neither their own cell members nor those in other cells.

On the event night they will locate their own cell's Safe House and be introduced to other cell members. Before the evening is over, they will meet with the other cells for worship and mutual encouragement.

A week before the event, underground leaders circulate special ID cards and bracelets to identify all believers (see Publicity below). ID cards are color coded by cell group with a small colored dot. Included with them is a map with the first of four clues that eventually lead to the Safe House for a particular cell group.

• **The task of underground members.** On the night of the event—armed with color-coded ID, bracelet, map, and the first clue—kids get their next three clues from three Contacts: two Street Persons and a Store Owner/Manager/Clerk (see Instructions for Underground Contacts). Participants must move about in groups of three or four. Groups smaller or larger than that are strictly forbidden.

When players approach someone they suspect is a Contact, they say the underground passwords, "Do you have any old newspapers to donate?" True Contacts respond, "Come walk on the water." Contacts then check kids' IDs, for they can give clues only to students with their color.

The fourth and final clue takes underground members to their Safe House where they'll be blindfolded and driven to the secret gathering at the Meeting House.

Believers need a total of four dots on their ID card to get into the Safe House. The bracelet identifies participants to Contacts and other believers. No one is allowed into a Safe House without a bracelet.

As they're searching for Contacts and clues, they must also elude the Secret Police, who are intent on breaking up the resistance movement and discovering the members of the underground. They are everywhere that night, and they have no identifying signs except that they are armed with Super Soakers. When the Secret Police catch believers, they remove their bracelets, blindfold them, and take them to prison.

• **Prison.** Prison is a darkened room at the church. While sitting in the darkened room, prisoners hear sounds of interrogation, torture, and guns firing blanks. Use good judgment as to how much realism is appropriate for your group. From time to time the Secret Police remove one of the prisoners from the room. These are taken to another darkened room, but the people in the first room don't know where their comrades are.

In the end underground commandos rescue their captured fellow believers and take them to the Meeting House, but the commandos act as if not everyone got out alive. Those who died can be memorialized at the worship service. Some groups make it so that the fatal circumstances of these martyrs resemble those of actual martyrs killed by repressive governments in our own day.

• **The clandestine celebration.** At each of the Safe Houses, students are blindfolded and transported by vans and buses to the secret Meeting House—a nearby church, chapel, camp, or retreat center.

Conduct the celebration service according to your group's tastes. A typical one consists of:

—Upbeat contemporary songs as well as some somber, meditative songs.

—The narration or reading of actual persecution around the world, both ancient and modern, intertwined with a few fictitious stories about underground members who were lost that evening trying to get to this meeting.

—A challenging message.

—Concrete take-home symbols—salvation bracelets, ID cards--reminders of the underground experience.

After the celebration students are transported back to the starting point to be taken home.

• **Publicity.** Here's how you can make this evening a big event—and even get some press coverage if you're lucky.

—Three weeks before the event. Youth group members each receive a flier that invites them to a secret underground gathering, with a warning to watch out for the Secret Police. Use the flier provided or design your own.

—Two weeks before the event. Polaroid photos of captured underground leaders—along with cassette tapes of their coerced confessions—are circulated at school. Run free radio spots on local stations inviting kids to Go Underground! Spots include the date, time, and starting location. Students receive a Secret Police flier with the photo of a captured underground leader (see the sample). The message is clear: *Don't* go underground.

—One week before the event. Students circulate underground bracelets and ID cards. Run a notice in your local paper warning residents that students will be participating in this adventure game. The Secret Police make home visits, warning kids not to go underground. Place signs strategically in neighborhood yards reading Go Underground! and Don't Go Underground! or Go Underground at Your Own Risk!

Skip Seibel

UNDERGROUND CHURCH

INSTRUCTIONS FOR PARTICIPANTS

We are now living in a police state. Christian gatherings are outlawed. Yet the underground has planned a clandestine meeting of area Christians and has circulated bracelets to identify all members.

UNDERGROUND BRACELET

You must locate the Safe House with your bracelet intact. From your Safe House you will be transported to the secret gathering at the Meeting House.

ID CARD AND COLOR-CODED ROUTES

You will be given an ID card with a colored circle and a street location. The street location will take you to your first contact, who will place a matching colored dot on your ID card—and give you another clue. From there you will continue your journey.

You must find a total of three Contacts, for a total of four colored dots on your ID card, before you will be able to enter your cell's own Safe House. There are many Safe Houses, but only one that will accept your color-coded ID card. Contacts can give clues only to underground church members whose cell color matches the dots they are carrying.

PASSWORDS

To identify Contacts ask, "Do you have any old newspapers to donate?" Contacts will respond, "Come walk on the water." They will then determine if your color-coded ID card matches the color they can give out. *Not all Contacts can give you your color dot.*

SECRET POLICE

On your way to the Safe House, you must elude the Secret Police. Beware! They are everywhere, and they are deadly! The Secret Police are armed with Super Soakers. If they kill you—that is, drench you—they will remove your bracelet and take you to prison. Once you are hit by water from a Super Soaker there is no escape. Safe Houses will not admit anyone who is wet, even if the person has a bracelet and ID card.

GROUP SIZE

You must move about in groups of three or four. Groups smaller than three and larger than four are strictly forbidden.

CAN'T FIND THE SAFE HOUSE?

You have until 7 p.m. to find your Safe House. If you don't find your Safe House by 7 p.m., return to the starting point immediately. We will transport you from there to the underground Meeting House.

UNDERGROUND CHURCH

INSTRUCTIONS FOR UNDERGROUND CONTACTS

Date of event: ______________ Time of event: ____________

Thanks for helping with Underground Church. We have 14 separate routes. Each one is color coded. Kids will come to you with an ID card with a colored dot on the back. Give clues or directions *only* to kids with your color.

The game part of the evening will begins at ____ p.m. and concludes at ____ p.m.

FIRST CONTACT: STREET PERSON 1

You can be anywhere on your assigned section of the street, doing whatever you like—loitering, reading, dumpster diving, talking with someone, talking to yourself, etc.

Underground members will ask you, "Do you have any old newspapers to donate?" Your response is, "Come walk on the water."

Check their ID card for your color dot. If the color is correct, place one of your dots on the ID card and give them the next clue. If they have a *different* color dot, give them neither one of your dots nor the next clue. (They must have four dots of the same color to be admitted to the Meeting House.)

SECOND CONTACT: STORE OWNER/MANAGER/CLERK

Whether an office, restaurant, or retail store—greet kids in a businesslike manner ("How can I help you tonight?" or "Table for how many?" etc.). When they ask, "Do you have any old newspapers to donate?" quietly respond with "Come walk on the water."

Check all IDs for your color, then follow the same procedure as above.

THIRD CONTACT: STREET PERSON 2

Your situation is similar to that of Street Person 1 (above); only be involved in something different. If Street Person 1 looks like a transient, for example, you may want to appear solidly middle-class, perhaps waiting for a bus or washing windows.

Follow the pattern explained above when kids approach you.

FOURTH CONTACT: SAFE HOUSE

To make it fun, you can respond in one of several ways:

Be suspicious and wary; don't immediately open the door when you hear the knock, but first peer through a window (but so the kids can see you) and perhaps even answer without opening the door, "Who is it?" or "What do you want?"

When the kids ask, "Do you have any old newspapers to donate?" *then* open the door and respond quietly with "Come walk on the water."

Answer the door nonchalantly. When underground members ask you, "Do you have any old newspapers to donate?" answer in a way that throws them momentarily off guard: "Oh, I'm sorry, we don't keep newspapers—but if you want, you can come walk on the water."

However you respond, admit only those underground members who are not wet (those who've avoided the Secret Police's Super Soakers), who have the correct number and color of dots on their ID card, and who are still wearing their bracelet.

In the Safe House kids are blindfolded, then driven by van or bus to the Meeting House.

Come Walk on the Water

GO UNDERGROUND

Date: ______________________

Place: ____________________

Time: ______________________

Beware of the Secret Police

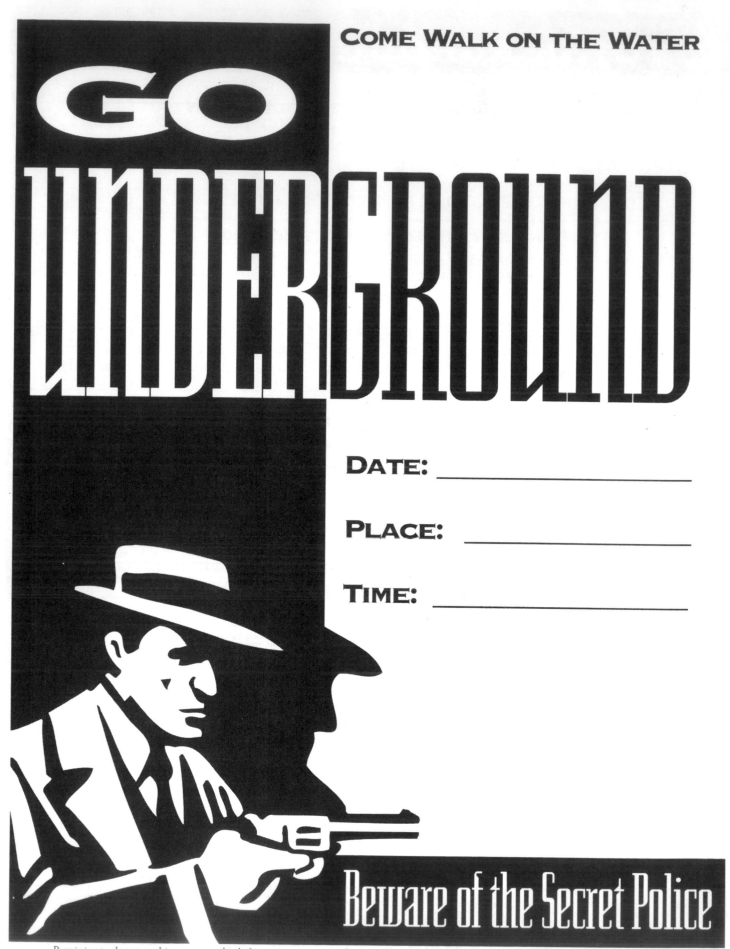

A WARNING FROM THE Secret Police

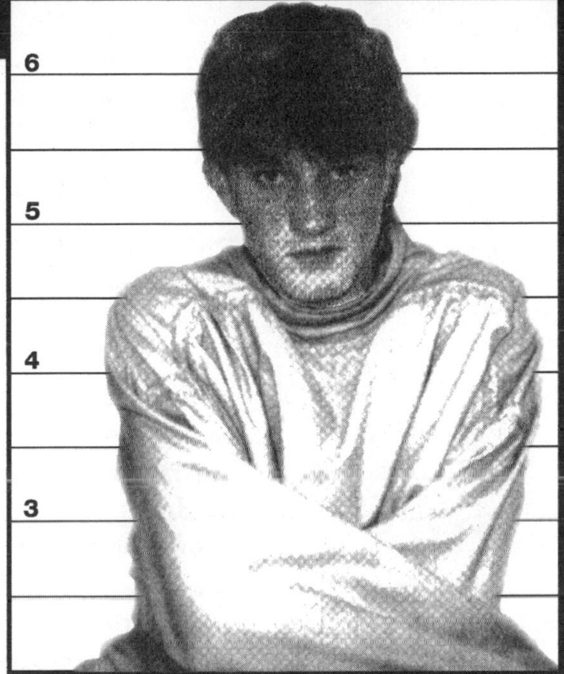

CAPTURED UNDERGROUND LEADER
THIS COULD BE YOU!

Don't Go Underground

DATE: ____________ **PLACE:** ____________ **TIME:** ____________

A message from your local Secret Police

ONE-POT POTLUCK SOUP-SUPPER

Here's an idea that's a great way to dramatize several issues like world hunger and how our small individual efforts can make the difference when added to the whole, and more generally, the meaning of the body of Christ as the union of all of the gifts and individual contributions of its members.

Before the meeting, have someone boil several soup bones. Add salt and herbs to make a hearty broth. This can be made well in advance and frozen but must be thawed completely. For best results, boil it rapidly at the very beginning of the meeting. Students bring one favorite vegetable or some grain or legumes. These are added to the broth. Make sure you add the beans and grains first, followed by the vegetables. The whole thing needs about one or one and a half hours to cook at a good pace. While the soup is cooking, have a film or speaker with the focus on world hunger, some crowd breakers, or community building exercises to dramatize further the nature of the body of Christ.

After an hour or so, serve the soup and see how amazed students are that their tiny offerings fit together so well to make a hearty and good-tasting soup. *James Ward*

RANDOM HUNGER

This idea can be used at a camp or at any church activity where a meal is to be served. Let the group know that the meal is going to be an experimental situation in which the food is divided according to the world population. For a group of 100 people, divide up this way:

Country	Number of People	Percentage of Food
North America	6	60
Europe/Middle East	16	20
Africa	10	
Central/South America	8	20
Asia	60	

Africa, South America, and Asia share 20 percent of the food.

Assign each continent a color. Decorate the tables by color (table cloths, napkins, or decorations) with enough places to accommodate the number of people for the continent. Cut one paper square for each person in the coordinating color. Put all the squares in a basket and let people choose a color as they come in the door. Direct them to sit at a table that matches the color of the paper they've drawn. Distribute the food proportionally according to the chart above. Let the kids determine what happens from there. Do not interfere with the process unless absolutely necessary.

Later discuss what went on and let the kids draw conclusions about the present world situation.

LOTTERY MEAL

This exercise is similar to the Third World Banquet but with an added ingredient to make it even more effective. The Lottery Meal can be held as part of a regular youth supper or, even better, as part of a weekend retreat. Either way, this semi-simulation game can help your youth understand better the frustrations of being poor in a rich society. In order for this to be effective, do not let the young people know that anything unusual will be happening at the dinner. Let them discover the lottery when they show up to eat.

Seal play money in plain white envelopes in amounts ranging from $2,500 to $50 (10 percent contain $2,500; 50 percent contain amounts from $1,500 to $500; 40 percent contain amounts from $300 to $50).

Place the envelopes in a box and have each person draw one envelope to use for purchasing the meal at a buffet dinner. In plain view near the buffet table should be a large menu and price list.

Milk $10
Soda $50
Cake $300 a piece
Cupcake $75
Steak $1500
Hamburgers $100 each
Plain spaghetti $40
Salad $250

Interaction will vary with each group during the meal, but watch for those who balk and refuse to ask for more money and those who will go to any extreme to get more money. And on the part of the wealthy you might observe those who make the have-nots grovel for extra cash and those who freely share their money. You might even find the wealthy pooling their money and forming a bank. The discussion possibilities are many, and you will have no trouble getting people to talk. Oh yes...after the discussion, you should arrange for everyone, rich and poor, to have a full supper.

• **Un-Dinner for World Hunger.** Here's a slightly different way to communicate world hunger to your kids. Create a sign of entrees and prices. Display it on the buffet. Explained that everyone can order whatever they choose—up to 13 cents worth of food. This represents the daily food budget of many in the world.

Here are some possible food choices and relative pricing:

Water—1 cent per cup
Coffee—6 cents per cup
Sugar—2 cents per serving
Milk—2 cents per cup
Saltines—1 cent each
Olives—2 cents each
Orange slices—8 cents each
Hard-boiled eggs—6 cents each
Carrots—3 cents per serving
Sweet pickles—2 cents per serving
American cheese—6 cents per slice
Radishes—1 cent per serving
Raisins—9 cents per serving
Cookies—3 cents each

Of course, the meal can be followed by a discussion of the problems of world hunger and one's own personal involvement. The price of a regular dinner can be charged as admission and the difference between it and the un-dinner can be given to World Vision for distribution. *Bob Lawrence and Randy Deering*

SMALL WORLD PARTY

This fun event will increase your students' awareness of the world around them. Advertise it as a Small World Party and give all the activities an international flavor. Here are some examples:

• **Name Tag Mixer.** As kids arrive they make a name tag representing their family's nationality. Emphasize creativity. Allow 15-20 minutes to make the tags. You might want to award prizes for the most creative tags.

• **Signature Mixer.** Give everyone a list similar to the sample. The object is to get a signature for each item.

• **Costume Fashion Show.** Have kids dress in international costume and have judges pick the most elaborate, the most creative, the funniest, etc.

• **Folk Games.** Find games played in other countries in a book at your local library. Play as many as you have time for. If possible, invite guests who are familiar with the games to lead them.

• **Snacks.** Keep these along the theme, too. Swedish meatballs, tortilla chips and guacamole, tiny pizzas, cheeses from other countries, etc.

• **Closing Devotion.** Celebrate each person's heritage and uniqueness, emphasizing how all are made one in Christ. *Nancy Wise*

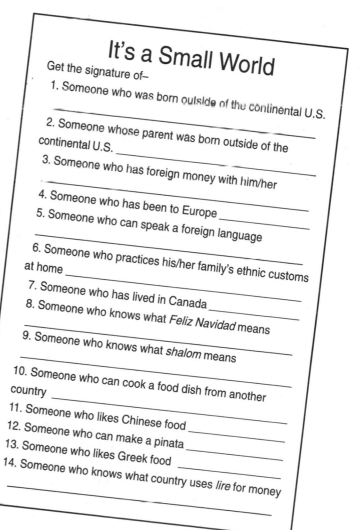

It's a Small World

Get the signature of–

1. Someone who was born outside of the continental U.S. ________
2. Someone whose parent was born outside of the continental U.S. ________
3. Someone who has foreign money with him/her ________
4. Someone who has been to Europe ________
5. Someone who can speak a foreign language ________
6. Someone who practices his/her family's ethnic customs at home ________
7. Someone who has lived in Canada ________
8. Someone who knows what *Feliz Navidad* means ________
9. Someone who knows what *shalom* means ________
10. Someone who can cook a food dish from another country ________
11. Someone who likes Chinese food ________
12. Someone who can make a pinata ________
13. Someone who likes Greek food ________
14. Someone who knows what country uses *lire* for money ________

GOURMET GORGE

To encourage more intimate, casual fellowship in your group and increase parent involvement, try a Gourmet Gorge each week. Everyone goes to one group member's home (a different one each week) to enjoy a dinner prepared by the youth and his or her parents. Each person pays a small amount to cover expenses.

The meals should be simple—hot dogs, tacos, or whatever. If no home is available on a particular Sunday, just stay at the church and order take-out food. After the meal you can sit around talking, watching a short movie, or playing a game. Keep it unstructured and spontaneous, and you'll find the time together perfect for relationship building. *Alan Hamilton*

TEN-MINUTE ALL-NIGHT PRAYER MEETING

All night prayer meetings are not very common among most youth groups these days. In fact they aren't all that common, period. But they can be meaningful and effective for the participants. The problem with long prayer meetings is endurance—or lack of it—and the fact that it is difficult to pray for more than two or three minutes at a time, let alone two or three hours. But this might be the answer to problems like these, particularly for youth groups.

Here's how it's done: Begin at midnight with a core group of kids. This could follow a youth group activity, a concert, or something similar. A Friday night is ideal.

Prepare kids for this adventure in prayer ahead of time by discussing scriptural guidelines for prayer and the power of prayer.

Each hour is then broken down into 10-minute segments. The first hour goes something like this:

- **12:00-12:10 Concern for the world.** Display a map of the world on the wall that shows all the major continents. Let volunteers throw darts at the map until they hit a country or continent. Provide information on the needs in that area of the world and pray for those needs.
- **12:10-12:20 Concern for each other.** Give each small group a different subject to pray about; family, school, friends, God's will, etc. Have kids within each group discuss their needs about the subject and pray for each other. During the next hour kids will form new groups.
- **12:20-12:30 Random needs.** Prepare ahead of time on small slips of paper a number of prayer requests. Get the requests from people at your church and from the news. Roll up the slips, slide them into balloons, inflate the balloons, and tape them to a wall or board. Let each student try to pop a balloon by throwing darts. Read aloud the prayer requests and spend some time praying for those special requests.
- **12:30-12:40 Teaching time.** At the half hour mark of every hour, have leaders conduct prepared 10-minute learning activities on the subject of prayer. Try segmenting the Lord's Prayer and discussing one segment each hour.
- **12:40-12:50 Youth group needs.** Emphasize special needs within the youth group, perhaps one per hour. You could follow the style of the "random needs" section. Or use your own creative approach. For instance, you could draw subjects from a hat, put topics in soda bottles and try knocking them over from a distance with a tennis ball, etc. Once the need has been selected, however, spend some serious time in prayer for that particular need.
- **12:50-1:00 Break.** Enjoy refreshments, play games, and have fun.

Begin the whole cycle again at 1:00 and continue until morning. The whole experience can be wrapped up with breakfast, perhaps prepared by some moms who get up early. *Spencer Nordyke*

MYSTERY PRAYER JOURNEY

Here's a creative field trip that will help your kids see the need for prayer in a new way.

Publicize the event as a mystery trip. Have your group arrive at the church or some other meeting point at a predetermined time. Teens won't know where they're going, but they'll be given clues along the way. The object of the trip is to encourage intercessory prayer.

Give kids their first clue at the meeting point—a Band-Aid, for example. Each person receives one Band-Aid and is encouraged to keep it. A leader reads an appropriate passage of Scripture, and the journey begins as kids move to the first destination—a hospital.

There, kids gather together at the entrance, in the chapel, or at some other appropriate place and pray for the sick, the lame, and the injured in the hospital. The young people are then given a clue to the next destination, where they pray again for the needs specified by the Scripture read en route.

At the end of the trip, tell the kids to keep the clues and use them as reminders to pray for the various needs that were identified on the trip.

Take advantage of your time at different institutions. At a hospital, military base, or correctional facility, for example, arrange ahead of time to have the chaplain join you for prayer. Or if a rescue mission is on your itinerary, plan to have the kids eat a meal there.

Praying on location can be done even within the church. Gather the group around the missions bulletin board and pray for the missionaries. Go into the pastor's study and pray for the pastor and his staff. Go into the sanctuary and pray for the church's worship services. Your kids will gain a new appreciation for the importance of prayer.

Below is a list of clues, destinations, Scriptures, and prayer needs that you can use. Add your own, too! *Randy Nichols*

MONDAY MORNING PRAYER BREAKFAST

If your church is located near a local high school, you can sponsor a free prayer breakfast every Monday morning at the church for anyone who wants to attend. Schedule it at least one hour before school starts and get a few adult volunteers to show up early enough to prepare the food. Have kids sing, listen to music, or play games until breakfast is served.

While the kids are eating, present a short devotion, and perhaps have several of the kids lead in prayer (ask them in advance). Get some sponsors to help cover the cost of the food (business people, church members, etc.) and make sure the food is good (no cold cereal or doughnuts).

As the breakfast becomes better known, you will find that more and more kids will come, making it a tremendous outreach program for your youth group. *Rick Wheeler*

MIDNIGHT PICNIC

Here's a Bible study idea that the kids will love. First, have the group look up information about star

CLUE OBJECTS	DESTINATION	SCRIPTURES	PRAY FOR–
Band-Aid	Hospital	Matthew 8:14-17 James 5:14-15	The sick, handicapped, injured
Paper clip, legal paper	Courthouse steps	Romans 13:1-7 1 Timothy 2:1-4	Local and national government leaders
Child's crayon drawings	Children's home	Matthew 19:13-14 James 1:27	Abused, neglected, orphaned children
Go to Jail Monopoly cards	Correctional center	Matthew 25:33-45	Prisoners, prison workers, chaplains
Toy soldiers	Military base	Luke 3:14-16 Matthew 8:5-8, 13	Military personnel, world tensions
Church bulletin	Church	Matthew 16:15-18 Acts 2:41-47	Church leaders, services, missionaries

formations and planets visible from the earth. Then, on a starry night, have a picnic at midnight. Each person should pack a lunch, a lantern, and a blanket. After eating, try to identify the star formations. You can even try to count the stars. Tie the evening together with some thoughts on how God created the stars (Genesis 1) and how God's handiwork is expressed through the heavens (Psalm 8 and Psalm 19). This activity can be done anytime after dark, but there is more of a sense of drama for the kids if it is done at midnight. *Alva Wiersma*

HANDICAPPED ALL-NIGHTER

To help your group gain a better understanding of the challenges faced by people who are physically handicapped, try an all-nighter like this. First, have a discussion about challenges faced by the handicapped. Then give each youth a disability for the rest of the evening. Design handicaps so that they are of maximum significance to each person: Star athletes, for example, can be confined to wheelchairs, given walkers, or restricted to crutches. This should include splinting legs or taping them together. Anyone in a wheelchair is not allowed to use the bathroom without two others to help. Your "motor mouth" can be given a stroke, simulated by a right leg splint, the right arm taped to the side, and mouth taped shut. Other active youths can be blindfolded or fitted with cardboard glasses that have off-center holes so only one side vision is possible. Some can be made to see through several layers of sandwich wrap to give clouded vision. Use your imagination.

Once everyone has a handicap, the evening proceeds like any other all-nighter, with dumb games, relays, skill activities, and mixers. Try making and eating pizza, with the youths doing all the work so that they must help one another to succeed.

Finally, have a Bible study focusing on several stories about Jesus healing. At midnight hold a Communion service. As each youth is given the bread and wine, each person can be "healed" of his or her handicap.

Follow with a discussion of what happened, what was easiest and most difficult about the experience, and what they learned. The rest of the night can be spent in the usual youth night activities. *Jon Erickson*

STIFF ARM PROGRESSIVE DINNER

As Christians it's imperative that we interact with and minister to each other. An excellent way to exemplify this need and have an enjoyable evening also is to have a Stiff Arm Progressive Dinner.

Arrangements are made for the progressive dinner in the usual manner (a different house or meeting place for each course of the evening's meal). However, when the people gather at a predetermined meeting place before going to the first house (for the first course of the meal), each person is fitted with removable cardboard bands that fit over their elbows. Before entering each house for the meal, they must slide this band over their elbows (each arm). This inhibits all bending of the elbow joint and therefore makes it rather difficult to feed yourself. If the individual wants to eat any food, he must depend on the rest of the people (who also depend on him) to feed him.

When leaving the house, the arm bands can be removed, but must be put on before entering the next house. At the end of the night, you can draw your own applications as to how we must depend on each other for our spiritual food and fellowship. *Larry Shelton*

HERE COMES THE BRIDE

Invite several couples to come speak to your senior high group about the difference between a wedding and being married. The couples selected to participate should have varying experience: one year, five years, 15 years, 25 years or more. Ask the ladies to bring their wedding gowns (if they still have them) and to model them (if they can still get into them).

Invite the kids to come to the meeting with wedding announcements. Have a big wedding cake, photographer, reception, and the whole bit. Assign all the parts to your kids—the bride, groom, wedding party, ushers, etc.

Have the pastor go through the wedding ceremony, explaining the various parts of it, why they are included, etc. After the reception have a discussion. Have the couples describe their wedding day and talk briefly about how their lives and their relationships have changed (or not changed) over the years. Then allow the kids to ask questions. You'll be amazed at how many they will have.

You can also draw the students' attention to our relationship with Christ. Distribute the worksheet on page 168 for kids to use as they reflect on the similarities between earthly and spiritual marriages. *Lenorah Chapman*

LOVE GROUPS

This exercise is a five-session project designed for more informal times with your youth group, although it could be used for Sunday school under certain conditions. The basic purpose is to let the youths be creative and imaginative about the subject of Christian love through many different activities. The teacher or youth leader acts as a traffic director and organizer and supplies very little direct lecture-type teaching.

The basic format of the five sessions has each youth working in an activity group for the first four sessions. Each of these activity groups is working on a project directly related to Christian love. During the class period (while the activity groups are working), the leader stops all the groups for one of a variety of give-and-take sessions including mini-lectures (three minutes), discussion, a short film, or whatever, all dealing with the subject of love. The fifth session is devoted to presentation of each finished product. Adults or other youth groups can be invited to see and hear the presentations.

Here are 10 sample love groups:

1. The Signs of Love Multimedia Show. This group shoots pictures of signs of love all around them, has them developed, and creates a video show with narration or music.

2. Drama. This group prepares a play on some facet of Christian love. It can be original or it can be a well-known Bible story.

3. The Multiple Listing Group. This group comes up with lists centered around Christian love, such as a list of "What love is," or "What it is not," or "Ways to demonstrate love," etc.

4. The Crossword Puzzle Group. This group designs one or more crossword puzzles based on the subject of Christian love.

5. The Poetry Group. This group writes original poetry about Christian love.

6. The Cartoons Group. This group publishes a booklet of Christian love cartoons. They can be original or from other publications.

7. The Bible Scholar Group. This group researches the concept of Christian love in the Scriptures, using commentaries and other books, and writes a report on the findings.

8. The Love Banner Group. This group needs to have some artistic or sewing ability, because they produce banners on the subject of Christian love.

9. The Song Writing Group. This group composes Christian love songs and performs them. They can be completely original or new words to familiar tunes.

5. The Love Object Group. This group produces love-related art objects to auction off or give away, such as jewelry, plaques, calligraphy, or paintings.

Each group should be supplied with the necessary items to complete their work, and the kids should be encouraged to work at home on their project as well. A textbook (such as Francis Schaeffer's *The Mark of the Christian*, published by Intervarsity Press) can be used during the class sessions as a common study guide. *Tim Doty*

REBIRTHDAY PARTY

Soon after a student has made a new commitment to Christ—the same day, if possible—celebrate with a Rebirthday Party. Get as many kids together as you can on short notice, pick up a cake, popcorn, and drinks, play well-known games, and then circle together and talk. Let the new Christian share his or her new faith, let experienced Christians encourage the new convert with what to expect and how to grow, and close with group prayer for the new believer and a song or two. *Michael O'Neill*

CHRIST IN THE MARKETPLACE

Here's a great program idea that helps youth think about and experience the fact that Christ is not just for Sunday, but can and should be found in our everyday lives, even in the bustling marketplace.

Have the group meet at the church at a predetermined time. At that time the youth leader gives a short recitation on the idea that Christ should be present in every sphere of life, no matter where you are or what you are doing.

The students are then transported to a large shopping mall. While there, they are to look for evidence of Christ in the midst of that busy place.

Here Comes the Bride!

Psalm 19:5	Isaiah 61:10	Isaiah 62:5	Jeremiah 33:11
Matthew 9:15	Matthew 25:1-10	Mark 2:19-20	Luke 5:34-35
John 3:29	Revelation 18:23	Revelation 21:2	Revelation 22:17

The Bride: The Church

The verse's main idea, in your own words	Comments

The Bridegroom: Jesus Christ

The verse's main idea, in your own words	Comments

They might find him in stores (paintings of Christ, sculpture, books) or on people (who have crosses around their necks, etc.). Students are given pencil and paper so that they can jot these things down.

When the kids get back to the church, talk about their findings in the shopping mall. This can be done in conjunction with a discussion of Christ in the marketplace. You'll be surprised to discover how observant the students can be and how many different ways they can recognize the presence of Christ in a place that's not considered to be very sacred.

> I simply argue that the cross be raised again at the center of the marketplace as well as on the steeple of the church. I am recovering the claims that Jesus was not crucified between two candles, but on a cross between two thieves; on the town garbage heap; at a crossroad so cosmopolitan that they had to write his title in Hebrew and in Latin and in Greek; at the kind of a place where cynics talk smut, and thieves curse, and soldiers gamble. Because that is where he died, and that is what he died about. And that is where the church ought to be and what the church should be about."
>
> —George McLeod
> a Scottish Presbyterian Minister

The sample sums up the point of this discussion. It might be a good idea to give each young person a copy of this quotation to hang up in his or her room. *Ron Scates*

TOMBSTONE TREASURE HUNT

A lot of kids are sheltered from the reality of death. Many have never been faced with death in their family and some have never even attended a funeral. The purpose of this idea is not to scare young people, but to help them realize that death is real and that all of us who are born will someday die. Here is an unusual but effective way to get youths thinking about death for a serious discussion.

Get permission from a cemetery to take your group on an outing there. Before the event, go there and make out 15 to 20 questions that can be answered by looking at the gravestones. For example:

- What state is William R. Baline, PFC, 66th Quartermaster Co., from?
- Who was "lost to memory! lost to love! who has gone to our Father's house above?"
- How old was Diane M. Ferrel?
- What Scripture reference is on Richard Keith's stone?

Make enough copies of the questions for everyone in your group. Take the students to the cemetery and have them look at the stones to find the answers. They may want to go in small groups. Some may just want to stay by the car. Encourage them to do the activity, but don't push them if they are really frightened. Remind them to be respectfully calm and to stay away from any mourners. When the students are finished or the time is up, gather them in a clear spot in or near the cemetery for a discussion. (Cemeteries are nice quiet places for discussions.) Go over the answers to the questions just for fun, then begin a discussion about their feelings. Some starter questions are:

- How did the game make you feel?
- What did you think about the people whose stones you were reading?
- What would you want written on your own tombstone?
- What bothers you the most about death?
- Have you ever thought about your own death?

Conclude with some remarks about death being the natural end to life here on earth, something that everyone does. We don't have to be afraid of death. John 6:47 is a good Scripture to use in building some thought about the Christian's triumph over death. Remind them that God loves them, and that he is preparing a place for his children. Remind them also what is promised to sinners, but resist the temptation to sell fire insurance at this point. This activity and discussion can get kids thinking about how to make their lives count. *Ray Houser*

COLLEGE SURVIVAL KIT SCAVENGER HUNT

Reach out to college students with this hunt.

Divide your teens into teams—one for each of last year's seniors now in college—and send them into the community to obtain items on the following list. When teens return with their completed collections, they write notes to mail to last years' seniors who are now in college, along with the survival kits they have assembled.

Here is a suggested list of items:

- **Cookies (various kinds to tickle their innards). Each team must get three dozen cookies, no more than six at any one house.**

• A discount coupon from a large pizza chain (very valuable to a college student!)
• Two tea bags (for mellow evenings)
• Two toothpicks (to hold their eyelids open after an all-nighter!)
• One package of instant soup (for those rushed lunches or boring cafeteria food)
• Hot chocolate (to drink as they're thinking of home)
• Kleenex tissues (in case they cry when they think of home)
• A flashlight battery (for late-night study)
• A stamp (so they can write and tell you how blessed they are)
• A church bulletin (so they know we're all still there)
• A quarter (so if they're lonely, they can call someone who really cares)
• Anything else you think would be appropriate.

Leroy Tucker

HOMELESS SCAVENGER HUNT

Expose your youth group to the plight of the homeless with this unusual spin on a pizza feed and scavenger hunt. It results in a surprise overnighter—outside—so parents should be made aware of this beforehand and then sworn to secrecy. Don't do this activity if the weather is severe.

Offer no details about the party but the date, starting time, and place. Begin the evening with a normal youth party. Play games, eat, and have fun. After an hour or two, begin the scavenger hunt. Send the teams out to find items *that can be donated to the homeless*. Assign point values: 10 points for a sleeping bag, five points for a blanket, 10 for a jacket, five for a big cardboard box, 20 for a tent, etc. When the teams have completed their hunt and returned to the church, tally the points and award the winning team with a prize.

This is where you describe what you really have in mind for the evening: a homeless experience. Explain that you are having an all-night lock-*out* and that the only things they can use are the items they just collected. The winning team gets to pick their blankets, jackets, boxes, and other supplies first. Then lock the doors and watch the kids adapt.

In the morning discuss what the group learned (usually a new appreciation for home!), then take the collected material to a donation center for the homeless. *Tim Brown*

WHERE'S BART?

Give your scavenger hunt a unique twist so that it will be beneficial to others by having your teens collect items that can stock a local food pantry. Before the meeting choose a mystery location for Bart and create clues to help your group members discover his whereabouts. When the group is assembled, give everyone a copy of Bart's Wish List on page 171. Be sure your group understands all the rules and send them off. *Terry Martinson*

SCRIPTURE SCAVENGER HUNT

This is a great way to combine a fun special event with some solid learning about the Bible. Teams go out and attempt to bring back items which can be found in the Bible. For example, they might bring back a stick (Moses' rod) or a rock (the stoning of Stephen) or a loaf of bread (the last supper), etc. Every item must be accompanied by a Bible verse to prove that it can be found somewhere in the Bible. The team that returns with the most items is the winner. Each team makes its presentation of all its items to the entire group. *Clifford Asay*

SHOPPING CART SCAVENGER HUNT

This event benefits the poor as well as provides fun for your group. Get permission from a grocery store to borrow enough carts to supply each team of four or so with one. Give each team a list of a couple dozen grocery items (ones that won't spoil and can be donated to a food pantry)—then release the kids into the neighborhood to scavenge for the food. Give a prize to the first team back, conclude the afternoon with a pizza dinner, and set a date to deliver the food to your local food bank. *David Landis*

WAY-OUT WEIGH IN

Divide kids into teams (car loads) and have them draw for street names or areas of town. They have one hour to try and collect as many canned goods or other nonperishable foods as they can from residents of the area which they drew. The teams report back and weigh-in the food they collected. The team that has the most (by weight) wins a prize of some kind, and all the food is then given to the needy.

Bart Is Missing!

The last we saw Bart, he was gathering groceries to help feed the hungry. We want to find Bart and help him. Collect as many of the following items as you can during the time limit. Everything should be unopened and usable.

Bart's Wish List:

- ❒ **Bar of soap**
- ❒ **Box of spaghetti**
- ❒ **Can of soup**
- ❒ **Can of tuna**
- ❒ **Can of vegetables**
- ❒ **Roll of toilet paper**
- ❒ **Can of fruit**
- ❒ **Box of JELL-O**
- ❒ **Toothbrush (in packaging)**
- ❒ **Package of elbow macaroni**
- ❒ **Microwave popcorn**
- ❒ **Spaghetti sauce**
- ❒ **Jar of baby food**
- ❒ **Can of cranberry sauce**
- ❒ **Box of tissues (Kleenex)**
- ❒ **Box of instant pudding**
- ❒ **Cake or brownie mix**
- ❒ **Jar of applesauce**
- ❒ **Can of baked beans**
- ❒ **Roll of paper towels**
- ❒ **Macaroni and cheese dinner**
- ❒ **Can of potatoes or yams**
- ❒ **Jar of jelly**
- ❒ **Can of ravioli or Spaghetti-O's**
- ❒ **Box of crackers**
- ❒ **Box of cereal**
- ❒ **Bottle or box of detergent**
- ❒ **Dry soup mix**
- ❒ **Box or bag of rice**
- ❒ **Jar of peanut butter**

Remember:

- This is not a race! Safety is our first concern. Please drive safely and act responsibly.
- The entire team must stay together. No splitting up.
- All items must come from homes of relatives, friends, and neighbors. You may not go to homes of strangers nor to stores.
- You may only get one item from each home.
- Only one of each item will count for your team. You may collect duplicate items to trade with other teams for things you need.
- All items should be unopened and usable.
- All items collected will be donated to a local food pantry.
- Every two items from Bart's Wish List that you bring back can be traded for one clue to help locate Bart. Bring all the items back at __________.
- Clues will be given out when the items are turned in. You will then have 10 minutes to figure out where Bart is.

You may want to restrict this to church members only, rather than soliciting food from strangers. However, if done during the Thanksgiving season, most people are willing to share with others. *Nat Burns*

SEARCH THE SCRIPTURES

The Bible passages below are clues to hidden treasures. Have students read the passages carefully to determine which word or words are clues. Hide treasure chests inside and outside the church, within reach so they can be seen without moving anything. See page 173 for a pattern. Put candy or other treats inside each chest.

For example, Ecclesiastes 1:6 says, "The wind blows to the south and turns to the north; round and round it goes, ever returning on its course." The key words "round and round" are the clue to look by the merry-go-round on the playground.

Philippians 3:8	garbage can
Proverbs 21:9	corner of the roof
2 Corinthians 7:11	alarm
Luke 2:16	manger
Acts 22:16	baptismal font
Ecclesiastes 12:12	library
John 15:2	branch
Proverbs 18:4	water fountain
Exodus 3:2	bush
Deuteronomy 6:9	gate
Daniel 3:6	furnace
Romans 15:20	foundation
James 1:23	mirror
Isaiah 61:3	oak tree
Malachi 3:2	soap
1 Peter 2:21	steps
John 2:4	clock
2 Corinthians 11:33	window

PEOPLE SHOPPING

Here's an activity patterned after a scavenger hunt that strengthens kids' concern for and awareness of others.

Take your group to a shopping mall and people-shop. Have kids go from store to store, observing people and following instructions on a shopping list you give them. The shopping list simply instructs kids to enter specified stores, select individuals in each store to observe for a minute or two, and then answer these questions:

1. Why did you choose this particular person?
2. What can you learn about this person by what they're wearing?
3. How does this person make you feel?
4. Do you think you could be friends with this person?
5. How do you think this person feels right now?

At the end of the people-shopping spree, the kids return and share their experiences, describing the people they observed. Some young people will reveal different observations about the same people. Emphasize the importance of noticing other people, caring about how they feel, and empathizing with them. Close by praying for all those who were observed during the activity. *Grant Sawatzky*

MISSIONS IMPOSSIBLE

If your church is in a large, ethnically diverse metro area, you have a microcosm of the world's mission fields at your door. To focus on some of the challenges missionaries face in ministering to people of a different culture, send your kids out as teams to encounter people of other religious faiths. Use a spy motif, preparing a packet for each team of six to eight young people.

Packets should include:

- **Instructions for the event on cassette tape (with background music from a James Bond movie or other spy movie)**
- **A written copy of the instructions**
- **A blank tape**
- **$2.00 in cash**
- **A pen**
- **A list of points to be earned**
- **A map of the area marked with the route to their destination**
- **A small paper bag**
- **Some evangelistic tracts**

When kids are assembled for their spy mission, give each group a packet, cassette player, and Polaroid camera. Make sure every group includes an adult.

The instructions should inform each group

Search The Scriptures Treasure Chest Pattern

- Copy onto heavy brown paper
- Cut on solid lines
- Fold on dotted lines
- Decorate as desired

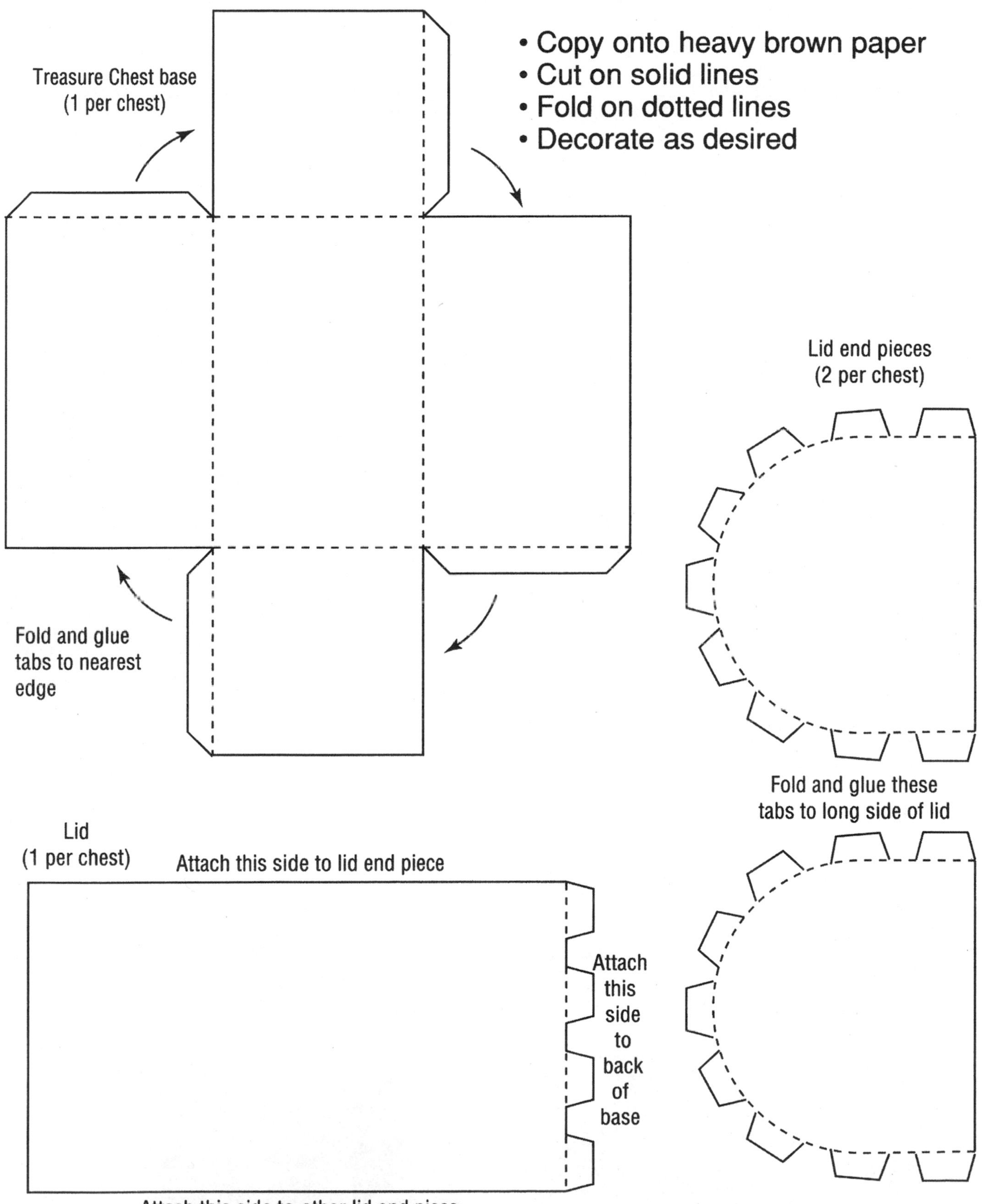

that they are being sent to a local temple of another faith to find out what the people who worship there believe. They will earn a designated number of points for accomplishing certain tasks you have chosen as meaningful ways to become acquainted with peoples of other cultures.

Here are some suggestions:

- 100 points for finding someone on the street who will say "Hi, how are you?" in a language other than English so that the group can record it
- 100 points for a photo of a priest or other religious professional from the temple they visit
- 500 points for a map of another country
- 100 points for every item they can buy with $2.00 that comes from another country and culture
- 1000 points for a taped or written statement from someone in the temple they visit, describing that person's concept of God
- 1000 points for their own taped or written statement telling how the person's concept of God differs from the biblical one, supported by specific scriptural texts

Add as many other point-earning tasks as you like. The team earning the most points wins. Caution the teams to be respectful of the people they visit. They will be seen as representatives of Christianity. Make sure you have personally spoken with the person in charge of each temple you send a group to visit, asking permission for the kids to find out more about their faith.

Tracts should only be given out on the street—not in a temple—and should not be forced on anyone.

Have a debriefing session when the teams return at the designated time. Talk about the team's strategies, how they felt as they approached people, how the people responded, what they thought of the temples, and any other significant aspects of the experience. They'll never forget it! *Dave Miller*

BEG, BORROW, OR STEAL LIBRARY

This works well on a college campus and might be worth trying on your high school campuses. Gather together from your teens, Christian paperbacks that they have read and been influenced by. Have them make a sign that says BEG, BORROW, OR STEAL. Then at school, before classes, at noon, or after school, they spread the books and sign out on a table in a crowded place. When persons stop to glance at the books, the teens staffing the library that day tell the onlookers to help themselves, the books are free. It's a good witnessing opportunity and a way of using books instead of leaving them to gather dust on bookshelves. It's best to have some small booklets, too, since many people feel inhibited taking a large book but will be glad to take a smaller one. Suggest to the takers that they pass them along to others after they read them or bring them back to the library and switch for another. *Dan Wilcox*

THEOLOGICAL ZOO GUIDE

Sometimes we take kids on excursions that are fun but end up wishing that we could have done or experienced something with a little more substance to it. Try handing out the Theological Zoo Guide on page 175 the next time you take a trip to the zoo. *Pierre Allegre*

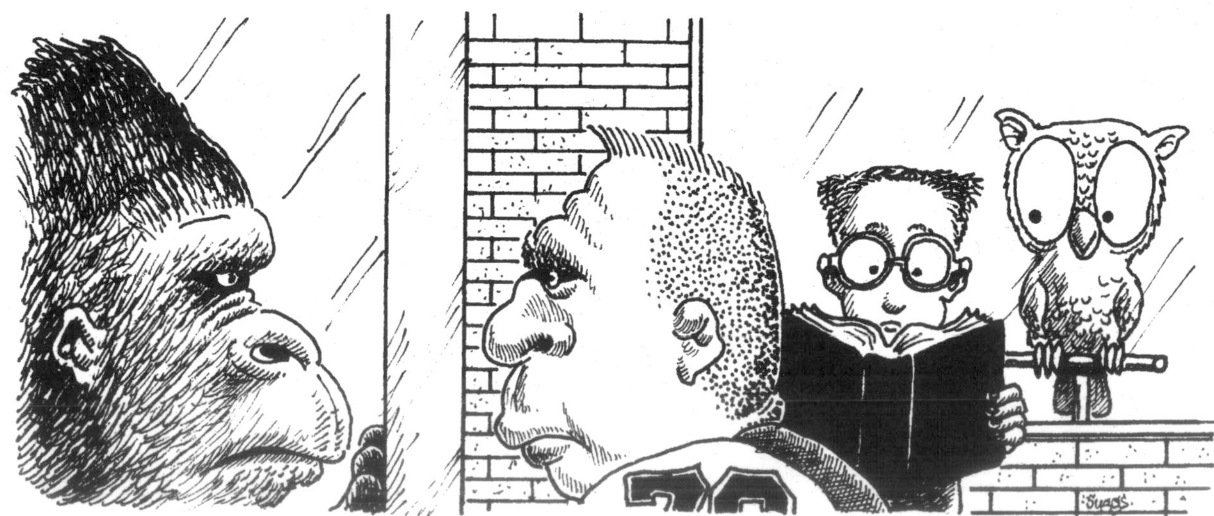

THEOLOGICAL ZOO GUIDE

- **PRIMATES.** Watch them monkey around. Does "monkeying around" describe your walk with God? What do you need to do to get serious about God in your life? (1 Cor. 9:24-27)
- **GIRAFFES.** Check out their necks, which help them to reach their food high in the trees. In your walk with God, are you stretching to reach spiritual food in the Bible, or are you only feeding off the crumbs on the floor? What are some things you can do to improve the reach of your devotional life? (Psa. 42:1-2)
- **HIPPOS.** Two words best describe these "water horses": lazy and fat! That's okay if you're a hippo, but Christians can't afford to get spiritually lazy and fat by failing to apply God's Word to their lives. How have you applied the Word to your life this week? (Prov. 13:4; Heb. 6:11-12; James 2:14-20)
- **ELEPHANTS.** These behemoths are a picture of strength and stability. As you consider your spiritual life, how strong and stable are you? What needs to happen in order for you to become a picture of spiritual strength and stability? (Eph. 6:10; 1 Cor. 15:58)
- **RAPTORS.** Although you probably won't see the bald eagle there in flight, you can imagine what a majestic sight that would be, wings outstretched and soaring freely. Do you feel strong and free in your walk with God, or do you feel like the eagle in the zoo, chained to a post and just sitting there? What is keeping you from soaring strong and free like an eagle in the wild? (Isa. 40:31)
- **OWLS.** Notice the different species. We traditionally think of owls as being wise. Are you listening to wisdom in your life, or do you live foolishly? What advice have you been ignoring that you should pay attention to? (Prov. 2)
- **TURKEY VULTURES.** They're valuable to the environment because they feed on dead and rotting carcasses. (Is it lunch time yet?) We can feed our minds rotten garbage if we're not careful about the things we watch or listen to. How pure is your mind? What changes do you need to make in what you allow to enter your mind? (Phil. 4:8; Psa. 101:3)
- **GORILLAS.** Good communication within a tightly knit social group is important for their survival in dense forest. Just like the gorilla, we need each other to survive in our jungle. How tightly are you knitted to the youth group at church? Are you committed to building love and unity in our group? What are some things you can do in order to make it a place where everyone feels loved and accepted and is encouraged to love others? (Heb. 10:23-25)
- **MOUNTAIN GOATS.** These are known for their sure, nimble footing in rocky, dangerous terrain. Spiritually speaking, how sure and nimble is your footing? Are there things in your life that are causing you to stumble? What can you do to remove or get around those obstacles? (Matt. 18:7-9)
- **LIONS.** How alert would you be if you were dropped in the middle of that cage? The Bible says that Satan is like a roaring lion, seeking to devour us. What are you doing to resist his attacks? (1 Pet. 5:8-9)
- **RETICULATED PYTHON.** Check out his size! Satan's first appearance in the Bible is as a serpent in the Garden of Eden, where he deceived Eve into eating forbidden fruit. Have you been tempted to believe a lie that Satan has thrown at you in order to deceive you? How can you guard yourself against his deceit and trickery? (Gen. 3:16, 13)

Time to test your creative thinking! Can you think of any other spiritual analogies related to any of the animals you saw today? Write down as many as you can think of.

PARKING LOT PALESTINE

Here's a creative way to add a new dimension to the events of the Bible. Have the youth group research and plan a large map of the Holy Land (to scale) that can be "painted" onto the parking lot of the church. Major cities and locations can be marked. Students can be assigned places to research. Displays, photos, and other sets can be put at each location (such as three crosses at Mt. Calvary, an ark at Mt. Ararat, etc.) Then the youth group can give guided tours to adults and children of the church with each guide telling about the events that took place in his or her area. With some creativity and a lot of work, this can be a very meaningful and worthwhile project. *Winifred Bartunek*

COLLEGE VISITATION

College. The mere mention of the word sets off stress for upper classmen who feel the weight of making a choice with life-long implications. But the church can do one better than the high school guidance office to defuse the threat. Provide college visitation weekends during which you not only visit former youth group members, but also expose juniors and seniors to various campuses within a day's drive of their hometown.

Plan trips to a variety of schools: public and private, large and small, Christian and secular, Bible and liberal arts. Contact the admissions office to arrange campus housing, tours, question-and-answer sessions, and written material. Most colleges are pleased to host potential students. If possible, attend several classes.

Before the trip contact any youth group graduates at the campus and arrange to visit them. Take advantage of their familiarity with the campus to break in the high schoolers to the college experience. This also assures the high schoolers that they won't be forgotten when they graduate, increasing the sense of community among both graduated and current members. Present the collegian with a care package put together by the youth group, and include their roommates in on fun activities. It may be their first experience with a Christian group of young people.

Groups such as Campus Crusade for Christ and InterVarsity Christian Fellowship generally have on-campus representatives as well as some sort of headquarters. Arranging for the kids to meet leaders of significant student ministries increases the likelihood of young people actually connecting with the group should they attend that college. Familiarize the students with recommended churches in the college community by driving by or by visiting a service.

Have fun on the trip. Bring lots of tapes to listen to as you travel, watch for roadside attractions for fun stops and photos, attend a college sporting event together, eat at the local fast-food favorite. You could even arrange with several college students to kidnap the high schoolers for a late night donut party. Help the word *college* to inspire something other than fear. *Kevin Turner*

NIKE NIGHT

A lot of kids have access to Nike athletic wear (whether bought or borrowed), so have them wear it on Nike Night.

Stage events such as creative races and other athletic competitions that everyone will enjoy.

Toward the end of the event, explain that the Greek word *nike* actually means *victory*. Talk briefly about victory using Scripture passages such as 1 John 5:4-5.

Your kids may never forget the new significance of Nike. *Richard Crisco*

POLITICAL ACTION NIGHT

Only a few items are needed for this stimulating evening of political action and discussion: stationery, envelopes, and postage stamps and a complete listing of the names and addresses of the politicians representing your government at the local, state, and federal levels. Obtain this list from your local public or college library or your county courthouse.

Give kids the opportunity to express their personal convictions about public issues in writing to congressmen and senators, city and county officials, or even the President of the United States. Letters cannot be written anonymously. Return addresses should be printed on the envelopes and in the letter itself. Kids sharing similar convictions can collaborate on one letter and send it to as many officials as they can.

Political Action Night should be promoted a few weeks in advance in your church bulletin or newsletter, making it clear to the congregation that the views expressed will not be those of any particular political persuasion, but rather those of the kids individually. The group may even want to invite the rest of the congregation to join them on the night of their letter writing to have fellowship and feedback from the adults' political points of view.

Leaders may want to come armed with information about both sides of hot issues to spark discussion and to help kids determine their stance.

In most cases, your kids will receive some kind of response, some of which may come from an official's assistant. Even if the responses are rather impersonal, you kids will have had an opportunity to become a small part of the political process.

Michael Bell

All-Night Bowling Party

This can be an excellent outreach activity that kids will really get excited about. Sell tickets in advance. Run an all-night blast at a bowling alley starting at midnight. The schedule can be as follows:

12:00-3:00 a.m.	Bowling
3:00-4:00 a.m.	Crowd breakers
4:00-5:00 a.m.	Devotional (singing group, film, speaker, etc.)
5:00-7:00 a.m.	More bowling
7:00 a.m.	Breakfast and go home

This special event is good for image-building, making new contacts, etc.

The doors should be locked at 12:30 and no one allowed to leave until 7:00 a.m. without calling parents and getting permission. Some kids want to go out and joyride, which could be dangerous. One group did this and tried for 300 kids; 700 showed up.

"Ike" Newsingham

Fifth Quarter

After high school football games on Friday night, rent an athletic club for the fifth quarter and let the kids have free run of the place for a couple of hours. Halfway through the evening, call them together in the basketball court for a five-minute, low-key evangelistic talk. The idea is not to call for a decision, but to open kids up to conversation about who Jesus is and what he wants to do in their lives. Your staff and several key youths can mix with the crowd during the second half of the evening and get some discussions going over soda and pizza. Extra adult staff is a must. *David Gilbert*

Bicycle Calling

"Calling" is the ecclesiastical term for visiting folks who have been missing from church for some reason or another. Most church rolls are full of people who are nonparticipators, many of whom are young people. Rather than making "calling" the youth pastor's job, allow the active kids to do it. One good way is to go out in pairs some Saturday, on bikes. Then meet back at the church later for refreshments and sharing of the day's experiences. *Jay Griffis*

Wanderlust

The following can be used as a special event or as a way to open up a good discussion on priorities, purpose, and direction in life.

- Have the kids meet at the church, house, etc., at a pre-advertised time, say 2:00 p.m.
- Divide the kids into cars, four or five kids per car.
- Supply each car with a die and a penny.
- Announce that this will be a Wanderlust experience involving driving around the countryside. Set a finish time, say 2:45 p.m. Announce that the goal is to see who gets the furthest away from the church, house, etc. in 45 minutes, following the conditions on the handout (page 178). Have the driver record the time to stop on the handout.
- Everyone returns to the originating location at that time and the car that got the farthest is the winner. Some will return earlier than others, so have games, refreshments, music or whatever for everyone until the entire group returns.
- To tie in with a learning experience, the event can

Wanderlust

When the signal is given, begin driving your car. You must make a decision at any of these three points along the road:

- **Four-way stop sign**
- **Traffic light**
- **Cloverleaf (interchange)**

If you come to one of the above points, throw the die. If the die reads:

- **1 or 2, go left**
- **3 or 4, go straight**
- **5 or 6, go right**

If you come to a dead-end, turn around. If you come to a place where you can't go straight (such as a T), then roll the die again. If it comes up an even number go left; if it comes up an odd number, go right. Proceed, driving the car in this fashion until __________.
TIME

STOP.

Record your location____

be likened to life and how many people do everything by chance. Many just go around in circles, hit dead ends or have no idea what the future holds. Discuss the feelings the group had while on the road and tie in with Scripture relating to how Christians receive direction for their lives from God.

Bob Stier

YOUTH VERSUS EXPERIENCE

In this parent-student event, kids compete against parents in everything from volleyball, softball, and basketball, to relays and food-eating contests. This can be an annual event, with a rotating trophy for the winning team each year. A wall plaque can display the names of past winners.

After the games, host a barbecue or potluck that lets parents get acquainted with the youth workers. This activity is particularly useful if parents don't regularly attend the church. *Brian Krum*

BEDROOM BLITZ

If handled with plenty of preparation, the Bedroom Blitz can be a great get-acquainted activity that allows kids to informally learn about each other, show other kids where and how they live, and permit the group to meet other kids' parents.

The event would begin at the church and either end at a home or the church for a special party or become a progressive dinner so the kids eat at each home they visit.

The kids then travel by car or bus to previously selected and prepared homes of young people in the group. Each young person should have a copy of page 180 and fill it in as each home is visited. At the last stop awards could be given away for the Messiest Room, the Funkiest Room, the Smallest Room, the Biggest Room, the Smelliest Room, and so on. *Bob Stier*

CARD PARTY

Here's a fun idea that you can use next time you would like to honor somebody in a special way on their birthday, anniversary, graduation, or whatever.

Get your group together for a Card Party in which you divide up into groups and create special birthday cards (or thank you cards, anniversary cards, etc.). Give each group some construction paper, a few old magazines, a pair of scissors, glue, marking pens, and anything else that you have available. Each group's assignment is to make a card, using word cutouts and photos from the magazines.

The words can be strung together ransom-note style and may say whatever the group would like to say. The only things written by hand should be the kid's signatures. The message should be made up of only word combinations from the magazine. If a photo from a magazine is appropriate, it can also be included. You'll find that the groups will have a lot of fun thinking up their cards, and the person who is honored will really appreciate them and probably cherish them much more than a commercially-bought card. *Jim Beal*

CHURCH CHALLENGE

If you've ever wondered why churches in your area don't do more things together, it's probably because no one ever bothered to set anything up. So why don't you? Invite three to five other youth groups in town to participate in a volleyball, softball, or basketball tournament. You could substitute other crazier games for any of those, of course, so long as they are fun and involve everyone. Award a trophy to the church that accumulates the most number of wins. This could turn out to be an annual event. Close with some refreshments, some singing, and give the kids a chance to get to know each other better. The rewards will be great. *Daniel Turner*

FROSH KIDNAP

Incoming freshmen can be made to feel welcome and a genuine part of their new group if the high schoolers kidnap them on a Saturday morning (having previously obtained their parents' permission, of course, and sworn them to secrecy). Bring them all to the church where parents make a big pancake breakfast for everyone, followed by a slide show and skits that introduce the freshmen to the high school program. Make a big deal of welcoming them during this time without embarrassing them too much.

Then off to an all-day activity—water slides, amusement park, a ball game, a Christian concert. By the end of the day, everyone will have

Bedroom Blitz

Questions	Bedroom of ________	Bedroom of ________	Bedroom of ________	Bedroom of ________
Walls: Painted? Wallpaper? (Describe)				
Bed and bedspread: Size? Design?				
Interesting posters, pictures on wall?				
Interesting objects in the room? Hobby? Craft?				
Awards, Honors, Trophies, Plaques?				
General rating of room: Would you want it? (0 NO! 10 YES!)				
Ten word impression, description of room: Size? Feelings about it?				
Rate neatness of room: 0 (slob-o-la) to 10 (neatnik)				

the chance to be on familiar and comfortable terms with each other.

A few details to make Frosh Kidnap successful:

• Have the freshmen's parents secretly pack day clothes for their kids, since the frosh will be taken to breakfast without much chance to change.

• Be sure not to leave any incoming freshman out. Not only will you avoid creating hurt feelings, but with a little attention the fringe kids in the junior high group may become active high school members. Keith Wright

MINI-POOL PARTY

Here's one way to have cool discussion on a hot summer day. Borrow or buy several inflated or hard plastic childrens' pools, one for every four teens in

your group. Scatter them around someone's backyard. Assign four kids to a pool, giving them some specific questions to ask each other. Every five or ten minutes, have the kids in rotate to different pools so that everyone has a chance to talk to everyone else. You might also want to play a few games and, of course, have lots to eat. Sharon Shaw

LONG-DISTANCE PARTY

Kids grow up and move away, go to college, or are just away at special times. One way for the dear departed to maintain contact with the old gang back home is to send them a Long Distance Party. It's simple. Just buy a cake mix, frosting, sprinkles, a party hat and some decorations. Put it all in a box and mail it to those far-away friends, along with letters of greeting from the group. This is especially appreciated by college students who really miss the support group back home.

Any occasion is suitable, but it would be most appropriate around a birthday. Instructions should be included, explaining that the group wanted to celebrate with them, but distance wouldn't allow it. Mark A. Simone

PROGRESSIVE VIDEO PARTY

An intergenerational get-to-know-you event, this activity can be played out among teams competing against a time limit or as a single group activity just for the fun of it.

Equip adult driver/chaperons with a camcorder and a collection of sealed envelopes, each containing a question such as the following: "What is your favorite Bible verse?" "When did you become a Christian?" "What is your most memorable church experience?" "In your opinion, what is the biggest problem facing teenagers today?"

The groups visit as many homes of church members as possible within one hour. At each home the occupant chooses one envelope, opens it, and responds to the written question while being videotaped.

At the end of the hour, all meet at a home or the church and show all the taped interviews. The videotape serves as proof that the mission was accomplished—as well as offering all the groups the chance to get to know some adult church members better. *Cheryl Ehlers*

NOSTALGIA NIGHT

Work in partnership on this event with your church's older folks. Together plan a Nostalgia Night, in which you lead your congregation in remembering the history of your church and thank God for what he's accomplished among you. Here are some ideas:

- Make a time line that runs the length of the room you use. On it note your congregation's major events.
- Ask members if you could borrow their old photos, bulletins, scrapbooks, home movies, etc., of church events. Some of these might be posted along the time line.
- Provide for everyone a brief written history of your church's formation and earliest meetings.

Cheryl Ehlers

TRASH ART

Scour the church's neighborhood for trash and clean it up—and have fun at the same time. Announce that you've scheduled an off-the-wall arts and crafts fair for a given day later in the week, that kids should wear their grubbies, and that the event will take a few hours to complete.

Then make sure you have these items before the day of the event:

- Heavy-duty trash bags
- Sealed envelopes, each containing one of the following written on a slip of paper: TYRANNOSAURUS REX, BRONTOSAURUS, GORILLA, ISUZU TROOPER, BARBIE, THE WHITE HOUSE, A GALAXY, etc.

When the day arrives divide kids up into groups of four to six and give each group a few trash bags, a sealed envelope, and instructions to pick up as much trash as possible in 30 minutes to an hour. Then they are to use every piece of trash to construct whatever item their envelope contains. Teams open their envelopes before they start. This way they know what they'll have to make and consequently pick up their trash accordingly.

When all teams have returned and finished the construction of their sculptures, take photos of the masterpieces with their sculptors and judge them. The day may provide discussion material later about what God has to work with in us. *Michael W. Capps*

THANKS, PASTOR

Give a progressive gift to say thanks to your pastors or youth workers. Send them a letter asking them to

reserve a certain evening for this activity—but give no details of what you have planned. If they need it, offer free baby-sitting for their children. Tell them only when and where to go on the given night. Only after they arrive will they learn what's next.

For example, you could ask them to meet at the church, where all the young people are gathered to roast their pastor with soft drinks in champagne glasses. Have fun, but also be serious in your gratitude so they understand that they are appreciated.

From there, send them to a location where they will find flowers, then to a restaurant where the youth group has already paid for an elegant meal, and maybe end up at a theater, bowling alley, concert, etc. (for which tickets have already been purchased). Choose activities that each honoree especially enjoys. *Cheryl Ehlers*

OUTINGS AND OVERNIGHTERS

OUTINGS AND OVERNIGHTERS

First, there's the general lunacy of taking a group of adolescents on a simple outing. Make that outing an overnighter, and you've achieved an even purer level of insanity. Here are plenty of trip ideas for you.

ARCADE LOCK-IN

Here's an idea that combines youth outreach, incredible fun, and fundraising. Arrange with a local video arcade to have an overnight lock-in for your

youth group. Contact the owner or manager and ask him to figure his cost for eight hours and the number of kids you expect to show up. Next, calculate what you need to raise, plus the cost of an all-you-can-eat snack bar and some video movies. Sell tickets at the adjusted price.

That night, every activity is included in the price of the ticket. You've already met your budget goal, so everyone can relax and have a good time. Not only that, there will probably be lots of new kids introduced to your ministry.

Andy Harvey

BIKE SIT

Since many people don't like to ride their bikes (only sit on them), this activity is designed to enable even the sitters to have fun. Most areas of the country have an extended downgrade of road. Simply truck all the bikes to the top of this downgrade and let them sit on their bikes all the way to the bottom. Some downgrades last for twenty miles! There can be variations, too. For those select teens who have a lot of energy, let them try to ride up the downgrade; or see who can coast the farthest without peddling. *Tim Doty*

CRAZY DAZE

Decorate a bus with poster paint, flowers, slogans, etc., or have kids decorate their cars in the same way. The wilder the better. Then on a Saturday or a holiday, spend the day as a group doing a variety of activities. Check out a museum, a giant slide, games in the park, a boat ride, free tourist attractions, etc. The more short activities, the better. Have the kids decorate the bus or the cars the night before or begin early in the morning.

Destination Unknown

Have kids meet at the church or some other location on Sunday morning around 6:30 a.m. to leave for a day of activities which are known only by the youth sponsors. It will include church as usual, but the other events make the day very different from the normal Sunday experience. A bus or car caravan can be used for transportation. Here is a sample schedule for a day such as this:

6:30 a.m.	Meet
6:45 a.m.	Go to nearby park
7:15 a.m.	Breakfast in park (prepared ahead of time by sponsors)
7:50 a.m.	Sunday School and morning worship at church
8:00 a.m.	Leave church
9:30 a.m.	Bowling (You can get it cheap at this hour)
12:30 p.m.	Lunch at restaurant
1:30 p.m.	Go to amusement park, beach, zoo, etc.
2:30 p.m.	Leave park
5:30 p.m.	Head for home or church for evening service

Jim Landrum

Five-Dollar Surprise

Announce to the group that on a certain Saturday you are going to have a Five-Dollar Surprise. The kids are to show up at the church with five dollars, with the understanding that the Five-Dollar Surprise will last from 8 a.m. until 3 p.m. (or whenever you decide). One group took everyone in buses down to the train depot, walked them to trackside just before the train was to leave and loaded them onboard. The buses then drove quickly to a train stop that was about one hour and a half away. The train arrived five minutes after the bus did. The kids got off the train and were bused to a park for a picnic and games. *Darryl Eisele*

Indoor Hayride

Here's a great idea for a way to have a hayride during lousy weather, or for a different way to go Christmas caroling. This way even groups in urban or suburban areas can still experience a hayride.

Secure a school bus without any seats, a panel truck, or a van, and dump two feet of loose straw inside. Add an old fashioned pump organ, banjo, or accordion for effect, and bring a supply of cider and fresh apples for eats. (Caution: make sure there are windows for ventilation. The dust gets very dense without it!) When you are done, back up to a trash dumpster and sweep it all away. *Brad Grabill*

Live-In Lock-In

Select a week during the school year when your entire youth group can have a weeklong lock-in at the church. Kids bring sleeping bags, pillows, alarm clocks, school books, Bible, a week's worth of clothes, trash bags for laundry, money for school lunches, etc.

Breakfast is provided each morning before kids leave for school. After school they return to church for recreation, study (with tutors, computers, etc., if needed), supper, an evening Bible study, and bed. If there's time include a service project, such as painting classrooms in the church building. And be sure to have an occasional outside activity, like bowling or a ball game.

A week together like this will go a long way in building community among your students.

Lock-Out

Instead of having a lock-in, have a lock-out outside your church, at a campgrounds, or in a barn. In addition to doing everything you would normally do at a lock-in, you can also stargaze, cook outdoors, and have a sunrise worship time. *Mark Evans*

Midnight Capture

Kids will buzz about this event for months. Just make sure you let parents in on the plans ahead of time—and swear them to secrecy.

On a predetermined Saturday morning at

3 a.m.—a night known only to your youth leaders and kids' parents—swoop down on the teen nearest your home, then map your way across town, picking up kids as you go until you reach your destination.

Rush into the teen's room and wake them up. Pull them from bed if you dare! Tell them they have only five to 10 minutes to dress—no time to shower, comb their hair, brush their teeth—got to get out quick! After you've hit a few homes, the teens you've already snatched will wake up enough to help you drag the rest of the kids from their beds.

Rush to your destination without talking or answering questions. Complete silence adds to the suspense. When you reach the party site, use the first minutes for a short devotional on the necessity of always being ready (for you know not the time nor the season), emphasizing Christ's soon return, the One who will come like a thief in the night. Or contrast the oppression of Christians in some countries with our freedom and the need for us to be thankful for our nation and its leaders. Allow time for discussion and questions.

Then let the party begin! After games and fellowship, award prizes for the scruffiest looking teen, the one who got out of bed and into the car the fastest, etc. Then on to a restaurant for breakfast. Or perhaps, since no one showered, you'll want breakfast catered that morning! *Candy Simonson*

Progressive All-Nighter

For your next all-night event, try a new twist on a familiar activity. Line up several homes to participate in a progressive party that lasts till morning. Each home hosts a different event: video games, board games, contemporary Christian videos, pizza feast, Ping Pong, conversation by the fireplace, backyard activities (swimming, snowball fights, games, whatever). The last home provides breakfast. Add your own ideas to this list. The fun part will be finding a family to take the 3 a.m. to 5 a.m. time slot! *Dave Mahoney*

River Ride

If you have access to a good creek or river that is somewhat uncrowded, have a tubing day in which kids bring inner tubes and sack lunches and float down the river in a long chain. Have transportation arranged to take the kids and sponsors up the river and let them float back down. A five-mile trip will take up most of the afternoon. While floating be sure to stop occasionally to keep the kids from getting too strung out. Also, one sponsor should be in the lead and one should bring up the rear of the floating procession. You can also hook the tubes together with rope to form a long line, or kids can hold hands as they float down. Prearrange a spot to get out and have cars there to pick up the kids. It's tiring, but a lot of fun. *Jim Hudson*

Tour de Beach

A daylong bike ride that culminates with a picnic at the beach or elsewhere is fun for both serious and casual cyclists in your group—and for their invited friends, too. It takes some advance work, though:

- Publicize it as an event to finish rather than an event to win.
- Solicit bike shops to sponsor the event—they may

have freebies for cyclists or may provide snacks, etc., for a little free publicity.
- Wear or print publicity for your church or youth group.
- Target a well-known destination that will be challenging to get to (45 miles can be pedaled in around five hours).
- Map out a safe route with periodic rest stops (preferably at parks with rest rooms), where fruit and drink stations can be set up.

• Inform your highway patrol of the tour's date and route, and ask for any regulations and suggestions.
• Set an early starting time—7 a.m. works well.
• Recruit servers for rest stops, experienced cyclists to ride along and supervise (and one to be a pacesetter), pickup truck drivers to follow the pack and give weary riders and their bikes a lift, and picnic organizers to set up the final destination.
• U-Haul-type moving trucks and bungee cords are convenient for transporting bikes back to church.
• Drill these rules into your cyclists: Obey the rules of the road (hand signals, stop signs and traffic signals, crosswalks, etc.), ride single file, pass on the left, do not pass the pacesetter, give cars the right of way, and stay in your own lane. *Gene Stabe*

20-MILE SKATE

For a different twist sometime, take the kids on a trip on Rollerblades or skates. It is unusual enough to get good news coverage. It can also be used as a fundraiser, with sponsors paying kids so much a mile to skate. If no street skates are available, maybe this can be done on a rented roller rink, determining how many laps make a mile and skating 20 or 30 miles without stopping. You might even consider a new skating world's record (see the Guinness Book of World Records). Don't forget helmets and padding.

TIME CAPSULE

Have a special overnight meeting and have as the last activity before bedding down for the night, a time to write notes about what that particular age group thinks about the world situation, their church, where they think the church will be in the next ten years, etc. Seal these along with a newspaper, personal items, and other such items in a plastic garbage bag and bury it at least three feet deep somewhere on church property. One could carefully remove the grass and dig a hole or a bare spot in the back. Be as secretive as possible (maybe let an elder or pastor know) and just plan to leave it. Maybe ten years from now some member of the group will remember and try to recover the items or you could call the evening "A.D. Two Million" and just let it stay and hope some archaeologist finds it a jillion years from now. *Don Maddox*

RACES & RALLIES

RACES & RALLIES

Your group have a need for speed? Whether it's cars, bikes, buses, or toilets—if it can be raced, you'll find an idea for it here. You'll also find rallies, which require team members to work together to complete an assignment and also a fair amount of driving.

AT THE SOUND OF THE BEEP, GET YOUR NEXT CLUE

Use the answering machine to add a new twist to a mystery journey.

Prepare five or so riddles that lead to pay phones at well-known locations around town. For example, the clue to Courtesy House/76 Truck Stop could be:

A big stop for your hungry truck or car
76 gas and a great salad bar.
Courtesy at this house means cleaning your plate,
And there are lots of gas pumps so you won't have to wait.

Then enlist people in your church to record the clues on their answering machines. Players access these clues by phoning from mystery locations to get the next clue and phone number. First team to reach the final destination wins.

Prepare a Journeyman's Packet of clues and phone numbers, event rules, and a diagram of the other teams' routes in case of an emergency. Designate an adult Journey Master who stays at the church with the same packet the drivers have in case of confusion or emergency.

Divide your group into teams, then give the driver for each team a Journeyman's Packet.

1. The teams receive the first clue at the starting point and must direct their drivers to the location they surmise from the clue.

2. Upon arriving at the correct pay phone, the driver pulls from the Journeyman's Packet the phone number to call. One of the team members calls to hear the recorded clue to the next stop. As proof that a team is actually calling from a correct location, callers must tell the number of the pay phone they're calling from and leave a silly message, just for fun.

Other details:

• The locations can be the same for each team, but in a different order.
• Give each team enough money for the number of phone calls required.
• Give participants a time limit.
• Lost or confused teams return to the church for help or call a designated emergency number. If all else fails, the driver may open up an emergency envelope marked DRIVER ONLY, which gives the clue to the last location. This final destination might be the church or the home of one of the kids or youth workers. *Paul Turner*

BIKE RALLY

This is a great competitive event that most junior high or high school groups will really go for. Advertise it well and make it open to anyone who has a bike. Offer some good prizes (you can get them donated) and it will lend to the success of the event.

Lay out a rally course all over your neighborhood or town using streets that are relatively safe. Divide the course into five sections that are about the same distance, maybe two miles each. Position an official at the end of each section of the race with a watch or timer that is synchronized with all the other officials.

Each rider gets a rally number to wear on his or her back. Riders must also have a watch with a second hand, a helmet, and a rally card. Everyone meets at the starting place at a certain time. When the rally begins, each rider is started at 30-second or one-minute intervals. When each rider is started, their exact starting time is written by an official on their rally card. They then have a certain amount of time to reach checkpoint number one (for example, three minutes, 22 seconds). Each rider must keep track of his or her time and try to arrive at the checkpoint exactly on schedule. The official at that checkpoint then records the arrival time on the rider's rally card, and also records the starting time for the next leg of the trip.

The object is not speed, but skill. Points are given for each second the rider arrives early or late, and at the end of the rally, the rider with the least amount of points is the winner. You can add other rules and variations as you see fit. *Ken Osborne*

HOT OR COLD CAR RALLY

This is a great car rally for small groups or junior high groups. Kids give directions to their adult driver. To avoid confusion, have the kids in each car elect one spokesperson. The driver will take directions only from the spokesperson, although all riders may have a part in the decision.

The driver knows the destination in advance, but the kids don't. Every quarter or half mile, the driver tells the passengers if they are getting hot or cold in relationship to the destination. When the car is getting closer to the destination, it may become necessary to reduce the clue times to two or even one-tenth of a mile in order to let the kids find the location.

To prevent cars from simply following each other to the destination, allow cars to leave the starting point at five minute intervals. Record their starting time and their arrival time at the final destination. Best time wins. *James L. Hamilton*

MYSTERY CAR RALLY

Kids must solve clues to get to their destination in this car rally. Leave out key words and numbers as shown here:

- **Take a right on ____________ street.**
- **Take the first left after you pass ____________.**
- **Go ________ blocks and turn right.**

Clues for filling in the blanks can look like this:

- **in the middle** *(answer: Central)*
- **____________, nickles, dimes, quarters** *(answer: J.C. Penney)*
- **144 divided by 6 minus 14 plus 2 times .5** *(answer: 6)*

As always, make sure a responsible person is in each car and that all traffic laws are obeyed and that safety precautions are taken. *Gary Nicholson*

TIMED CAR RALLY

This rally emphasizes the importance of following directions rather than being speedy. Map out a course ahead of time and write out a detailed set of directions for each vehicle. Make it complicated; try using 50 to 100 instructions. Here's a sample:

1. Go east to the first stop sign.
2. Turn right.
3. At the traffic light, turn left, then go straight.
4. At the first traffic light, turn right.
5. Proceed under the trestle at 25 m.p.h.
6. Confirm water tower and the red building on the left.
7. Turn left at the next stop sign.
8. Make a U-turn at the first opening in the middle divider.
9. Turn right at the stop sign.

Emphasize that this rally is not a race. However, each car will leave at five minute intervals and will be timed. Explain that the course has been previously and accurately timed by the leaders, and that the winner will be the carload of people that comes closest to that predetermined time.

Drivers must observe posted speed limits or drive at the speed specified in the instructions. This speed will help them to arrive at the right time. You can include some landmarks for the group to confirm (see item 6 in sample directions) just to make sure that they are still on the right course.

Have the rally end up at an ice cream shop or at someone's home where you can reveal the winning car, award prizes, and serve refreshments.

Bob Miller

Snowmobile Rally

For those who live in the colder climates and have a lot of snow on the ground, this event is a natural.

Take a car or bike rally idea and try it on snowmobiles. Make sure that all safety precautions are taken, like helmets, proper clothing, keeping the snowmobiles on a safe course, etc. If a race of some sort is to be run, then it would be best to have the snowmobiles leave at two minute intervals so that the course does not get crowded or collisions occur. Snowmobiles would race against the clock rather than against each other.

Tim Wise

Blind Car Rally

This is a great activity that combines both youth and adults in a fun learning experience. Divide the group into threes and fours and assign each group to a separate car. Blindfold each of the kids, put them in their assigned cars, and then give the drivers maps of the routes they are to take. Each driver should be given a different location than the others but each location should be approximately the same time and distance from the starting point.

As each car travels its preassigned route, the driver is not allowed to converse with anyone in the car in any way. The blindfolded kids in the car can converse and guess all they want as to where they are going. Once a car reaches its destination, the passengers are taken out of their cars, walked around them twice, then driven back to the starting point. The kids then remove their blindfolds and the groups each try to identify on a map the exact routes traveled. The group that determines the greatest number of streets actually traveled wins a prize.

Gene Poppino

Car Rally Starter

Here's a clever and frustrating way to begin a car rally or treasure hunt. Before you give the teams their first instruction or clue, give them sheets like the one shown here. Teams must complete the sheets before beginning the rally. *David Beguin*

Ready, Set, Go!

To receive your first clue, follow these instructions:

1. Please read all directions on this sheet before doing anything else.
2. Total the ages of everyone in your group: ______.
3. List the middle names of everyone in your group: ______, ______, ______, ______, ______, ______, ______.
4. Have someone in your group do ten push-ups.
5. Have everyone in your group yell "We're number one!" three times.
6. Write one Bible verse of your choice here: ______
7. Don't do items1–6. Just turn in this sheet with an X in the upper right-hand corner, get your first clue, and take off. Good luck!

CRAZY CAR RALLY

The group is divided into carloads, each with a car and a driver. Each car is given a sheet of questions that must be answered. The location indicated in the last question on every sheet is a checkpoint where each car and time is recorded and a new route sheet is given. Each car also receives an emergency envelope that is not to be opened until a specified hour. Drivers receive a handout of instructions (page 195). Winners will be judged by time, mileage, and the number correct. The emergency envelope contains the location of the after-rally party. If the cars finish all the route sheets, then the last location will be the address of the party. The first car to arrive wins. *Bob Griffin*

Route Sheet Questions

1. Who made the light pole on Costello and Broadway? ______________
2. What color is the sign on the Executive Car Leasing in Encino? ______________
3. What are the Saturday hours for the Hillview Market?______________
4. How many lights are on the KMPC towers? ______________
5. Who donated the gumball machine in Ralph's in Sherman Oaks? ______________
6. How many pitching machines are at Buddy's Bat-A-Way? ______________
7. When was Pinecrest School founded, and by whom? ______________
8. In total, how many fountains are there at Coast and Southern Federal Savings? ______________

CROSSWORD CAR RALLY

This is a great car rally or scavenger hunt idea which incorporates the completion of a crossword puzzle in order to win (see sample below). You will need to create your own puzzle, but it's not too difficult to do. Divide into teams (or car loads), and give each one a printed copy of the puzzle, with clues similar to the ones below. *Dick Gibson*

GIANT MONOPOLY

This event combines the standard game of *Monopoly* with a car rally. In Giant Monopoly, the whole youth group plays *Monopoly* using real houses around the community as the properties on the game board. Here's how it works:

First, line up enough homes around town to be all the properties on the game board (Baltic Avenue, Boardwalk, and so on). If you want to cut

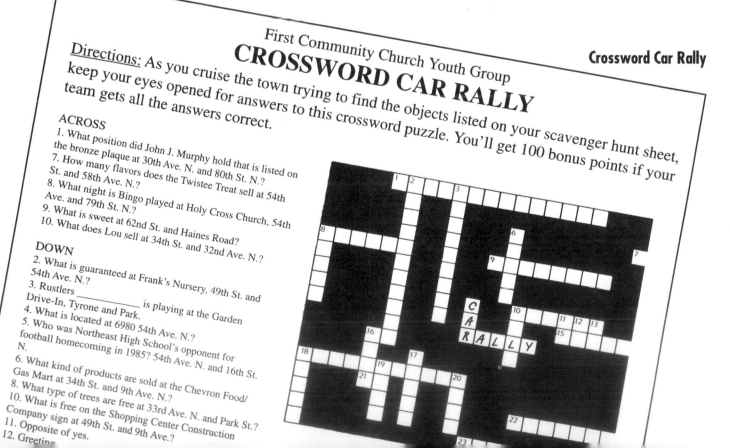

First Community Church Youth Group

CROSSWORD CAR RALLY

Directions: As you cruise the town trying to find the objects listed on your scavenger hunt sheet, keep your eyes opened for answers to this crossword puzzle. You'll get 100 bonus points if your team gets all the answers correct.

ACROSS

1. What position did John J. Murphy hold that is listed on the bronze plaque at 30th Ave. N. and 80th St. N.?
7. How many flavors does the Twistee Treat sell at 54th St. and 58th Ave. N.?
8. What night is Bingo played at Holy Cross Church, 54th Ave. and 79th St. N.?
9. What is sweet at 62nd St. and Haines Road?
10. What does Lou sell at 34th St. and 32nd Ave. N.?

DOWN

2. What is guaranteed at Frank's Nursery, 49th St. and 54th Ave. N.?
3. Rustlers ____________ is playing at the Garden Drive-In, Tyrone and Park.
4. What is located at 6980 54th Ave. N.?
5. Who was Northeast High School's opponent for football homecoming in 1985? 54th Ave. N. and 16th St. N.
6. What kind of products are sold at the Chevron Food/Gas Mart at 34th St. and 9th Ave. N.?
8. What type of trees are free at 33rd Ave. N. and Park St.?
10. What is free on the Shopping Center Construction Company sign at 49th St. and 9th Ave.?
11. Opposite of yes.
12. Greeting

Crossword Car Rally

Crazy Car Rally

Instructions to Drivers

1. You have a sheet of questions which must be answered in order. You will get a new sheet at each checkpoint.
2. The location of the last question on each sheet is a checkpoint. Here your mileage and time will be taken down by an official and you will be given your next route sheet.
3. Any questions you may have during the rally may be asked at the checkpoints.
4. When you left the starting point, you received an emergency envelope. This is not to be opened until ________ (TIME)
5. If by ________ (TIME) you haven't finished your last sheet, open your envelope and follow the instructions inside. Do not complete the route sheet.
6. Your envelope will be checked at every checkpoint to make sure it hasn't been opened.
7. Winners will be judged by time (the first to arrive), mileage (the least mileage possible), and the number of correct answers on your route sheets.

Crazy Car Rally

Instructions to Drivers

1. You have a sheet of questions which must be answered in order. You will get a new sheet at each checkpoint.
2. The location of the last question on each sheet is a checkpoint. Here your mileage and time will be taken down by an official and you will be given your next route sheet.
3. Any questions you may have during the rally may be asked at the checkpoints.
4. When you left the starting point, you received an emergency envelope. This is not to be opened until ________ (TIME)
5. If by ________ (TIME) you haven't finished your last sheet, open your envelope and follow the instructions inside. Do not complete the route sheet.
6. Your envelope will be checked at every checkpoint to make sure it hasn't been opened.
7. Winners will be judged by time (the first to arrive), mileage (the least mileage possible), and the number of correct answers on your route sheets.

Crazy Car Rally

Instructions to Drivers

1. You have a sheet of questions which must be answered in order. You will get a new sheet at each checkpoint.
2. The location of the last question on each sheet is a checkpoint. Here your mileage and time will be taken down by an official and you will be given your next route sheet.
3. Any questions you may have during the rally may be asked at the checkpoints.
4. When you left the starting point, you received an emergency envelope. This is not to be opened until ________ (TIME)
5. If by ________ (TIME) you haven't finished your last sheet, open your envelope and follow the instructions inside. Do not complete the route sheet.
6. Your envelope will be checked at every checkpoint to make sure it hasn't been opened.
7. Winners will be judged by time (the first to arrive), mileage (the least mileage possible), and the number of correct answers on your route sheets.

down on the number of houses you use, have one house represent all the properties of the same color on the board. On the day or evening that the game is played, all the owners of these houses will need to be at home and know what to do. You will also need to arrange cars and drivers for each team.

To play, use a regular *Monopoly* game. Divide into teams of four or five kids per team. (They must all ride in the same car together.) Distribute *Monopoly* money to each team as follows:

6 x $500 bills
6 x $100
6 x $50
18 x $20
15 x $10
15 x $5
15 x $1
(Total: $4,500)

Place $1,000 in the middle of the board. Roll the dice to see which team goes first. Most of the regular Monopoly rules will apply, like collecting $200 every time you pass Go.

But here's where the game really differs. If you're the first one to land on a property, you may either buy it or allow it to go to the highest bidder. If someone owns the property you land on, then your team must get in the car and go to that property and pay the fee. The owners at the home will collect the fee and give you a receipt. Then you return to the game so that you can roll again. While you're gone, the other teams can continue to play until they also have to leave for whatever reason. When there are other teams present at the game board, you must take your turn in order, but if no one else is there, you may roll more than once at a time.

Other rules:

- **Chance or Community Chest.** You must pick a card and do what it says.
- **Railroads.** You must get in the train car and go for a train ride—one mile out and one mile back. Then you must pay the conductor (driver).
- **Utilities.** You must go to the house designated as the utility office and pay.
- **Jail.** You must go to jail if you land on the *Go to Jail* space or draw the *Go to Jail* card. The jail can be a room in the building. You can get out of jail by paying $100, rolling doubles on your next turn, or sitting in jail for three minutes.
- **Free Parking.** Landing on this gives you all the money in the middle of the board.
- **Luxury Tax.** You pay $75 to the middle of the board.
- **Income Tax.** You pay $200 to the middle of the board.
- **Mortgages.** These are administered by the bank.
- **Out of Money.** If you are running short on cash, you can take your title deed to your owner's house and collect your money (if there is any) any time.
- **Selling Property.** You may sell to another group or trade with them as you choose.

The game is over at the end of the designated time. At that time each team must gather up all its money and assets and turn them into the bank. The team with the most money and accumulated property value wins.

Obviously, this event will need to be carefully planned and well thought out before you do it, but it's worth the effort. The idea of playing *Monopoly* with the whole town as your board is crazy enough to generate a lot of enthusiasm and participation. *Scott Welch*

PHONE BOOK BIKE RALLY

For this event each kid is instructed to bring a phone book and a bike. Kids may also need backpacks or baskets to carry the phone books while

Phone Book Bike Rally

1. Ed Saldin's Drug Store: What hours are posted on the front door? ________
2. Yo Yo's Cafe: What number telephone pole is directly behind the building? ________
3. Loving Day Care Center: What kind of animals are on either side of the front door? ________
4. San Marco Apartments: What product is advertised on their sign? ________
5. Guthrie Cabinet and Millwork Shop: How many panes of glass are there above the sign on the front of the building? ________
6. Spratt's Metal Works: What does the traffic sign directly in front of the building say? ________
7. Anderson's Grocery: What kind of flour is stacked in the front window? ________
8. Yakima Ambulance and Towing: How many trees are growing in front of the building? ________
9. Hobbit Shoppe Antiques: Name the farm implement hanging over the front door. ________
10. Apple Tree Gift Shop: The display in the front window features glassware and what? ________
11. The Walter J. Farnsworthy home: What kind of flowers are in the front yard? ________

riding. A list of locations is passed out to everyone (on separate slips, so that each person will take them in a different order) and each kid must obtain the information asked for. No phone calls are allowed. Each location must be visited. You obviously will need to select places in your own city that can be looked up in a phone book. The first person to complete their list within the time limit is the winner. This can also be done in cars. *Sonny Salisbury*

SAKAYAMANASHIMIYA-COPASHIROGEEITIS

This game's name is simply a synthesis of family names of a specific church. You can use this name or you can have fun making up a name synthesized from families in your church—and then trying to pronounce the name.

It's basically a sophisticated relay race relying heavily on teamwork. At any point during the race a team can easily come from behind. We have reprinted below a sheet explaining the game that each person would receive. The map, or course, would be different for your church.

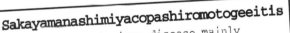

Sakayamanashimiyacopashiromotogeeitis is a highly contagious disease mainly characterized by rapid deterioration of brain tissues. Symptoms include the severe paralysis of the arms and legs, rapid loss of weight and strength, and terminal idiocy.

There are two methods of treatment available. The traditional method of treatment is the quick and immediate removal of the head by decapitation. The other known treatment of this horrendous disease is the administration of a special antidote. This antidote is hot dog of the Der Wienerschnitzel variety, type: mustard, taken orally with liquid. Warning: If this antidote is not given to the patient quickly enough, the traditional method of treatment must be administered!

Personnel

3 airplanes (one must be female)
1 helicopter (blindfolded)
1 patient (must be female)
1 radar
1 nurse

One member of your team has contracted the hideous disease, Sakayamanashimilyacopashiromotogeeitis. With all of your determination and strength of will, your main objective is to get the special antidote to your dying team member. The antidote must be flown by plane, transferred to a helicopter, and taken to the hospital where the patient lies. The sequence is as follows:

1. Airplane No. 1 takes off from the starting point and gives the prescription to Airplane No. 2 at the transfer point.

2. Airplane No. 2 flies to the pick-up point, receives the antidote and returns to the transfer point. The pilot must exchange the prescription for the antidote.

3. The antidote is transferred to Airplane No. 3 (female) and flown back to the church accompanied by Airplane No. 1.

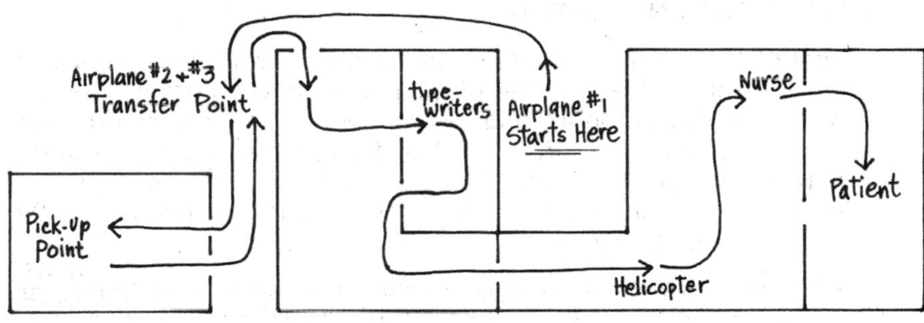

4. Before entering the airport (social hall), Airplane No. 2 must type the name Sakayamanashimiyacopashiromotogeeitis. Typewriters are located in Burnett Hall. The airplane must enter the church through the stairs.

5. The antidote is given to the helicopter and brought to the hospital. Note: the helicopter encounters bad weather and must fly to the hospital blind. The pilot is guided by radar.

6. At the hospital, the antidote is given to the nurse. Before this can transpire the pilot must sign special authorization papers and give his name, address, phone and social security number to the nurse. The nurse must write down the information on the chalkboard for identification purposes.

7. The nurse takes the antidote to the patient and assists her in taking the antidote. The first patient to eat the hot dog and the drink will save their patient and be declared the winner.

Here are a few other hints:

- Airplanes fly by running. The race is started when the radar person pops a balloon.
- The antidote can be any food; hot dog, hamburger, taco, etc.
- The patient's hands and legs are tied together to represent paralysis.
- When the helicopter takes the antidote in, there could be a maze of chairs to represent a heavy storm. The game could even be wilder by having blindfolded thunderclouds disrupting helicopters.

Milton M. Hom

WORLD CHAMPION TOILET RACE

Each team must build a nonmotorized toilet-mobile with the requirement that the bowl and tank be present on the machine. This weird-looking go-cart-type machine is then raced down a long street against other toilet machines from other teams to determine the world champion. You can also race separately against a clock, or in one giant pack. After the main event a destruction derby can be held. The old toilets can be purchased at a nominal fee from any old junkyard that handles such things.

Ronald Wells

OTHER PARTIES & SPECIAL EVENTS

OTHER PARTIES & SPECIAL EVENTS

Name a theme, any theme, and you have an excuse for a party. Heck, anybody can throw a birthday party—but it takes a special kind of weirdness (which is highly attractive to teenagers, by the way) to throw a party that commemorates canine birthdays (page 203) or the passing of summer (204).

BROAD SIDE OF A BARN

Try this idea on a warm balmy summer night. Show a movie on the side of a building, barn, or storage building. You can do this at camp also. Works great and the kids really like it. *Jim Allard*

BUS DRIVE-IN

Take your group to a drive-in movie in a bus. Simply park in the back parallel to the screen and have the kids sit on top of the bus to watch the show. (It is probably best to go during the week when the drive-in is not crowded.) Just pull the sound boxes up and hang them off the bus windows. *Ben Mathes*

BUS WASH

Fill water balloons with soap and water. Fill others just with water. Throw them at the bus while washing it. Use mops to scrub the top and sides. You can even have a water balloon fight inside the bus with teams at each end (no soap, though, it gets in the eyes). This helps make a big job fun! *Mark Reed*

CHURCH ZOO

Here's an all-church event that the youth group can organize. Have everyone bring a pet to church and set up a church zoo for a few hours. All can show their pets, demonstrate any tricks the critters might be able to do, and compete for an award presented to the pet which looks the most like its owner. This could be tied in with a lesson for the children on Noah's ark. Encourage everyone to participate. Any pet is allowed (yes, even goldfish). Make sure people bring leashes and cages when necessary. *Gary N. McCluskey*

THE CYCLOTRON

Here's how you can make a chilling, breathtaking amusement park thrill ride for your youth group. For a little time and money you can create a safe Cyclotron that they will want to ride again and again.

Materials: You need a large wooden spool, available from your phone company or water and power department. Some power companies sell used spools very cheap. The best dimensions are those shown. Make sure it's sturdy. You also need sections of 2-inch galvanized pipe cut to size and threaded, two 2-inch side-outlet elbows, and four 2-inch caps.

Other materials: Two 3/4-inch pipe lengths (for hand grips), four 3/4-inch flanges, plenty of 16d common nails, two heavy-duty seat belts, a lot of foam rubber, and various bolts and handles.

Now follow these simple instructions:

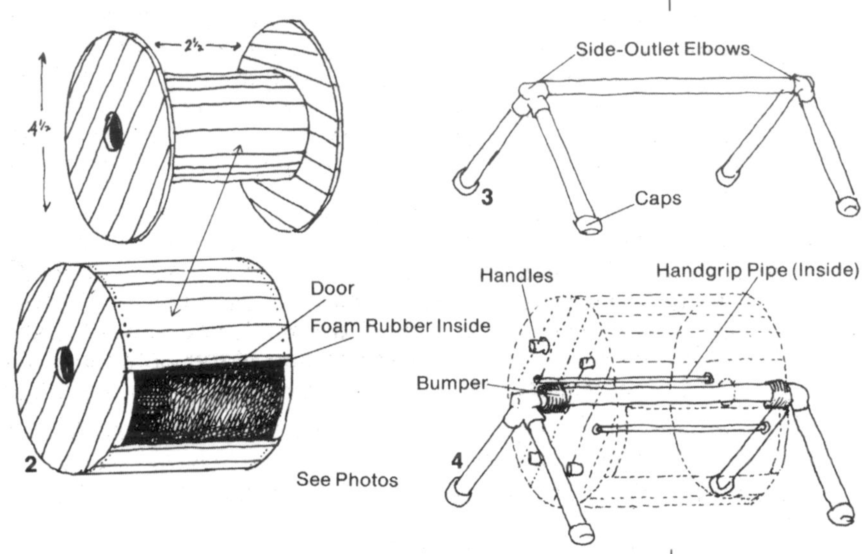

1. Take out the horizontal boards of the inner part of the spool.

2. Nail these same boards around the outer edges of the wheels, forming a large cylinder. Nail each board securely with three or four nails at each end. You will probably need more boards the same size from another spool. Nail them close together. Leave an opening about two feet wide for getting into and out of the Cyclotron.

3. Pad the entire interior with thick foam rubber.

4. The pipe framework will look as shown, but don't assemble it first. Put the horizontal pipe through the Cyclotron first, through the holes in the large wheels, then attach the other pipe fittings. The legs should be long enough to lift the Cyclotron a few inches off the floor (it depends on the size of the spool you start with). The Cyclotron should now roll vertically on the sturdy pipe framework.

5. Bolt the seat belts into the interior so that when people are sitting inside (with their heads completely in), the belts will fasten firmly across their waist.

6. Bolt the hand-grip pipes and flanges in a position where the riders can hang on tightly, a few inches from the center pipe and directly in front of them when they're sitting inside.

7. Fasten some handles securely to the outside of the large wheels so that it can be turned.

8. Cut some pieces from a thick cardboard tube (about 3" in diameter) and mount them on the horizontal pipe near the side-outlet elbows, as bumpers.

9. Test everything carefully before anyone uses it to make sure it is SAFE. Seat belts especially should be firmly bolted, and all pipe fittings should be tight.

How it works: The Cyclotron can hold two adults or four children. If two ride, one steps in first and fastens his seat belt securely. Then the other person goes around to the other side. Roll the entrance opening toward him and let him step in while you hold it still. Make sure both fasten their seat belts tight and hold on to the hand grip with both hands. They are sitting facing each other. One can spread his feet apart and the other can have feet together.

Keep everybody clear and use only dependable operators who care about safety. Grab the handles or wherever you can get a good hold, and begin spinning the Cyclotron around. The riders travel around and around inside, going upside down. After it goes a short while, let it slow down, then change direction and spin it the other way, so that each rider gets to go both head-first and feet-first.

Operating tips:

- Put a little motor oil on the horizontal pipe where the Cyclotron rests on it. It will spin easier. Oil it every few rides.
- The main danger is someone falling out the opening by not being fastened in securely. Double check the seat belts before operating every time. Enforce the rule that riders are not to unfasten the seat belts until given permission to do so. Be sure their heads are well inside.
- At the end of the ride, you can hold the riders in an upside-down position for a while.
- Choose an agreed-on word or signal the riders can give for emergency stopping.
- If possible build your Cyclotron in a place where it

can be locked up when not in use to prevent someone using it without a leader present and getting hurt.

The Cyclotron can be an asked-for attraction at your youth meetings. Their enjoyment of it will last longer if you don't overuse it—maybe open it once a month or make them earn tickets for rides. Paint it in bright colors and make it as fun as you can. Don't force anyone to ride, but most teens will try it if their friends urge them to. *David Coppedge*

Disappointment Party

So you had to cancel your lock-in or scavenger hunt due to a minor flu epidemic or other illness in your group? Maybe some of your disappointed kids won't be so disappointed if you promise a Disappointment Party.

That's right—invite all who had preregistered for your original event to a pizza party or similar get-together (by which time everyone's recovery should be complete). That will soften the frustration of missing a big event and may also give the afflicted some incentive for a speedy convalescence. *Margaret Brown*

Hangin' Party

Sometimes kids just need a place to hang, so have a party at a location where kids will feel comfortable. Provide music, a TV, some videos, card or board games, snacks, and inconspicuous chaperones. Encourage kids to bring a friend, a favorite game to play, or even homework.

This event requires little preparation or expense, yet meets a genuine need for teens. *Dave Shaheen*

Group Birthday Party

If your kids enjoy celebrations, don't overlook the anniversary of your first group meeting. If you need to, do a little research on the history of your group and try to pin down a specific date. Otherwise just choose a day to celebrate the existence of your group. Then make it a point to celebrate that anniversary with a party every year. Order a cake from the local bakery with appropriate decoration or make one of your own if you have baking skills. You can even go so far as to decorate with streamers and balloons and give everyone party hats and favors.

For games you might want to play a different version of the old favorite, Pin the Tail on the Donkey. Each person can write on a paper tail a headline for a news item. The headline must describe an event from the previous year in your community or the world that was not good news or that was a shortcoming. (For example, Family Sees Twister Movie Then Lives Through Real Thing.) Then teens try to pin these tails to the donkey's posterior while they are blindfolded. Voting may decide the single most donkey event of the year with prizes given for the best ones.

To carry on the first anniversary theme, award prizes to the *first* teen to stand and correctly spell a theological term of your choice, the *first* person to identify the make and model of a youth leader's vehicle, the *first* to remember the name of any hymn sung in church during the past month, or the *first* to guess the number of praises in the song, "Praise Ye the Lord."

At this time you can also solicit ideas for the upcoming year that would benefit the group. Have kids list books of the Bible or topics they would like to study, fundraising ideas, or event or retreat ideas. Read and discuss each idea. Award prizes in different categories such as most helpful idea, most fun idea, most creative, etc.

Since presents are usually opened last at birthday parties, have the youth leaders say something they appreciate about each person in the group, as a gift to the kids. Give kids time to describe favorite memories about the group. Or if you wish the youth leaders can use this time to present group with a gift from the leaders or from the church such as athletic equipment, a game, or something else that can be used by the group for years to come. *Albert Frederico*

Happy Birthday, Dear Doggy

If you know the birthday of your dog or a student's dog—or if you want an excuse for a party and are willing to falsify a birth date—throw a doggy birthday party. Use wall and ceiling hangings and paper plates, cups, and napkins that carry dog pictures. Display photographs of the birthday dog (in puppyhood, at one year, etc.), invite the kids to bring inexpensive gifts (dog biscuits, a new collar, balls, chew bones, etc.), and conduct the following games to get your kids into an appropriately doggy disposition.

- **Tether Cat.** Buy a stuffed toy cat and tie it to a tetherball pole and rope. Play by normal rules.
- **Water the Tree.** A dog's favorite pastime is watering the neighborhood trees, right? So assign one player the doggy role, give him a squirt gun, and inform the other players that they're trees. Staying within boundaries, the dog chases the trees, trying to mark them—that is, squirt them with water. Players marked are out of that round of the game. Last person marked wins.
- **Championship Ball Fetching.** Divide the group into two teams, each of which stands in single-file lines, front to back. The two lines stand end-on to each other so that the first players on each team are facing each other, separated by five feet or so. The first players in each line simultaneously throw a playground ball (the inexpensive kind found in supermarkets and drugstores work great) far behind the opposing team. Those same two players must run and fetch the ball thrown in their territory and return it to the opposition's second player to throw again, and so forth.
- **Bite the Mail Carrier.** Play this like Pin the Tail on the Donkey—except that students pin the face of an angry dog (instead of a tail) to a picture of a mail carrier (instead of a donkey). The object is to pin the dog's mug on or close to the mail carrier's derriere. *Jack Hawkins*

HOBBY SHOPS

Here's an idea for getting large groups of junior or senior highers into small groups. Have them vote on a list of hobbies they'd like to learn more about. Take the top five or six and have everyone choose a group. Find interested adults in your church who will help out one evening a week for six weeks. Generally the most effective leaders are those who are not professionals, but are fairly expert in their hobby field. Possibilities are endless: cooking (guys love this), drama, auto repair, chess, model building, gymnastics (borrow equipment from the YMCA or a local school), crafts (woodwork, rubber stamps, etc.), photography. The kids will come up with their own ideas.

On the seventh week, have an Appreciation Dinner. Invite all your teachers and their spouses, your minister, and anyone else who might be interested. Each Hobby Shop group shows what it's been up to. The cooking group could make part of the meal. The drama group performs a one-act play. The chess group might demonstrate a few power plays on a gigantic board. Use your imagination. Kids learn something new and become close friends with those in their group. *Barbara Nelson*

ONCE-A-YEAR BIRTHDAY PARTY

This idea is excellent for groups of all ages.

Decorate a large room for a birthday party. Arrange 12 tables and decorate each according to the events of that particular month in the year, e.g., swimming in June, Halloween in October. Make a birthday cake for each month and set it at the appropriate table along with ice cream and party favors.

Invite each person in the group to sit at the table corresponding to their birthday month. The program could include awards recognizing the oldest person, the youngest, the person with a birthday on a holiday, etc. *Deanne Smith*

PERSONALIZED T-SHIRTS

As a special event, have a get-together in which each person brings a plain white or colored T-shirt. You provide liquid embroidery pens, lettering stencils and cardboard to make other patterns from, and then create personalized custom T-shirts. Kids can design a statement of their faith, or an emblem for their youth group, or simply a crazy design with their names. They can be done large or small. It's easy, fun to do, and fun to wear. *Ellen Sautter*

SUMMER WAKE

Around Labor Day announce a wake for summer, at which they'll mourn the passing of summer and the beginning of school. Tell them to wear dark clothes and bring money for dinner. Then gather an old swimsuit, a towel, sneakers, tanning lotion, sunglasses, a water ski—anything that symbolizes summer to your group. Place the objects in a crate that looks like a casket or, better yet, in a realistic casket that you build from plywood.

On the evening of the event, arriving teens are escorted into the viewing room where they can pass by the casket and pay last respects to summer.

Then comes the memorial service. The kids are seated, you or another leader eulogizes the deceased summer (and includes the highlights of your summer's activities), and the casket is sealed. Supply a box of tissues to each row.

Afterwards go out to eat—to recover from grief and mourning, of course. *Jim Smith*

PORT-A-PARTY

Please and surprise even your longtime youth group members by showing up at a regularly scheduled meeting with a suitcase filled with party items. For any outrageous reason or for no reason at all, stage an instant party by bounding into the room with your party hat and your suitcase filled with a cake, ice cream, bowls, spoons, napkins, streamers, everything. You can do it for random birthdays or in celebration of some obscure event. (National Pickle Week, maybe?) You might even try taking a Port-a-Party to kids' houses at 6:00 a.m. on their birthdays. Use your own imagination for the reason and time, and your surprise party will be talked about for a long time by some quite thrilled kids. *Jan Augustine*

SNOW CARVING

First you need some snow. Second, create snow-carving teams of three or four kids each. Then assign a theme such as food and have the kids create large snow carvings of all kinds of food for judging.

To make the carvings more realistic, provide spray bottles of water colored with ordinary food coloring, and allow kids to paint their masterpieces. It works great and looks terrific.

Encourage creativity. One group, using the food theme, carved a 20-foot hot dog (complete with mustard and catsup), a bag of french fries, a banana split, a bowl of spaghetti with meatballs, and a giant taco.

Award prizes, take pictures, and serve snow cones for dessert. *Dave Washburn*

SWIDEO

This is a great idea for a swimming party. While the kids are swimming in the pool, show continuous videos at one end of the pool—stuff like Laurel and Hardy, W.C. Fields, even home movies. Hence the name: a swideo. *John Coulombe*

SECRET SUNDAY NIGHT

Once a month this activity will keep your group looking forward to the after-church party. Contact the parents of one of the members of the youth group and secretly arrange to have an after-church party complete with refreshments. Try not to let the children of the host-family know.

After church load up the kids for the hunt to the secret location making sure to lead the kids on a wild goose chase while they try to guess the location of the house.

When you arrive, some may have guessed the location, but most will be surprised. Kids will look forward to this activity. *Rhett Payne*

THEATER IN THE ROUND IN REVERSE

This is dinner theater with a dramatic difference. Serve a delicious meal with tables set up in the middle of the room, leaving plenty of space on all sides of the room. Then surround the diners with drama. Use several areas of the room, making the

kids wonder where the actors will come from next.
John Peters

Sunday School Tailgate Party

Tailgate parties are popular at sports events in some parts of the U.S. People show up hours before the game in their motor homes, cars, campers, or trucks, and cook hamburgers, visit with other tailgaters, toss a football around, and so on. So why not try a tailgate party for your church?

Just have everyone come an hour or two before Sunday school and cook breakfast over a grill or camp stove. Serve coffee and orange juice, sausage and eggs, pancakes, and whatever else sounds good. People can bring lawn chairs, Frisbees, and guitars to relax and have a good time before Sunday school.

One church has made this an annual event and advertises a few weeks in advance. Lots of people come who normally don't show up for Sunday school. It has become a favorite event for the church. *Dan Craig*

Wednesday Night at the Movies

Change the day in the title as needed. Kids bring personal family videos or videos of favorite movies. Try to have several videos playing at once and let kids mingle and choose what they want to watch. Set up a soda fountain where kids can get free popcorn, soda, candy, etc. The results are fantastic.

Y'no

Y'no how everybody says y'no all the time? Well, here's a good way to take advantage of that. Next time you have a party or special event, y'no, you just call it Y'no, which stands for Youth Night Out. It's a pretty simple idea, y'no, but the group will love it.
Robert Crosby

YOUTH SPECIALTIES TITLES

Professional Resources

Administration, Publicity, & Fundraising (Ideas Library)

Developing Student Leaders

Equipped to Serve: Volunteer Youth Worker Training Course

Help! I'm a Junior High Youth Worker!

Help! I'm a Sunday School Teacher!

Help! I'm a Volunteer Youth Worker!

How to Expand Your Youth Ministry

How to Speak to Youth...and Keep Them Awake at the Same Time

One Kid at a Time: Reaching Youth through Mentoring

A Youth Ministry Crash Course

The Youth Worker's Handbook to Family Ministry

Youth Ministry Programming

Camps, Retreats, Missions, & Service Ideas (Ideas Library)

Compassionate Kids: Practical Ways to Involve Your Students in Mission and Service

Creative Bible Lessons in John: Encounters with Jesus

Creative Bible Lessons in Romans: Faith on Fire!

Creative Bible Lessons on the Life of Christ

Creative Junior High Programs from A to Z, Vol. 1 (A-M)

Creative Meetings, Bible Lessons, & Worship Ideas (Ideas Library)

Crowd Breakers & Mixers (Ideas Library)

Drama, Skits, & Sketches (Ideas Library)

Dramatic Pauses

Facing Your Future: Graduating Youth Group with a Faith That Lasts

Games (Ideas Library)

Games 2 (Ideas Library)

Great Fundraising Ideas for Youth Groups

More Great Fundraising Ideas for Youth Groups

Great Retreats for Youth Groups

Greatest Skits on Earth

Greatest Skits on Earth, Vol. 2

Holiday Ideas (Ideas Library)

Hot Illustrations for Youth Talks

More Hot Illustrations for Youth Talks

Incredible Questionnaires for Youth Ministry

Junior High Game Nights

Kickstarters: 101 Ingenious Intros to Just about Any Bible Lesson

Memory Makers

More Junior High Game Nights

Play It Again! More Great Games for Groups

Play It! Great Games for Groups

Special Events (Ideas Library)

Spontaneous Melodramas

Super Sketches for Youth Ministry

Teaching the Bible Creatively

Up Close and Personal: How to Build Community in Your Youth Group

Wild Truth Bible Lessons

Worship Services for Youth Groups

Discussion Starter Resources

Discussion & Lesson Starters (Ideas Library)

Discussion & Lesson Starters 2 (Ideas Library)

4th-6th Grade TalkSheets

Get 'Em Talking

High School TalkSheets

High School TalkSheets: Psalms and Proverbs

Junior High TalkSheets

Junior High TalkSheets: Psalms and Proverbs

Keep 'Em Talking!

More High School TalkSheets

More Junior High TalkSheets

What If...? 450 Thought-Provoking Questions to Get Teenagers Talking, Laughing, and Thinking

Would You Rather...? 465 Provocative Questions to Get Teenagers Talking

Clip Art

ArtSource Vol. 1—Fantastic Activities

ArtSource Vol. 2—Borders, Symbols, Holidays, and Attention Getters

ArtSource Vol. 3—Sports

ArtSource Vol. 4—Phrases and Verses

ArtSource Vol. 5—Amazing Oddities and Appalling Images

ArtSource Vol. 6—Spiritual Topics

ArtSource Vol. 7—Variety Pack

ArtSource Vol. 8—Stark Raving Clip Art

ArtSource CD-ROM (contains Vols. 1-7)

Videos

EdgeTV

The Heart of Youth Ministry: A Morning with Mike Yaconelli

Next Time I Fall in Love Video Curriculum

Understanding Your Teenager Video Curriculum

Student Books

Grow For It Journal

Grow For It Journal through the Scriptures

Wild Truth Journal for Junior Highers